IDA

IN RETROSPECT

IDA
IN RETROSPECT

THE FIRST TWO DECADES OF THE
INTERNATIONAL DEVELOPMENT ASSOCIATION

PUBLISHED FOR THE WORLD BANK □ OXFORD UNIVERSITY PRESS

Oxford University Press

NEW YORK OXFORD LONDON GLASGOW
TORONTO MELBOURNE WELLINGTON HONG KONG
TOKYO KUALA LUMPUR SINGAPORE JAKARTA
DELHI BOMBAY CALCUTTA MADRAS KARACHI
NAIROBI DAR ES SALAAM CAPE TOWN

All the photographs in this book illustrate projects supported
by IDA credits. Photographs appearing at the openings of
chapters are identified as follows: (Chapter 1) surveyor on
the construction site of a dam in Pakistan; (Chapter 2) local
mason constructs a school in the Yemen Arab Republic;
(Chapter 3) workers in a rice paddy on an irrigation project
in Sri Lanka; (Chapter 4) laborers compact the sides of an
irrigation canal in Upper Volta; (Chapter 5) workers build
low-cost housing outside Calcutta, India; and (Chapter 6)
stacking wheat for storage in Ethiopia. World Bank photographs by Kay Chernush, cover, page 43; Yosef Hadar, page
35; James Pickerell, page 57; Tomas Sennett, cover, pages 1,
9, 19, 70; and Ray Witlin, pages 40, 50, 61, 65, 74, 77.

Library of Congress Cataloging in Publication Data

World Bank.
  IDA in retrospect.

  1. International Development Association.
I. Title.
HG3881.W584 1982   332.1'53   82–14224
ISBN 0–19–520407–7
ISBN 0–19–520408–5 (pbk.)

Foreword

Established in 1960, the International Development Association (IDA) has been a major channel of concessionary assistance to low-income developing countries. This report describes IDA's origins and its evolution, reviews its activities, and assesses its place in development finance. It is offered in response to the growing uncertainty about the future of IDA, and the feeling that IDA's record is not sufficiently known.

This report was prepared by Bank staff working together with a number of outside contributors. The team was asked to undertake a frank and objective review of IDA's accomplishments and failures. The report has been reviewed by a wide range of readers both inside and outside the Bank and from both the industrial and developing countries. Its purpose, content, and conclusions were discussed in four seminars held in Washington, Paris, London, and New York. These outside comments and views are reflected in the text. The judgments expressed, however, do not necessarily reflect the views of the Bank's Board of Directors or the governments they represent.

IDA is an integral part of The World Bank; it is therefore difficult to separate its work from that of the Bank itself. A unique feature of IDA is that it is funded entirely by contributions by member governments. One purpose of this study, therefore, is to report to members on what these funds have achieved.

As IDA has grown in size, it has naturally come under closer scrutiny. Donors have become increasingly concerned about the size of IDA, the allocation of contributions among donors, and the allocation of credits to developing countries. Questions have been raised about the quality of IDA's projects, the terms of its loans, and its ability to reach the poor. While recipients have generally welcomed IDA's projects, they have often been unhappy with long procedural delays in financing projects and have disagreed at times with the technical and policy solutions proposed by IDA. Another purpose of *IDA in Retrospect,* therefore, is to deal frankly with these concerns.

Reviewing IDA's history has proved a valuable experience. No institution is or could even hope to be perfect. Both IDA's shortcomings and achievements are evident in various parts of this report. What is most striking, however, is its record of solid achievement and its ability to learn from past mistakes. In its 20-year life, IDA has become one of the strongest, most effective bodies for promoting development. It stands as a symbol of multilateral cooperation and worldwide commitment to development. While substantial progress has been made, the poorest countries of the world remain in desperate need of further assistance. IDA now stands in the front line of this struggle against world poverty; it continues to need the support of both traditional and new donors.

A. W. CLAUSEN
President, The World Bank

July 1982

This study was written by a team consisting of Norman Hicks (team leader), Robert Ayres (Overseas Development Council), Barbara Herz, Jeffrey Katz, Danny Leipziger, and Josefina Valeriano. Other World Bank staff members making major contributions include: Michel Beguery, Ramesh Chander, Emmanuel D'Silva, Chandra Hardy, Kandiah Kanagaratnam, José Olivares, Ossie Rahkonen, and Hans Rothenbuhler. The study was also assisted by Stephane Baile and Carol Rosen. Among the outside consultants contributing to the study were Robert Asher (independent consultant), Edward Fried (Brookings Institution), Robert Cassen (University of Sussex), and Paul Streeten (Boston University).

The cooperation and assistance of various departments of the Bank is also acknowledged, including the Economic Analysis and Projections Department, the financial staff, and the staff of the various regional departments throughout the Bank. In addition, extensive use was made of the reports of the Operations Evaluation Department.

The study was directed by a Steering Group comprising Shahid Javed Burki (chairman), Percy Mistry, and Alexander Shakow.

Contents

Map: IDA Donor and Recipient Countries

Text Tables

Text Figures

Boxes

Definitions

The principal country groups used in the text of this report are defined as follows:

• *Developing countries* are divided into: *low-income economies*, with 1980 gross national product (GNP) per person of $410 and below; and *middle-income economies*, with 1980 GNP per person above $410. Developing countries are also divided into *oil exporters* and *oil importers* (see below).

• *Oil exporters* comprise Algeria, Angola, Bahrain, Bolivia, Brunei, People's Republic of the Congo, Ecuador, Egypt, Gabon, Indonesia, Iran, Malaysia, Mexico, Nigeria, Oman, Peru, Syria, Trinidad and Tobago, Tunisia, and Venezuela.

• *Oil importers* comprise all other developing countries not classified as oil exporters.

• *Industrial market economies* are the members of the Organisation for Economic Co-operation and Development (OECD, see below) apart from Greece, Portugal, and Turkey, which are included among the developing economies. This group is commonly referred to in the text as *industrial economies* or *industrial countries*.

• *Nonmarket industrial economies* include the following developed European countries: USSR, Bulgaria, Czechoslovakia, German Democratic Republic, Hungary, and Poland. This group is sometimes referred to as *nonmarket economies*.

• *Least-developed countries* are Afghanistan, Bangladesh, Benin, Bhutan, Botswana, Burundi, Cape Verde, Central African Republic, Chad, Comoros, Ethiopia, Gambia, Guinea, Guinea-Bissau, Haiti, Lao People's Democratic Republic, Lesotho, Malawi, Maldives, Mali, Nepal, Niger, Rwanda, Somalia, Sudan, Tanzania, Uganda, Upper Volta, Yemen Arab Republic, People's Democratic Republic of Yemen, and Western Samoa.

• *DAC*. The Development Assistance Committee of the OECD (see below) comprises Australia, Austria, Belgium, Canada, Denmark, Finland, France, Federal Republic of Germany, Italy, Japan, Netherlands, New Zealand, Norway, Sweden, Switzerland, United Kingdom, United States, and the Commission of the European Communities.

• *OECD*. The Organisation for Economic Co-operation and Development comprises Australia, Austria, Belgium, Canada, Denmark, Finland, France, Federal Republic of Germany, Greece, Iceland, Ireland, Italy, Japan, Luxembourg, Netherlands, New Zealand, Norway, Portugal, Spain, Sweden, Switzerland, Turkey, United Kingdom, and United States.

• *OPEC*. The Organization of Petroleum Exporting Countries comprises Algeria, Ecuador, Gabon, Indonesia, Iran, Iraq, Kuwait, Libya, Nigeria, Qatar, Saudi Arabia, United Arab Emirates, and Venezuela.

Other terms used throughout this report:

IBRD means International Bank for Reconstruction and Development.

IDA means International Development Association.

World Bank refers to the combination of the IBRD and IDA operating as a single institution, and often referred to simply as "the Bank."

FAO means Food and Agriculture Organization.

GDP means gross domestic product.

GNP means gross national product.

ILO means International Labour Organisation.

IMF means International Monetary Fund.

ODA means official development assistance, sometimes referred to as foreign aid.

SDR means special drawing right.

UNDP means United Nations Development Programme.

WHO means World Health Organization.

Years used in this report are World Bank fiscal years when referring to data relating to the operations of the IBRD or IDA, and run from July to June of the calendar year. Fiscal 1982 ended on June 30, 1982.

Economic and demographic terms are defined in the technical notes to the Statistical Annex of this volume.

Billion is 1,000 million.

Tons are metric tons, equal to 1,000 kilograms or 2,204.6 pounds.

Growth rates are in real terms unless otherwise stated.

Dollars are United States dollars unless otherwise specified.

Symbols used in the text tables are as follows:

    (.) Less than half the unit shown.
    – Not applicable.

All tables and figures are based on World Bank data unless otherwise specified.

Summary

The International Development Association (IDA) was established over 20 years ago to provide concessional assistance to low-income countries. Its origins lay in the recognition that, for many of the poorest countries, private capital and existing aid arrangements were not adequate. The World Bank, which had led the multilateral aid effort after World War II, could not lend to the poorest countries without damaging its own credit position in international capital markets. Furthermore, the low-income countries could ill afford to take on loans carrying high interest rates and short maturities to finance projects with long payback periods and earning little or no foreign exchange. India became a particular problem in the late 1950s, when its ambitious development plans were thwarted by a rising debt burden and growing food shortages.

Donor governments agreed to the establishment of IDA because, in its affiliation with the World Bank, they saw an assurance that concessional loans would be used to finance Bank-type projects. They also saw IDA as a body that could coordinate assistance among donors, encourage new donors, and help to depoliticize foreign aid. While IDA did not emerge as the large, independent, soft-loan agency sought by several countries, its establishment was a compromise that they all welcomed. IDA has helped to expand the Bank's role from that of a financial institution into a development agency as well. Without IDA, the Bank would not have been able to take the lead in coordinating aid to most low-income countries and in offering them resources and policy advice. It would have been unable to tackle some of the most critical development problems of the past two decades, in countries such as India, Indonesia, and Bangladesh.

IDA and Aid

During the past 20 years the developing world has made tremendous progress, but the pace of development has been much slower in the low-income countries, which constitute the bulk of IDA's current recipients. These countries remain highly dependent on official development assistance (ODA) from the industrial countries, and IDA is an important part of this assistance. In 1980, ODA financed 65 percent of the deficits of the low-income countries, with IDA accounting for 16 percent of total ODA. By contrast, the middle-income countries are able to rely much more heavily on private capital flows; these financed 70 percent of their deficits in 1980 (compared with only 9 percent in the low-income countries).

The level of aid flows has grown rapidly in the past two decades, even allowing for inflation. In 1980 it equaled $36 billion, a real growth of about 4 percent annually since 1960. About one-fifth of ODA comes from OPEC countries, another fifth from the United States, while Europe and Japan together provide most of the balance. The share of DAC assistance channeled through the multilateral agencies has grown dramatically, from 13 percent in 1960 to 35 percent in 1980; about one-third went to IDA in 1980. The growth of multilateral aid agencies reflects the perception that they have certain comparative advantages in giving long-term development assistance.

Despite a worsening world situation, aid provided by DAC countries remained a stable proportion of their combined GNPs during the 1970s (about 0.35 percent). A significant portion of the increase in ODA has come from the OPEC countries, whose aid exceeds 1 percent of their combined GNPs. Among the DAC countries, aid performance has declined in the United States and the United Kingdom, but improved in some others, particularly the Netherlands, the Nordic countries, Japan, and the Federal Republic of Germany. With the current world recession and tight budgetary conditions prevailing in most countries, however, donors are taking a more discriminating view of all types of aid.

IDA's Finances

In the course of various replenishments, the money pledged to IDA has increased to a cumulative total of about $30 billion, of which $23 billion had actually been paid in by the end of 1982. Contributions have taken the form of non-interest-bearing notes; as of June 1982, only $14 billion had actually been drawn against these notes. IDA's replenishments have never been easy to negotiate, and the problems they have encountered often recur. The central issues concern the size of replenishments and the way they are shared among donor countries, the problem of handling delays in contributions, and the eligibility of recipients. Other questions, such as maintaining the value of contributions and procurement, have also been important.

As IDA has grown, so has the number of its donors. The initial subscription involved 17 industrial countries; today there are 33 donors, including nine developing countries. Over the years, shares have

changed to reflect the changing economic circumstances of the donors. The combined share of the United States and the United Kingdom has declined from 59 percent of the initial subscription to 37 percent of the sixth replenishment (IDA-6), while Germany, Japan, and Saudi Arabia have markedly increased their shares. About 6 percent of IDA's total resources have come from profits transferred from the Bank itself.

IDA's Credits

During its first 22 years, IDA committed $27 billion to finance 1,302 investment projects in 78 countries. Although IDA remains small compared with the IBRD (disbursements of $2.1 billion versus $6.4 billion in 1982, respectively), this is offset by the larger debt-service payments received by the IBRD on its lending. Net of debt service, the IBRD and IDA transfer about the same amount of resources (in 1982, $2.4 billion compared with $1.9 billion).

While IDA's overall purpose to assist development has remained unchanged, there have been important shifts in its operations and the economic background against which it operates. The needs of the low-income countries for concessional finance have remained sizable; since 1973 particularly, changes in the international environment have made these needs even greater. Nevertheless, low-income countries have made real progress. Their per capita incomes have grown, albeit slowly; literacy and life expectancy have increased. Progress can be gauged by the fact that 27 countries have "graduated" from IDA, including such countries as the Republic of Korea, Indonesia, Tunisia, and Turkey. As more countries have graduated, IDA has been able to devote itself more to Sub-Saharan Africa and Asia and has increasingly focused on the poorest developing countries. In 1980, 80 percent of IDA's net disbursements were to countries with per capita incomes of less than $410, compared with 34 percent for bilateral programs.

Per capita income is only one of several criteria that have determined the allocation of IDA lending. Others include a country's lack of creditworthiness and access to commercial borrowing, its economic performance, population, and the availability of projects. Applying these criteria has required a considerable amount of judgment rather than the mechanical use of a formula. And, regardless of the criteria, small countries (those with populations of less than 2 million) tend to receive more on a per capita basis than larger ones. India's share for IDA has been held to 40 percent, even though it has had over half the population of IDA countries.

IDA's Projects

While the terms of IDA credits are soft, its projects are generally identical in scope and rigor to IBRD projects. Because IDA countries are less developed, however, a larger proportion of IDA lending (37 percent, compared with 22 percent of IBRD lending) has financed agriculture and rural development. IDA credits have tended to finance a larger share (44 percent) of total project costs than IBRD loans (35 percent), and this share has been higher in the poorest countries. The remaining share of total IDA project costs (56 percent) has been financed partly by the recipients and partly by other donors. In general, about 30 percent of IDA credits have gone to finance local costs—a larger share than in IBRD projects, because IDA projects typically involve more local costs and because IDA finances a higher share of total project costs.

At its inception, IDA concentrated on infrastructure projects—transportation, power, ports, and the like. These projects account for about 30 percent of total lending. As development thinking evolved during the 1960s, it was recognized that agriculture was being comparatively neglected in many countries, resulting in food shortages and growing food imports. In the late 1960s, IDA therefore shifted to a greater involvement in agriculture. In 1973, growing more concerned about issues of employment and income distribution, the Bank extended this emphasis to rural development. Projects have been intended to raise the productivity of small farmers, as a way of both reducing absolute poverty and increasing total agricultural output.

Much of IDA's lending has helped to boost agricultural production in South Asia, spreading the technologies of the "green revolution" and realizing their true potential. As a result of these achievements, India is now able to meet its own food needs for the first time in decades. IDA has been particularly active in financing irrigation facilities and agricultural credit. Over the years, IDA has shifted away from large irrigation works to privately owned wells and pumps, and to more emphasis on distribution systems and on-farm water management.

The agricultural transformation that is occurring in South Asia is difficult to repeat in Sub-Saharan Africa. Countries there are among the world's poor-est in infrastructure, human capital, and agricultural development. In addition, African agriculture is almost exclusively rainfed, so that workable packages for farmers are harder to devise and involve higher risks. Nevertheless there are countries where IDA's efforts have produced encouraging results, notably Malawi and Kenya.

IDA has increasingly been concerned with urban poverty and employment problems. It has pioneered programs to find affordable solutions to urban shelter problems. Industrial lending has favored small and medium-size firms as a way of increasing employment. Water-supply projects have increasingly stressed simpler systems. All these changes are part of an effort to reach the poorest people within poor countries and to design projects that will benefit them directly. Experience has shown that raising the productivity of the poor means more than providing them with productive assets. It also means increasing their skills and strength through education, health programs, and other services. IDA's education lending, for example, has given increased emphasis to primary schooling, as well as vocational and technical training.

One way of measuring the effectiveness of projects is by their rate of return. For several reasons—weather, government policies, mistakes in project design and operation—rates of return expected when projects are appraised often differ markedly from final results. Overall, IDA's projects appear to have about the same average rate of return as IBRD projects, about 18 percent in both cases. Rates of return vary widely among regions, however, averaging 14 percent in Africa and 22 percent in South Asia. There is wide variation within these averages, however, and wide variation between expected and actual rates.

Although these figures refer to only a limited sample of IDA's completed projects that have been audited and for which recalculated rates of return are available, they indicate the risky nature of development projects in low-income countries, particularly in Africa. Despite these risks, the high average return suggests a fairly successful record. Furthermore, in pioneering new approaches a certain number of project failures are almost inevitable before a successful design can be developed. And the lessons learned from one region or country are often not suitable for immediate adoption in another country. Projects are also affected by factors outside IDA's control, such as weather and political disruptions. Many projects experience difficulties because they have been insensitive to complex sociocultural situations in recipient countries. Other problems often result from the failure of governments to do their part in terms of price incentives, procurement policies, or financial support.

Many IDA projects have important benefits that are difficult to quantify. For instance, projects assist in developing local institutions, in establishing procedures for cost recovery, and in improving efficiency and management. In many cases, IDA has supported institutions that are capable of taking over some of IDA's lending to individual projects; this has allowed IDA to become more of a wholesaler of credits and has increased the ability of intermediaries to play an independent role in development. This has been particularly true of industrial and agricultural credit. Programs aimed at cost recovery reduce price distortions and reduce the burden of operating expenditures that would fall on the recipient's budget. In the past decade, IDA projects have been increasingly successful in improving the productivity of the poor either directly or by increasing their access to basic services, such as health and education. Experience suggests that these "poverty focused" projects have been successful in reaching the poor without sacrificing the quality of projects.

Policy Dialogue

Despite its growth, IDA remains a relatively small contribution to development finance in most countries. Its loans have never exceeded 2 percent of total investment in its recipient countries overall, although it is more important in some—particularly the small countries of Africa—and in certain sectors within countries. But IDA's impact is not necessarily determined by its share of total investment. Its influence is often related to the help it gives in building enduring development institutions and to the advice it offers on macroeconomic and sector policies. Those activities, though hard to quantify, have a much broader impact than even a series of successful projects.

IDA can help to influence policy in a variety of ways. Countries that receive IDA credits benefit from the World Bank's economic and sector assessments. These are designed to identify development constraints and establish investment priorities. As economic and sector reports are prepared, IDA discusses the issues they raise with the government; these reports in turn lay the groundwork for iden-

tifying and preparing projects. Similar discussions occur in the context of program and "structural adjustment" lending, in which IDA credits are used to support a general development program, rather than particular projects. They are tied to particular policy reforms designed to help the country adjust to new circumstances and make better use of its resources. Likewise, project lending gives an opportunity to discuss policy issues affecting a particular sector, such as public utility tariffs, institutional reforms, and investment programs. Overall, it is difficult to judge the impact of IDA on policy changes through these discussions; often its influence is indirect and takes place over a long period.

Conclusions

At least four conclusions emerge from this study:

- First, IDA lending has been effective in promoting development. This can be seen not only by the high rates of return on IDA projects, but from its impact on policy reforms and the development of institutions. However, it would appear from a review of project experience that IDA's success is greater in South Asia than in Africa. But this does not mean that IDA was less effective in Africa; lower rates of return on projects in Africa, for instance, reflect lower levels of institutional development, relative shortages of trained manpower, and other factors.
- Second, IDA has demonstrated a tremendous capacity to grow, not only in size, but in understanding through learning by doing. It has gradually shifted its lending to the least developed of the poor countries and to poor people within these countries; it has incorporated the lessons learned from past mistakes into better project designs.
- Third, despite divergent levels of public support for aid in donor countries, IDA has been remarkably successful in attracting an increasing amount of financial support. But with its growth, it has also become the subject of closer scrutiny and criticism.
- Fourth, even though many countries have graduated from IDA's rolls, the need for concessional development assistance remains as great as ever. IDA has a key role to play in laying the groundwork for long-term development in the poorest countries in the world.

1 History and Background

The International Development Association (IDA) was created in 1960 as an affiliate of the World Bank, to make concessional long-term loans to the world's poorest countries. The initial fund of just under $1 billion has been replenished six times, making a total of about $30 billion by the end of 1980. To those closely involved in negotiating IDA's replenishments and allocating its loans, its history has never been smooth. But the creation of IDA was in at least three ways an important landmark in the history of international relations. It strengthened efforts to establish a multilateral system of world trade and payments. It made poverty a major concern of the world's richest countries. And, at the international level, it institutionalized the giving of concessional finance to promote economic development.

The Bretton Woods Agreements

In July 1944, the world's major countries assembled at Bretton Woods to agree on the principles of a postwar international financial system. The purpose of the conference was to prevent any repetition of the anarchy and protectionism that had such disastrous consequences between the first and second world wars. To support this goal, the participants agreed to the creation of the International Bank for Reconstruction and Development (IBRD), which became known as the World Bank, and the International Monetary Fund (IMF).

Most of the developing countries were still colonies in 1944, so only a handful—mostly the independent nations of Latin America—had attended the Bretton Woods conference. Even if more of them had been there, the results would probably have been the same; the overriding concern was the reestablishment of an open world economy and a stable system of exchange rates, not the financing of development. Most of the discussion therefore concerned the Fund rather than the Bank.

By the time the Bank and Fund began operations in 1946, it was clear that the reconstruction needs of Europe and Japan were more than either institution could finance. The United States felt that growing international tensions demanded a rapid European recovery, and enacted the Marshall Plan in 1947. Between 1948 and 1952 it provided aid to Europe equivalent to 1 percent of America's GNP. Since no government could foresee how long recovery would take, the aid was provided mostly as grants (about $47 billion in 1981 dollars). There were few restrictions on where or how the grants were to be spent; the needs were many and the

1

United States was the only country able to meet them. The United States did insist on a collective recovery program and not an uncoordinated series of national programs. It also pushed strongly for regional integration.

Once European recovery was under way, more attention was paid to the question of development finance. The membership of the Bank was expanding to include the newly independent countries, so this new emphasis could no longer be delayed. The prevailing theory of development stressed that low-income countries, having high population growth rates and low savings rates, could not invest at rates sufficient to accelerate growth in per capita incomes. They needed foreign capital to supplement domestic savings, to boost investment and hence output. The Bretton Woods agreements supposed that finance for development would come either directly from private investors or via private capital funneled through the World Bank to productive, revenue-producing projects. The money was to be spent on capital-goods imports and would be limited—it was believed—only by the availability of sound projects.

However, the developing countries needed to strengthen their infrastructure as well—and not only ports and railways, but also human skills and administration. The benefits of such investments would be slow to mature and were not always going to produce revenues of their own. They were the kinds of projects not attractive to private investors; potentially, therefore, they should be financed by the World Bank. However, many productive projects, such as in education, produced benefits that could not be exported and converted into the hard currency needed to repay Bank loans. Furthermore, the Bank could not lend to countries that were deemed uncreditworthy without jeopardizing its own ability to borrow in capital markets. Many of the poorest countries were therefore excluded from Bank lending and needed concessional aid to develop.

The Build-up to IDA

Although Western Europe and Japan had regained their prewar levels of production by the mid-1950s, the United States still dominated the world economy. With only 6 percent of the world population, it produced 40 percent of world output, and its average income was three times higher than Europe's, nine times higher than Japan's, and 50 times higher than incomes in the developing world. The United States therefore played a crucial part in all new initiatives designed to promote development.

The success of the Marshall Plan and the tensions of the cold war encouraged the United States to set up aid programs for the developing countries. Those programs clearly had political, strategic, and military objectives, as well as economic ones. The first major effort, the so-called Point Four, was established in 1951 by President Harry Truman. It made a major effort in technical assistance (through the provision of advisers and training, for example), but left the job of capital funding largely to private investors and the Export-Import Bank.

The deficiencies in this approach soon became apparent. In 1957, the United States set up the Development Loan Fund to provide concessional long-term project and nonproject loans. Some European countries gradually established similar programs, initially aimed at assisting former colonies to make the transition to independence. Over the years, these and other noncolonial powers developed aid programs for countries with which they had close commercial, trade, and strategic links. For instance, in 1950, the United Kingdom established the Colombo Plan to finance technical assistance and advice for the Commonwealth countries of South and Southeast Asia. By 1960, 40 percent of concessional aid was being provided by Western Europe and Japan.

In the United Nations, the developing countries, their numbers bolstered by the newly independent former colonies, pressed their case for new sources of international development finance under UN auspices. The Bank, they argued, could not make a significant contribution to their massive investment requirements; even if it could, the terms and conditions of its lending were restrictive. In 1949, a UN economic development agency funded by donors was proposed, which would make low-interest loans for a variety of development purposes. The United States replied that developing countries should look primarily to private investors, with the Bank assisting on projects that were less attractive to them. The Bank's Board and senior staff concurred. In their view, the functions being proposed in the United Nations either were not needed or could be performed by the Bank. Any softening of Bank terms would amount to intergovernmental grants, they thought, and would change the financial character of the institution.

Throughout the 1950s academic and official circles actively studied and debated the financing of development. In the United States, a report to President Truman in 1951 concluded that some important projects could not be financed entirely by loans. The report recommended the creation of an International Development Authority, managed by the Bank and receiving and making grants. This view gained considerable support in the United Nations, which called for an Authority that could eventually make grants of $3 billion a year largely to finance industrialization. Despite opposition, the idea continued to be debated and refined, and reemerged as a proposed Special United Nations Fund for Economic Development (SUNFED). For the most part, the Bank continued to resist these suggestions. Some industrial countries supported the creation of a body like SUNFED, but were wary of its being controlled directly by the United Nations. The search for alternatives eventually led to the establishment of IDA.

Support for a multilateral aid agency stemmed from the growing recognition that a real problem existed, particularly in the Asian subcontinent. In India, the Second Plan, which emphasized rapid industrialization, had failed to produce the expected economic benefits. Food shortages reflected growing population and stagnating agricultural production. The growing size of its debt made India unable to borrow the funds for additional food imports, and there was little growth in export earnings despite the industrialization effort. In 1958, the concerned donors formed the India Aid Consortium, chaired by the Bank, in order to establish a cooperative effort for international assistance, followed shortly by a similar effort for Pakistan. It was clear that the situation could only be helped by a large influx of concessional assistance.

In the United States, there were three other factors that continued to give impetus to the establishment of IDA:

- A desire to share the "aid burden" more widely. The United States felt that it was financing a large proportion of defense spending that covered the other countries of the West, in addition to providing the bulk of foreign aid. Rising balance-of-payments deficits increased the American determination to place more responsibility for both aid and defense on the reviving economies of Europe and Japan. In 1960, it initiated the establishment within the OECD of the Development Assistance Committee (DAC) to help ensure the coordination of aid programs and the monitoring of other countries' aid efforts.
- A growing feeling that aid should be channeled through multilateral agencies, so that it would become less political and more effective in promoting development. In 1959, the United States became the main contributor to the establishment of the Inter-American Development Bank, and later channeled a large amount of concessional aid through its Social Progress Trust Fund.
- A large American stockpile of the currencies of developing countries prompted new ideas on how to use it. In 1954, a law (widely known as PL480) was passed authorizing the United States administration to dispose of surplus agricultural production to developing countries and accept repayment in the recipient's own currencies. The Development Loan Fund could also accept repayment in local currencies.

In February 1958, Senator Mike Monroney proposed that these and other resources, including contributions from other governments, should finance the creation of IDA. The new body's purpose would be to make long-term loans at low rates of interest to the developing countries, operating as an affiliate of the World Bank. Eugene Black, then President of the World Bank, welcomed the proposal, dropping his previous opposition to concessional loans. The Japanese supported the idea, as did most developing countries. The European reaction, however, was mixed. Germany and the United Kingdom opposed the plan initially, on the grounds that it would undermine the Bank's credit standing. France felt it was already giving enough concessional aid on a bilateral basis.

After some discussion and modification of the original Monroney proposal, the United States Treasury proposed the establishment of IDA, and this was endorsed by the Bank's Governors at the Annual Meeting in October 1959. The Executive Directors were given the task of drawing up Articles of Agreement for the new institution, guided by the American proposals, which envisaged a separate body within the Bank. An alternative would have been to amend the Articles of Agreement of the Bank itself to accommodate IDA, but there was a danger that this would open the way for further amendments which the United States and others wished to avoid. Although IDA was conceived as a separate legal entity, it would operate under the Bank's management and share the same staff and procedures.

The United States proposed an initial fund of $1 billion, to be subscribed by the 68 members of the Bank in proportion to their share of the Bank's capital, which had in turn been determined by their relative shares of world trade and reserves in 1947.[1] Although several European members felt that some formula based on ability to pay would be fairer, the subscription formula prevailed. The Nordic countries and the Netherlands wanted an IDA that was larger than $1 billion, that was open to countries that were not Bank members, and that could give grants. These suggestions were rejected, largely because the United States administration felt it would be impossible to obtain congressional approval for a larger, more open institution.

The Establishment of IDA

The final Articles of Agreement for IDA were completed in January 1960 and became effective in September, when the agreement of 80 percent of the industrial-country members was attained. It is clear that the new Association was intended as an integral part of a broader international framework. A "... healthy development of the world economy and balanced growth of international trade," stated IDA's Articles of Agreement, will be "conducive to the maintenance of peace and world prosperity." The acceleration of economic development in the less-developed areas was seen to be in the interest of the international community as a whole. The role of the Association was to promote development through the provision of "... finance to meet their important development requirements on terms which are more flexible and bear less heavily on the balance of payments than those of conventional loans ..." thereby furthering the objectives of the Bank itself. IDA had thus emerged as a facility that allowed the Bank to make project loans in countries not suitable for normal Bank borrowings and not having recourse to other sources of finance.

In other ways, including organization and membership, the Articles parallel those of the IBRD. Finance, for instance, shall "... except in special circumstances, be for specific projects," wording similar

to those in the IBRD's Articles. As with the IBRD, the staff was left free to interpret "special circumstances" and "specific projects." The report by the Executive Directors indicates, however, that IDA was intended to be somewhat more flexible than the IBRD about the types of projects it financed. The Association was to support anything of high developmental priority "whether or not the project is revenue-producing or directly productive." Specific mention is given to possible projects in such areas as water supply, sanitation, and housing, although "it is likely that a major part of the Association's financing is likely to be for projects of the type financed by the Bank."

The Articles called for an initial capitalization of $1 billion, with $763 million coming from the industrial countries. They were to pay 100 percent of their subscription in convertible currency or gold, while the developing countries paid only 10 percent in convertible currency and gold and the rest in local currency. All countries were given a minimum of 500 votes (0.25 percent of the total) regardless of their subscription. In this way, the developing countries acquired 31 percent of the voting rights without having to put in more than a token amount of hard currency.

The Articles clearly foresaw the need for additional subscriptions, although they were expected only once every five years. The Articles also allowed for the possibility of supplementary finance from members, and for IDA itself to borrow money and guarantee loans or securities. All developing countries that were members of IDA were eligible to receive credits; there was no specific restriction to low-income countries, and the allocation of lending was left to the staff and the Executive Directors to work out.

Although IDA was financed by grants, its founders felt that it should make loans rather than grants, since this would ensure that the money would be used more productively and would tie IDA's operations more closely to the IBRD. However, the Association was allowed to "... provide financing in such form and on such terms as it may deem appropriate." The Articles of Agreement did not specify repayment terms; indeed, they permitted repayment in local currency, which would have had the effect of making a loan very much like a grant. Concerned about accumulating large amounts of local currency, however, the staff of IDA proposed terms that were repayable in foreign exchange but extremely concessional. IDA credits, it was decided,

---

1. Although the United States' holdings of other currencies had been instrumental in generating support for IDA, they could not be used to meet the capital subscription. Special donations of the currencies of other countries could be made with the approval of the issuing country and acceptance by IDA, but in fact none have been accepted or offered.

would have a 50-year maturity and repayments would begin after a 10-year grace period. Loans would carry no interest, but a service fee of 0.75 percent on the disbursed balance would be levied to cover IDA's administrative costs. Although IDA members discussed the possibility of varying terms to suit individual borrowers or certain projects, this was not done—in part because it was recognized that more advanced low-income countries could receive a "blend" of IDA and IBRD lending (discussed in more detail in Chapter 3).

The Replenishment of IDA

IDA officially came into being in September 1960. By the end of its first fiscal year (June 1961), it had made four loans—for highway development in Honduras, India, and Chile and for an irrigation project in Sudan. Fears that there would be a dearth of adequately prepared projects proved groundless; the demand for IDA was so great that by 1962 it was clear that it would need more money much earlier than expected. Members therefore began negotiating a replenishment for the three fiscal years 1965–67, thus establishing the practice of preparing replenishments at three-year intervals.

Since 1965, IDA has been replenished six times, each time by enough to boost the real value of its annual commitments (see Table 1.1). The objective of increasing the real value of IDA's finance has always been widely shared, but accelerating inflation in recent years has meant that the real increase has been less than what was intended. The size of each increase has often been the subject of intensive bargaining, but no formula for deciding it has ever been agreed on. For IDA-6, donors agreed to contribute the same proportion (0.046 percent) of their

Figure 1.1. Composition of Contributions to IDA
(percentage)

GDP as they had provided in the previous replenishment, thus tying the real growth in IDA to the expected real growth in GDP.

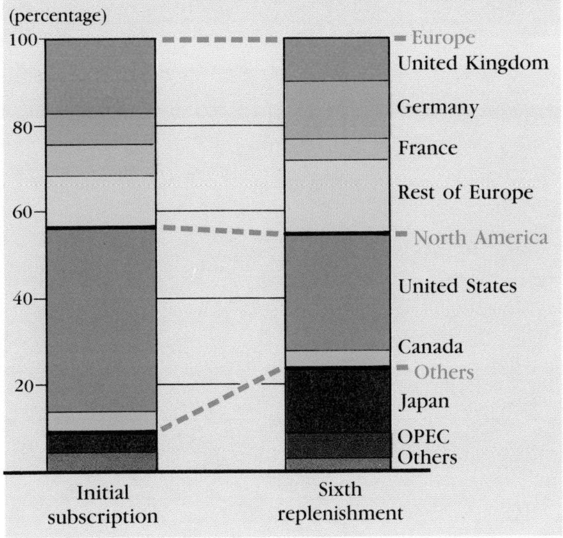

The replenishment process has never been easy, being dogged by the problem of burden sharing and by delays in payments by the United States. Other issues that have complicated replenishments include the adjustment of voting rights, the maintenance of the value of contributions against changes in exchange rates, the balance-of-payments impact of IDA contributions, and the allocation of IDA's funds among the developing countries.

Burden Sharing

In general, IDA has followed the practice that donors would more or less maintain their shares of previous replenishments. Although requests for significantly smaller shares have generally been opposed (since that would mean larger shares for the other donors), adjustments have been made for changes in relative economic strength. Thus, on one hand, the U.S. share fell from 42 percent of the original subscription to 27 percent of IDA-6 (see Table 1.2 and Figure 1.1), while the share for the United Kingdom declined from 17 percent to 10 percent. On the other hand, Japan's share has increased from 4 percent to 15 percent over the same period, and the German share has risen from 7 percent to 13 percent. (This issue is discussed further in Chapter 6.) Over the years there have also been voluntary increases and special contributions by several countries in excess of their normal shares.

Table 1.1. Replenishment of IDA Resources, 1961–83
(millions of dollars)

	Current dollars	1981 dollars
Initial (1961–64)	757	3,128
IDA-1 (1965–68)	745	2,844
IDA-2 (1969–71)	1,271	3,466
IDA-3 (1972–74)	2,441	4,495
IDA-4 (1975–77)	4,501	6,200
IDA-5 (1978–80)	7,732	8,688
IDA-6 (1981–83)	12,000	11,204
Total	29,447	40,025

Table 1.2. Shares for Major IDA Donors, 1961–83
(percentage of total contributions)

	Initial (1961–64)	*IDA-1* (1965–68)	*IDA-2* (1969–71)	*IDA-3* (1972–74)	*IDA-4* (1975–77)	*IDA-5* (1978–80)	*IDA-6* (1981–83)
United States	42	42	38	39	33	31	27
United Kingdom	17	13	12	13	11	11	10
France	7	8	8	6	6	5	5
Fed. Rep. of Germany	7	10	9	10	11	11	13
Canada	5	6	6	6	6	6	4
Japan	4	6	5	6	11	10	15
Italy	2	4	4	4	4	4	4
Nordic group	4	4	10	7	7	7	6
OPEC	1	—	—	—	1	8	6
Others	11	7	8	9	10	7	10
Total	100	100	100	100	100	100	100

These special contributions have often helped to resolve disputes on burden sharing. Under IDA-2, for example, when some countries requested a reduction in their shares, five other countries—Canada, Denmark, Finland, the Netherlands, and Sweden—offered supplementary contributions totaling $17.5 million. A special supplementary contribution of $5.8 million, not carrying voting rights, was made by Sweden and repeated in subsequent replenishments. Switzerland, which is not a member of the Bank and is therefore not eligible for membership in IDA, made a SwF52 million interest-free loan to IDA-2 followed by a similar loan of SwF130 million under IDA-3. A proposed loan of SwF200 million for IDA-4, however, was defeated by the Swiss electorate in a special referendum.

Over time, a growing share of the burden has been taken up by the more advanced developing countries. Under IDA-3, Ireland, Spain, and Yugoslavia agreed to make contributions in usable currencies totaling $10 million. Israel, Spain, and Yugoslavia made supplementary contributions in convertible currencies to IDA-4. In IDA-5, the Republic of Korea, Saudi Arabia, and the United Arab Emirates joined the ranks of hard-currency contributors, and Kuwait increased its contribution in line with the industrial countries.

Voting Rights

To avoid adjusting voting rights, IDA-1 and IDA-2 had been replenished by supplementary contributions (which did not carry voting rights) rather than by increases in subscriptions. As a result, by 1971 some countries' votes had come to differ substantially from their cumulative share of total contributions. Members therefore agreed under IDA-3 that the voting rights of industrial countries would be determined by their cumulative share of the total finance provided. To avoid a reduction in their voting power, developing countries were also allowed to make additional subscriptions payable entirely in their own currencies. The voting-rights system established in connection with IDA-3 has basically been followed ever since (see box on voting rights).

Maintenance of Value

For the first three replenishments, all contributions to IDA had been expressed in 1960 U.S. dollar equivalents. After the devaluation of the dollar in December 1971 (by 18 percent against the currencies of its major trading partners) and the switch to floating exchange rates, this system became increasingly unwieldy. Under IDA-4, members therefore agreed that industrial countries would make their contributions in a stated amount of their own currencies, without any obligation to maintain the value of these payments in the event of exchange-rate changes.[2] This system was maintained in IDA-5 and IDA-6, but in the latter, donors were also allowed to express their contributions in dollars or SDRs. This has complicated the management of IDA's funds, since changes in exchange rates can alter the amount of money at IDA's disposal. The donors have agreed,

2. Actually donors negotiate their subscriptions in terms of U.S. dollars, and then convert their contributions back to their own currencies using the exchange rates prevailing at some agreed date.

Voting Rights

For their initial subscriptions, original IDA members received 500 membership votes, plus one additional subscription vote for each $5,000 (1960 dollars) they subscribed. This formula meant that the distribution of voting rights in IDA was approximately the same as in the IBRD. But the voting power of smaller members, which had been diluted in the IBRD because of successive capital subscription increases, was strengthened in IDA by giving members relatively more membership votes, in comparison to the total votes available, than was the case in the IBRD at that time.

Under IDA-1 and IDA-2, members made supplementary contributions not having voting rights. During negotiations for IDA-3, it was agreed that the voting rights of the industrial countries should be adjusted to reflect the relative size of their cumulative contributions. Short of amending the Articles of Agreement, the only way for effecting such an adjustment was to give additional votes to the donors by authorizing them to make additional subscriptions to IDA. But this also raised difficulties. Under the Articles of Agreement, developing-country members had to be given an opportunity to increase their subscriptions so as to maintain their relative voting power. These "preemptive rights" to make additional subscriptions would indeed preserve the voting power of the developing countries, but only if it could be done without substantial financial cost.

Accordingly, the voting power of industrial-country members was adjusted to correspond (except for membership votes) to their respective shares of their combined, cumulative contributions. IDA-3 subscriptions carried additional subscription votes at the rate of one vote for each $80 (1960 dollars) contributed. For IDA-4, IDA-5, and IDA-6, the rate was set at $25 (current dollars) per subscription vote.

To avoid diluting the voting power of the smaller (mostly developing-country) members, extra membership votes were also accorded. The total of each country's membership votes is maintained at 0.25 percent of the total potential subscription votes. As a result, the number of membership votes available to each country has now increased from the original 500 to 9,900.

Nominally, both industrial and developing countries get their additional subscription votes at the same rate. But developing countries are authorized to make their extra subscriptions entirely in their own currency. Furthermore, industrial countries pay a much higher effective "price" per subscription, because their much larger additional contributions do not carry voting rights. Under IDA-6, for example, for each $25 entitling them to one subscription vote, they have to make a contribution of $10,279.60 that does not carry any voting rights.

From a practical point of view, voting rights may not seem all that important. Most matters are decided by consensus, and formal votes of the IDA Executive Directors are rare. Nor does the composition of IDA's Board of Executive Directors depend on members' voting rights, since the Executive Directors of the Bank are ex officio the Executive Directors of IDA. However, the considerable efforts devoted to setting up and reviewing IDA's elaborate voting-rights system reflect its symbolic significance in the eyes of IDA members. IDA is both a financial and a cooperative institution; its current voting system represents an attempt to do justice to both these characteristics. It combines and tempers a weighted voting structure dependent on capital contributions—an important principle for many donors—with safeguards that recognize the need for all members to be adequately represented (see Annex Table 1 for details on past and current voting rights).

---

however, that shortfalls in resources under one replenishment could be covered by contributions under subsequent replenishments.

Procurement

Because of growing balance-of-payments deficits in the 1960s, the U.S. administration requested that its contribution to IDA-2 should be tied to the amount of American goods and services bought as the result of IDA loans. Instead, it was finally agreed that the drawdown of the United States contribution would initially be limited to the amounts that American suppliers would receive from IDA-connected procurement; the other donors would make up the difference in the form of increased drawdown on their contributions, with the United States then making good its total subscription later. With the easing of U.S. balance-of-payments problems after 1971, this arrangement did not have to be continued in subsequent replenishments.

Country Allocations

During IDA-2 negotiations, members raised the important issue of the allocation of IDA's funds among countries. Although some early credits had gone to middle-income countries, chiefly in Latin America, members generally agreed that IDA should concentrate on the low-income countries (roughly, those with per capita incomes of less than $300 in 1968). Above this level there would be a "strong presumption against" further IDA lending, though not an absolute bar. Under the initial subscription and first replenishment, however, about 70 percent of IDA's resources had been allocated to the two largest borrowers, India and Pakistan. While this share was not unreasonable considering the large populations in these countries, there was considerable pressure to reduce it so as to favor others not as well served by bilateral aid. Thus the management recommended, and the donors agreed, to a limit of 40 percent for India and 12.5 percent for Pakistan.

These guidelines were adjusted again after the emergence of Indonesia and Bangladesh as IDA borrowers.

Procedural Delays

For each replenishment to become effective, countries must commit a combined total equal to 80 percent of the replenishment. Delays by the U.S. Congress, which authorizes and appropriates the funds, can therefore hold up the entire replenishment process, because the United States has always contributed more than 20 percent of each replenishment. Unlike the European parliamentary system, the U.S. executive branch does not automatically receive the support of the majority party in the legislature. The authorizing legislation for IDA-1 was voted down by the House of Representatives, and the executive branch had to mount a major effort to restore it. As a result, the American contribution was delayed, and the replenishment became effective three months later than planned.

The protracted negotiations for IDA-2 and the subsequent delay in obtaining congressional approval of the U.S. contribution created a slowdown in IDA operations in 1968. Continuation of lending was accomplished through the willingness of most donors to put some or all of their contributions at IDA's disposal, even though the replenishment was not at the time legally effective and notification by the largest contributor was not ensured. As a result, IDA commitments, which had been rising fairly steadily between 1961 and 1967, dropped from $354 million in the 1967 fiscal year to $107 million in fiscal 1968, and a number of projects were financed by IBRD loans instead of through IDA. Similar delays and advance contributions occurred under IDA-3.

The authorization bill for IDA-4 was initially de-feated in the House of Representatives, but this was later reversed after an intensive lobbying effort, and IDA-4 was able to begin on time. The United States intended to spread its contribution over four years, however, and payment of the United States contribution was not completed until 1981. Thus the United States began IDA-5 while still having to complete payments on IDA-4, and this further complicated the approval of its IDA-5 contribution. While the Carter administration succeeded in having Congress pass the IDA-5 authorization on time, and also make good the arrears, the appropriation of the actual funds was delayed.

In an attempt to prevent delays over IDA-6, other donors initially agreed to make their contributions available in proportion to the share contributed by the United States. Indeed, the U.S. Congress did not authorize the $3.24 billion that the administration had originally pledged to contribute, nor did it appropriate the first installment by the time IDA-6 was to become effective, in July 1980. Without this contribution, IDA lending would have had to be interrupted until fresh funds were made available. Despite their pro rata stipulation, many other donors therefore agreed to pay their first installments in full so that IDA could continue its work. Nevertheless, they agreed that the pro rata provisions would apply to the second and third tranches.

When the second American installment fell short of the expected contribution, the application of the pro rata rule limited IDA's commitment authority in the 1982 fiscal year to $2.6 billion, about $1.5 billion short of the program earlier approved by the Board. The first two installments from the major shareholders were thus only 60 percent of what had initially been agreed. Faced with this shortfall, some donors decided in 1982 to release their second installments in full.

2 IDA in Perspective

This chapter looks at IDA's role over the past two decades in the development efforts of low-income countries and the aid efforts of donors. In particular, it considers how IDA has helped meet the developing countries' needs for external resources and how it fits into the donor countries' programs of bilateral and multilateral economic assistance.

Development and IDA

Independence came to much of the developing world less than 20 years ago and economic development has been a formal goal for a relatively short time. Nevertheless, considerable progress has already been made. Among today's middle-income countries, average per capita output rose almost two and a half times in real terms in the past 30 years, from some $570 in 1950 (1980 dollars) to $1,400 in 1980. This is much better performance than industrial countries achieved in similar periods of their own development. Many middle-income countries that have advanced rapidly in this period are former IDA recipients—countries such as Colombia, Indonesia, the Republic of Korea, Thailand, and Turkey.

But among today's low-income countries, where IDA commits more than 80 percent of its resources

and where some 700 million people live in poverty, per capita income rose by about one-half, from $150 (1980 dollars) in 1950 to $230 in 1980. This is a gain of only $80 per person in 30 years—though significant gains have been made in combating illiteracy, improving education and health, and lowering mortality and fertility (see Figure 2.1).

The low-income oil-importing countries depend heavily on export earnings and foreign capital to finance their investment programs, and they have been seriously affected by the deteriorating international environment. Most export primary commodities, for which demand has grown more slowly than demand for manufactures. Thus, the volume of their exports has grown at an annual rate of only 4 percent since 1970, compared with 7 percent for the middle-income countries. Moreover, these countries suffered a substantial deterioration in their terms of trade. While export prices rose at an annual rate of 11 percent after 1970, import prices rose at an annual rate of 16 percent, thus offsetting the small gains in export volume.

These changes adversely affected the balance of payments of low-income countries. Current account deficits of low-income oil importers rose from $1.7 billion in 1970 to over $12 billion in 1980, a considerable real increase. These deficits represented

Figure 2.1. Progress in Income, Health, and Education, 1950–80

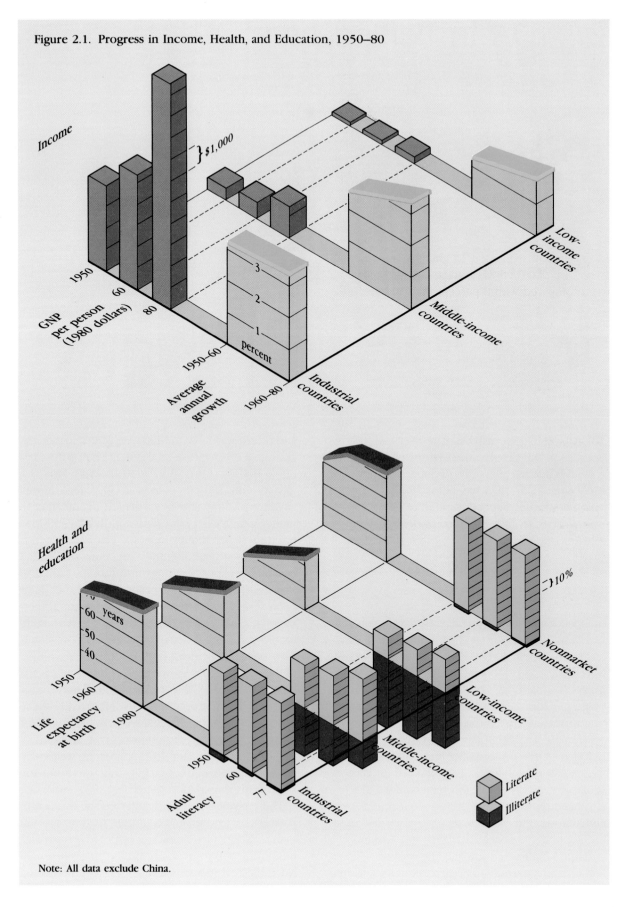

Note: All data exclude China.

4.7 percent of GNP in 1980, compared with 1.9 percent in 1970.

A large current account deficit reflects availability of funds but is an inadequate measure of needs. While middle-income countries can rely on private capital to finance 70 percent of their current account deficits, private loans and direct investment cover only 10 percent of these deficits of low-income countries. They are thus more dependent on official development assistance (ODA) from bilateral and multilateral sources. In 1970, ODA flows covered more than 90 percent of the current account deficits of low-income countries, while in 1980—despite increases in ODA—they covered only 65 percent. IDA's own role expanded. In 1980, IDA represented 16 percent of ODA flows going to low-income countries, compared with 8 percent in 1970 (see Table 2.1). Thus IDA, which financed about 10 percent of the current account deficit, is an important element in the balance of payments of these countries, although by no means the dominant or the most critical one.

It is difficult to define the "needs" of the low-income countries for assistance. However, the fact that in 1980 low-income countries drew down their foreign-exchange reserves by $2.6 billion to pay the higher cost of imports suggests that available financing was less than what was required. Drawing down reserves is, obviously, a short-term solution. Unless the low-income countries can find ways to accelerate export earnings or find new sources of concessional capital, they will have to reduce im-

Table 2.1. Balance of Payments of Low-income Countries, 1970 and 1980
(millions of dollars)

	1970	1980
Current account balance[a]	−1,675	−12,115
Direct private investment, net	142	154
Private loans	1	1,010
Official development assistance, net	1,570	7,945
Of which: IDA	128	1,245
Other capital	230	426
Changes in reserves[b]	−268	2,580
Current account balance as a percentage of GNP	1.9	4.7
IDA as a percentage of ODA	8.1	15.7

Note: Excludes China.

a. Balance of trade in goods and services plus private transfers.

b. Negative sign indicates an increase.

Table 2.2. IDA's 10 Largest Borrowers, 1961–81

	IDA commitments, 1961–81 (millions of dollars)	Gross IDA disbursements as a percentage of gross domestic investment		
		1970	1975	1980
India	9,566.2	0.6	2.4	1.6
Bangladesh	1,788.2	—	16.8	13.1
Pakistan	1,446.9	1.7	1.5	1.8
Egypt	981.2	—	1.1	0.9
Indonesia	931.8	0.8	1.6	0.3
Tanzania	631.5	2.8	3.6	3.1
Sudan	595.5	(.)	2.2	3.6
Sri Lanka	536.6	0.3	2.3	1.5
Kenya	458.3	1.6	1.8	1.5
Ethiopia	443.1	2.0	7.6	7.9
IDA average for all recipients	—	0.8	1.4	1.1

ports in the future, with a consequent reduction in output and growth.

As IDA has grown, it has become a more important source of finance in recipient countries, not only for the balance of payments, but also for total investment. In aggregate terms, however, it has never constituted more than 2 percent of total investment in these countries (see Table 2.2), although it has been relatively more important in the smaller countries. IDA inflows are a large share of total investment, for example, in Burundi, Rwanda, Benin, Mali, the Gambia, Senegal, Guinea, the Central African Republic, Nepal, and Haiti.[1] Of the countries in which IDA disbursements have exceeded 5 percent of domestic investment, almost all are designated as "least developed" and most are in Sub-Saharan Africa. But of IDA's 10 largest recipients, only Bangladesh and Ethiopia rely on IDA for more than 5 percent of their investment.

In particular sectors, such as agriculture, transport, and power, IDA has been a more important source of finance, particularly in some of the smaller countries. As shown in Chapters 4 and 5, however, it would be erroneous to judge IDA's impact by the size of its contribution to investment financing. IDA's influence on policy reform, on creating viable development institutions, and on general economic and sector analysis is perhaps its most important contribution to development in member countries.

1. These IDA clients accounted for only $1.4 billion in total commitments (1961–81), however.

Table 2.3. Net Official Development Assistance, 1960–80
(billions of 1980 dollars)

	1960	1970	1980	Average annual percentage change 1970–80
DAC countries	15.8	18.2	27.3	4.1
OPEC	—	0.9	7.0	22.3
Others	—	2.5	1.8	−3.0
Total	15.8	21.6	36.1	5.3
Amount of ODA to multilaterals	2.0	3.3	10.0	11.6
Amount of ODA to IDA	0.5	1.5	3.1	7.4
Percentage of ODA to multilaterals	12.6	15.5	28.1	
Percentage of ODA to IDA	3.3	7.1	8.7	

Note: Data are based on note deposit contributions to, not disbursements by, multilateral organizations.
Source: DAC.

Aid and IDA

Over the last 20 years the volume of official aid flows has increased significantly, as has the number of countries giving aid and the share of aid going through multilateral channels. Official development assistance more than doubled in real terms between 1960 and 1980 (see Table 2.3). Of the $36 billion of assistance in 1980, 75 percent came from DAC countries and 20 percent from OPEC countries. Over the period, the share of ODA going through multilateral agencies rose sharply, from 13 percent to 28 percent; IDA's share rose from about 3 percent to 9 percent, so that it accounted for roughly 30 percent of all multilateral aid.

The United States and the OPEC countries each provided a fifth of all ODA in 1980; Japan, Germany, and France each provided about half that much (see Figure 2.2). This distribution reflects a major shift over the preceding two decades: although the United States remains the single largest donor in absolute terms, its share of total ODA dropped from about 55 percent in 1960 to 20 percent in 1980, while the shares of Germany, Japan, and the OPEC countries

Table 2.4. Official Development Assistance for Selected Countries

	Total ODA 1980 (millions of dollars)	ODA as a percentage of GNP			Multilateral aid as a percentage of ODA 1980	IDA as a percentage of ODA 1980
		1960	1970	1980		
Australia	667	0.37	0.59	0.48	27.4	11.8
Belgium	595	0.88	0.46	0.50	24.0	—
Canada	1,075	0.19	0.41	0.43	38.3	13.7
Denmark	474	0.09	0.38	0.73	45.9	9.4
France	4,162	1.35	0.66	0.64	17.3	4.0
Fed. Rep. of Germany	3,567	0.31	0.32	0.43	35.3	14.6
Italy	683	0.22	0.16	0.17	89.2	46.4
Japan	3,353	0.24	0.23	0.32	40.6	18.7
Netherlands	1,630	0.31	0.61	1.03	25.5	6.0
Norway	486	0.11	0.32	0.85	42.6	8.9
Sweden	962	0.05	0.38	0.79	26.8	—
United Kingdom	1,851	0.56	0.41	0.35	*44.8*	*22.8*
United States	7,138	0.53	0.32	0.27	38.8	15.0
DAC total	27,256	0.51	0.34	0.38	35.2	13.2
Kuwait	1,188	—	5.81	3.88	*16.2*	*6.7*
Saudi Arabia	3,040	—	5.02	2.60	*26.1*	*15.2*
OPEC total	6,978	—	4.04[a]	1.47	19.2	7.0

Note: Data in italic are for 1979.
a. For aid-giving members only.

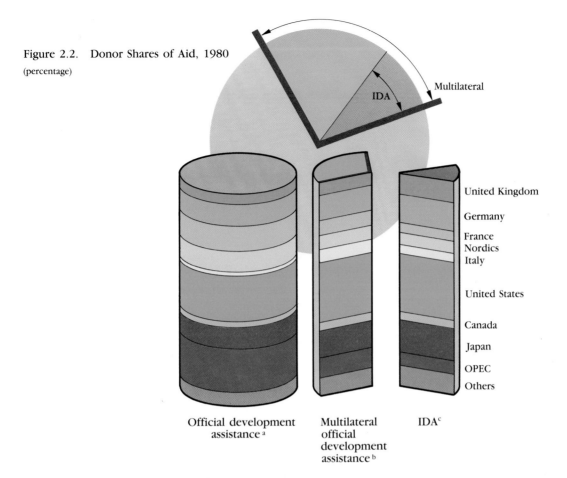

Figure 2.2. Donor Shares of Aid, 1980
(percentage)

IDA

Multilateral

United Kingdom

Germany

France
Nordics
Italy

United States

Canada

Japan

OPEC

Others

Official development
assistance [a]

Multilateral
official
development
assistance [b]

IDA [c]

a. Data represent net disbursements of DAC and OPEC countries.
b. Data represent net disbursements of DAC and OPEC countries; demand notes are recorded on the basis of date of issue.

c. Data represent shares in the sixth replenishment of IDA as negotiated, thus they are not strictly comparable with disbursements in the other parts of this figure.

increased. Much of this shift reflects changes in relative economic strength among donor countries (see Chapter 6).

Although ODA has increased substantially in the past two decades, GNP has also grown rapidly. As a result, ODA declined in relative terms—from about 0.50 percent of GNP in the early 1960s to 0.35 percent by 1970; it has fluctuated around 0.35 percent during the past decade (see Table 2.4 and Figure 2.3). The aid given by OPEC countries increased markedly in the late 1970s, averaging 1.47 percent of their GNP in 1980. For the Arab members, who provided most of the OPEC aid, assistance exceeded 2 percent of their GNP.

What is of concern to most governments is not the ratio of aid to GNP, but the level of aid in relation to their budgets. While there has been increased concern with the "affordability" of aid, it has remained a small share of most donor governments' expenditures. Aid now represents about 1 percent of DAC governments' budgets on average, ranging from 0.3 percent in Italy to 2 percent in Canada, Norway, and Sweden. Over the past 20 years, this share has generally declined, with the notable exception of the Nordic countries.[2]

Any government's capacity to increase its aid is determined partly by economic conditions and partly by public opinion. Seen in that light, the 1970s were not a propitious time for aid. Weak balance-of-payments positions—particularly pronounced in the United States and the United Kingdom—imposed constraints on some countries' willingness to expand their aid. Conversely, Japan's large external surpluses were made an argument for increasing assistance, an argument that the Japanese government itself accepted.

Even more fundamentally, slower growth and faster

2. This ratio is also influenced by the variations in the size of government expenditures over time and among countries.

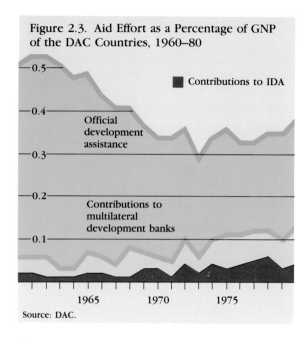

Figure 2.3. Aid Effort as a Percentage of GNP of the DAC Countries, 1960–80

■ Contributions to IDA

0.5

0.4

Official development assistance

0.3

0.2

Contributions to multilateral development banks

0.1

1965   1970   1975

Source: DAC.

inflation put new strains on government budgets, while unemployment increased spending required by social programs. The result was that foreign aid faced tough competition for funds. Governments naturally found it hard to run far ahead of public opinion, which in many countries favored cutting aid rather than other programs "closer to home" when economic conditions were difficult (see box on public opinion). Nonetheless, in many countries budgets for aid have been maintained or even increased.

Looking toward the future, several countries, including Canada, France, Germany, and the United Kingdom have announced their intention to move toward the UN's target that ODA should reach 0.7 percent of GNP. Japan's target is to double its aid in dollar terms in 1981–85 compared with the previous five years. Italy, which gives much of its ODA funds to multilateral agencies, plans to increase its previously modest levels of aid. The Nordic countries and the Netherlands, whose performance exceeds the UN target, seem intent on maintaining or even increasing their strong support for ODA, despite some economic difficulties and debate over the effectiveness of aid.

Trends in Multilateral Aid

Multilateral assistance has increased sharply, especially during the 1970s, when aid generally stag-

nated as a proportion of GNP (see Figure 2.3). The share of ODA from DAC countries going through multilateral organizations, chiefly the multilateral development banks (MDBs), climbed from 12 percent in the early 1960s to about 20 percent in the early 1970s and 34 percent in 1980. The share of OPEC aid going to multilateral organizations was 12 percent in 1980, of which about 40 percent went to Arab- or OPEC-dominated organizations. In absolute terms, MDB support grew from $582 million in 1960 to about $10.0 billion in 1980. In part, this reflects the establishment of several new channels for multilateral assistance—the Asian Development Bank, the International Fund for Agricultural Development, the African Development Fund—as well as the expansion of several existing banks.

The rising share of multilateral aid in total assistance comes at a time of generally stable or declining aid performance. Indeed, it is possible that the rise in allocations required to support the new multilateral institutions has helped to stabilize aid performance during the past several years. The rise in popularity of multilateral institutions reflects the view that aid channeled through these institutions can be particularly effective in promoting long-run development (see box on U.S. Treasury study). From the viewpoint of recipients, multilateral aid is considered somewhat more removed from shorter-term political concerns that may color bilateral aid programs. The larger multilateral development banks, including IDA, are considered able to engage in a meaningful policy dialogue and help coordinate aid efforts among donors.

But the emphasis donors place on multilateral assistance varies, as Table 2.4 suggests. Four of the five major donors—the United States, Germany, Japan, and the United Kingdom—generally contribute at least the DAC average of one-third of ODA through multilateral development banks. Other donors, such as France and the OPEC countries, have relied more heavily on bilateral assistance.

Trends in Bilateral Aid

Almost all donors maintain some bilateral aid programs, no matter how high their multilateral share. Bilateral aid programs also offer certain advantages, particularly a visible political impact. Through bilateral programs, donors can also favor certain countries or sectors, which may not be so favored by multilateral institutions.

Public Opinion

While public opinion on foreign aid varies from country to country, some broad points of similarity emerge: most favor helping poor people in poor countries but feel that current efforts are already sufficient or too large, and that problems "at home" should take priority. They are skeptical about the effectiveness of official agencies, less skeptical of private ones.

The United States

A detailed poll in 1972 showed about 80 percent of respondents regarded assistance as "morally right" and about two-thirds (up from half in the 1960s) favored development aid in principle, primarily on humanitarian grounds. But 43 percent of those asked favored cutting aid programs; roughly three-quarters believed the United States was doing more than its "fair share" in aid compared with other wealthy countries.

In a 1979 poll covering 12 government programs, "foreign aid was not only one of the three items that the public feels we are spending too much on, it was an easy first. . . . Seventeen times as many Americans (69 percent compared with 4 percent) feel we are spending too much as feel we are spending too little on foreign aid. . . ." The poll indicated that people often doubted aid's ability to gain allies and maintain peace. In addition, they felt aid went to the wrong countries and did little to relieve poverty. A remarkable 91 percent felt that "too much of our foreign assistance is kept by the leaders of poor countries and does not get to the people." Over three-quarters regarded such organizations as the Peace Corps, Red Cross, CARE, and UNICEF as effective, while the World Bank received the lowest rating of 43 percent—lower even than American corporations.

The United Kingdom

The only available detailed poll, done in 1971, showed a strong concern for problems, particularly hunger, in the developing world. Eighty percent of those asked supported the principle that wealthier countries should help poorer countries; about three-fifths believed Britain itself should help "at the moment." But only about two-fifths thought British aid levels were appropriate or should increase, while an equal number favored cutting aid. About a third actually knew roughly how much aid Britain provided; about 40 percent underestimated and about a quarter overestimated.

Most people believed aid should be adjusted to reflect affordability: arguments for aid "are not likely to have much influence against fears that the economy is in immediate danger." Two-thirds thought the United Kingdom provided more than its fair share of aid, though some 40 percent indicated willingness to reduce living standards to feed the world's poor. But the vast majority thought efforts to relieve poverty in Britain should take priority, and almost 90 percent thought most of the problems in the poorer countries could be solved if the rich people in those countries helped their own people more.

France

Public support for aid is not conspicuous in France, but public opinion polls suggest quite broad underlying support. About three-quarters of those asked in a 1975 poll regarded aid as a moral obligation; two-thirds believed it preserves cultural and political ties with France; half thought it benefited France generally; about two-fifths approved current aid levels and would even increase aid; but about a third thought the neediest may not benefit sufficiently.

Germany

In response to an opinion poll by the Ministry of Economic Cooperation in 1981, 67 percent of those questioned favored development aid in principle (against 71 percent two years earlier), while 20 percent were fundamentally opposed (against about 18 percent earlier). Although, in 1979, 53 percent approved the government's development policy, by 1981 only 47 percent did. The ministry attributed this decline to a worsening economic situation—while only about 24 percent of those questioned in 1979 found the economic situation poor, in the latest poll 74 percent found it to be so. Interestingly, 40 percent thought German aid exceeded its exports (exports were actually about DM70 billion, aid DM6 billion). In a 1974 poll, about two-thirds of those asked had singled out aid as something to cut if budget cuts were needed. Similar results were reported in a 1977 poll, when only about a tenth of those asked favored increasing aid, while the overwhelming majority thought priority should go to programs providing unemployment benefits, health care, pensions, and other benefits at home.

The Nordic Countries and the Netherlands

Development issues and aid enjoy unusually strong public support—which may help explain the high commitment of these countries to aid. Lively debate on development and aid occurs in schools and universities, trade unions, religious groups, the press and political circles. Aid is advocated largely on humanitarian grounds, to ease poverty and help meet basic needs, though political and economic interests are not absent. Less than one-quarter of the population favors reducing aid, as opposed to almost three-quarters in some other countries. Support for aid has actually grown in some countries.

In Norway support for aid has grown over the past decade; in 1980, 77 percent supported the idea of giving aid. Nineteen percent of those polled indicated that aid budgets should rise, an increase from 10 percent in 1972, despite the fact that aid performance had increased substantially over the same period. Polls from Denmark also show strong and rising support: in 1975, about half of those asked were willing to "make sacrifices for aid" despite problems of unemployment and recession—the strongest support since 1960.

Support in Sweden is also strong, though concerns have been expressed lately (by Nobel Laureate Gunnar Myrdal, for example) about the difficulties of achieving rapid development. About 50 percent of those asked in 1980 approved existing aid levels (against 60 percent in 1979), while about 15 percent favored increasing aid (about the same as in 1979).

Polls from the Netherlands indicate sustained support for aid. A decade ago, almost half of those asked favored increasing aid even though it already amounted to over 0.6 percent of GNP, and support remains strong today despite economic difficulties and some concern for aid's effectiveness and appropriate focus.

Most bilateral donors have favored countries and regions with which they have long-standing economic, political, and cultural ties. More than 40 percent of France's aid in 1980 went to its Overseas Departments and Territories. The United Kingdom has continued to direct a substantial bilateral aid to former territories in South Asia and Africa (above all India, but also Bangladesh, Pakistan, Kenya, and

Table 2.5. Net Disbursements of IDA and Bilateral Official Development Assistance by per Capita Income of Recipient
(percentage)

Per capita income of recipient [a]	IDA[b]			DAC bilateral aid			OPEC bilateral aid	
	1970	1975	1980	1970	1975	1980	1975	1980
$410 or less	72	71	80	41	41	34	24	20
$411–730	14	22	18	18	20	28	47	10
$731–1,275	5	2	1	12	11	8	2	11
$1,276–2,200	9	5	1	20	12	11	21	54
Over $2,200	—	—	—	9	16	19	6	5
Total (percentage)	100	100	100	100	100	100	100	100
Total (billions of dollars)	0.2	1.1	1.5	5.1	8.8	16.0	4.8	5.8

a. GNP per capita in 1980.
b. Fiscal years.

Table 2.6. IDA and DAC Bilateral Aid Commitments by Sector
(average percentage, 1979–80)

	Basic infra-structure	Industry	Agri-culture	Social sectors	Other[a]
IDA[b]	24	12	43	13	8
DAC bilateral aid, total[c]	28	10	18	29	15
France	15	3	8	61	13
Fed. Rep. of Germany	36	20	15	22	7
United States	15	3	36	28	18
Japan	54	16	15	8	7
United Kingdom	25	6	10	18	41
Netherlands	30	7	27	29	7
Canada	38	5	16	8	33
Sweden	11	35	21	26	7
Others	18	13	17	19	33

a. Includes nonproject loans, technical assistance, and flows unspecified by sector.
b. IDA figures based on fiscal 1980–81.
c. Excludes commitments not allocable by sector.
Source: DAC.

Zambia). Germany provided about 14 percent of its bilateral assistance to Turkey and substantial amounts to countries in Africa. In 1980, half of all OPEC aid went to Syria, Jordan, and Morocco. The United States has heavily assisted Israel, Egypt, and a number of other countries of key strategic interest. And about half of Japan's recent assistance has gone to Asia, particularly East Asia.

Most of these bilateral links are with the better-off developing countries. Middle-income countries with per capita incomes of more than $730 (1980) received about 38 percent of DAC bilateral aid in 1980 (see Table 2.5), but almost nothing from IDA. By contrast, 80 percent of IDA's lending in 1980 went to countries with per capita incomes of less than $410; these poorer countries received only a third of the bilateral aid from DAC donors (see Figure 2.4). This contrast has grown over the years. IDA's lending has been increasingly concentrated in low-income countries and, within that group, in countries designated as least developed (their share rose from 16 percent in 1970 to 25 percent in 1980). During the same period, the share of DAC bilateral loans going to low-income countries has fallen. OPEC countries, which became important donors in the mid-1970s, directed 20 percent of their bilateral assistance to low-income countries in 1980.

In addition, bilateral aid programs may have sectoral priorities different from those of multilateral programs, reflecting in part the views of individual

donors on development. For instance, IDA devotes 43 percent of its loans to agriculture, compared with only 18 percent of the bilateral aid of DAC countries (see Table 2.6). The share of social sectors, particularly health, family planning, and education, was far higher for bilateral aid than for IDA—29 percent as against 13 percent. The traditional areas of basic infrastructure absorbed about equal shares of IDA and bilateral aid as a whole. But IDA devoted a far higher share of its resources to basic infrastructure than did the United States, France, and Sweden, although notably less than Japan.

If donors perceive that multilateral agencies have

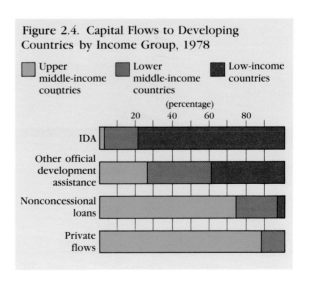

Figure 2.4. Capital Flows to Developing Countries by Income Group, 1978

a comparative advantage in a particular sector, they may tend to concentrate their aid in other areas. Over the years, the World Bank has earned a reputation for undertaking sound infrastructure and agricultural projects in low-income countries. It has not done as much, nor been as successful, in such areas as population, nutrition, and health. In some areas, bilateral donors have moved to compensate for these perceived deficiencies; to the extent that they can offer a different mix of technical assistance, training, and capital, their emphasis may suit their comparative advantage. Most donors have increasingly concentrated on reaching poor people, as well as increasing food production. To the extent that governments see IDA successfully working toward the same goals, they recognize its efforts as being complementary to, rather than in competition with, their own.

3 IDA Operations, 1961–82

During its first 22 years, IDA approved 1,302 credits amounting to $26.7 billion to 78 developing countries. Disbursements for these credits totaled $14.7 billion. Throughout, IDA's purpose has remained unchanged: to support the economic development of low-income countries by providing finance on concessional terms. However, there have been important shifts in IDA's operations, in the sources and uses of its funds, and in its role compared with other sources of finance for developing countries.

- The scale of IDA's lending, after remaining largely unchanged in real terms during most of its first decade, rose by about 11 percent a year in the 1970s.
- The sources of IDA's funds expanded as the number of contributing countries rose from 18 in IDA-1 to 33 in IDA-6.
- IDA's recipients have changed, as 27 countries "graduated" to other sources of finance, while 56 countries (most of them not sovereign nations when IDA was established) were added to the list of recipients. Only eight of IDA's current borrowers received credits during its initial operations in 1961–64.

This chapter first reviews where IDA's funds have come from. It then discusses the growth of its lend-

ing, the policies it uses to allocate funds, the patterns of its allocations, and the similarities and differences between IDA and the IBRD.

The Financing of IDA

As of June 1982, the cumulative resources available to IDA exceeded $25 billion. These resources have been provided by:

- Subscriptions to its capital and contributions from member countries ($23.6 billion).
- Transfers of net income from the IBRD ($1.6 billion).
- Repayments of credits and IDA's own net income ($280 million).

In addition, Switzerland, which is not a member country, made two interest-free loans to IDA, in 1967 and in 1973. In 1981, these loans, equivalent to $51 million, were converted to grants (see Table 3.1 and Figure 3.1).

Subscriptions and Contributions

At present, 33 countries contribute to IDA. While most of these are industrial countries, the list includes some developing members of IDA—Brazil,

Table 3.1. Resources Available to IDA for Commitment, 1961–82

(cumulative total in current dollars as of June 30, 1982)

	Millions of dollars	Percentage
Total subscriptions and supplementary resources from members	23,582[a]	92.6
United States	7,603	29.8
Japan	2,773	10.9
United Kingdom	2,766	10.9
Fed. Rep. of Germany	2,706	10.6
France	1,231	4.8
Canada	1,230	4.8
Sweden	800	3.2
Italy	747	2.9
Netherlands	699	2.8
Saudi Arabia	611	2.4
Australia	472	1.9
Belgium	370	1.5
Kuwait	365	1.4
Denmark	264	1.0
Norway	257	1.0
Others	688	2.7
Contribution by Switzerland	51	0.2
Transfers from IBRD	1,564	6.1
Other sources	280[b]	1.1
Grand total	25,477	100.0

a. Excludes $4,812 million of contributions to the sixth replenishment, and $217 million of Part II members subscriptions provided in their own currencies, that are not available for commitment. For a definition of Part II members, see the technical notes to Annex Table 1.

b. Includes repayments of $250 million, and accumulated net income through fiscal 1979 of $30 million. Does not include accumulated deficits of $198 million incurred in fiscal 1980, 1981, and 1982.

Greece, Mexico—as well as two former recipients— the Republic of Korea and Colombia.[1]

Subscriptions and contributions (also referred to as supplementary resources) provided 93 percent of the total resources available to IDA for commitment between 1961 and 1982. As of the end of fiscal 1982, $23 billion had been received from donors, including $5 billion of the $12 billion agreed to be provided under IDA-6. Upon the completion of IDA-6, contributions will total $30 billion.

Contributions have been paid largely as non-interest-bearing notes deposited with IDA. These are cashed only when money needs to be disbursed. As a result, almost $9 billion of the $23 billion that

1. A complete list of current contributors is in Annex Table 1.

donors had deposited with IDA remained uncashed at the end of fiscal 1982, pending disbursement. The large amount of uncashed contributions reflects the long lead time between IDA commitments and disbursements, which postpones the ultimate impact on the donors.

Until IDA-6, IDA's credit commitments to its borrowers were in dollars. Since the elimination of maintenance-of-value arrangements for donors' contributions after IDA-3, contributions (which in most cases are made in national currencies) have at times diverged from the value of IDA's credits as a result of exchange-rate movements.[2] To reduce the impact of currency fluctuations, credits under IDA-6 have been denominated in SDRs.

Transfers from the IBRD

Since 1964, IDA has received regular support from the IBRD. The IBRD has decided annually to transfer some of its net income to IDA following a general policy that allows such transfers if the funds are not needed for the IBRD's own purposes and thus might otherwise be available for distribution as dividends. By the end of fiscal 1982, the IBRD had authorized transfers to IDA of $1.6 billion (6 percent of IDA's total support), making the IBRD the fifth largest contributor to IDA. As with contributions from countries, actual cash drawings are made only when IDA needs the money for disbursement. IBRD contributions are drawn last, however, after the donor contributions have been exhausted. Through fiscal 1982, IDA had encashed $817 million of the funds transferred from the IBRD.

Internal Funds

Since IDA credits are highly concessional, net income and repayments have been only a minor source of funds. By the end of fiscal 1982, $250 million had been repaid. Repayments are due to accelerate as IDA's portfolio matures—$519 million is to be repaid between 1983 and 1987. Although repayments do not provide any extra resources to IDA's borrowers as a group, they allow lending to shift from former to current borrowers.

IDA's net income, after being in surplus through

2. As of June 30, 1982, the value of credits approved by IDA's Board ($26.7 billion) exceeded the value of its resources available for commitment by $1.2 billion. This difference was largely due to the impact of exchange-rate movements on the dollar value of resources provided in other currencies.

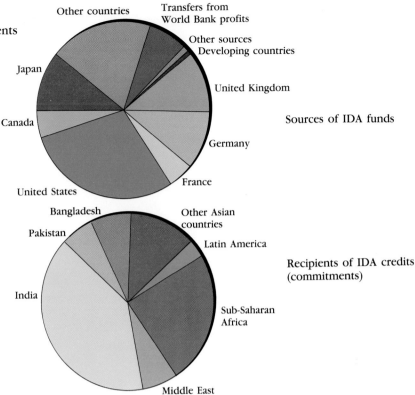

Figure 3.1. Sources and Recipients
of IDA Funds, 1961–82

(percentage based on cumulative
amounts in current dollars)

its first 15 years, turned negative in fiscal 1976 and
has remained negative. The cumulative net loss was
$168 million at the end of June 1982. Until the mid-
1970s, IDA earned substantial income on donor
contributions, which were held as investments
pending disbursement. Income from this source
declined after 1974 when donors' contributions began to be made largely in the form of non-interest-
bearing notes. Since that time, IDA's income has
been derived almost entirely from the service charge
of 0.75 percent a year it levies on the disbursed
outstanding balance of its credits. However, most
of IDA's expenses for a project are incurred just
before and after a commitment is made. This is
usually several years before the bulk of a credit is
disbursed and income from service charges is received. Although this mismatch in the timing of expenses and fee income has existed throughout IDA's
history, it has only resulted in negative overall net
income since IDA's other source of income largely
ended.

IDA's expenses are entirely in the form of a management fee paid to the IBRD, representing IDA's
share of the costs generated by the operations of
both institutions. As IDA is precluded by its Articles
from borrowing funds from the IBRD, and it wanted
to avoid using donors' contributions to meet its

administrative expenses, in 1982 IDA began to charge
its borrowers a commitment fee of 0.5 percent per
year on the undisbursed balance of new credits.

The Growth of Lending

IDA's growth has been determined by the size of
the contributions agreed among the donor countries. Between 1961 and 1968, IDA's annual commitments fluctuated between $100 million and $360
million, and averaged $229 million a year. They then
increased to an annual average of $525 million in
1969–71, and rose more than sixfold to $3.8 billion
in 1980 (see Table 3.2). A large part of this growth
reflects inflation. In constant (1982) dollars, IDA's
annual commitments more than doubled between
1970 and 1980. So did the annual number of credits,
which rose from 49 in 1969–71 to 114 in 1980. The
average size of credits fluctuated around $30 million
(in 1982 dollars) during the 1970s, about half the
average of the 1960s when nonproject lending was
more prevalent.[3]

Reflecting slower-than-anticipated contributions
from IDA-6, lending declined in 1982 to a level 30

3. Nonproject lending is discussed in detail in Chapter 4.

Table 3.2. Summary of IDA Operations, 1961–82
(millions of dollars)

	Annual average					1980	1981	1982	Total 1961–82	Average annual growth 1969–71 to 1980 (%)
	1961–68	1969–71	1972–74	1975–77	1978–80					
Credit amounts										
Current dollars	229	525	1,151	1,513	3,057	3,838	3,482	2,686	26,738	22.0
1982 dollars	976	1,523	2,277	2,257	3,656	4,396	3,728	2,686	43,362	11.2
Average size of credits										
Current dollars	14	11	14	19	28	34	30	26	21	11.9
1982 dollars	61	31	28	29	33	39	32	26	33	2.3
Disbursements										
Current dollars	192	211	488	1,192	1,232	1,411	1,878	2,067	14,657	20.9
1982 dollars	690	715	1,078	1,894	1,393	1,452	2,026	2,067	24,716	7.3
Number of credits	16	49	80	78	111	114	116	104	1,302	8.8

Note: Constant price data calculated using the Bank's commitment and disbursement deflators. Data for 1982 are preliminary.

percent below that of 1980. This reduction was accommodated partly by substituting some IBRD funds and partly by scaling back projects. The average size of IDA credits fell in 1982 to $26 million (in 1982 dollars).

IDA's funds are disbursed gradually, matching the progress of the projects for which they are committed. Between 1961 and 1982, disbursements in current dollars were just over half of commitments. Some $9.2 billion had been fully disbursed for 608 credits. The remaining credits were under disbursement as projects were being implemented; for these, disbursements had already totaled $5.4 billion, with more than $11 billion committed but still undisbursed (see Table 3.3).

The lag between commitments and disbursements means that the level of disbursements in any one year reflects commitments made years earlier. The ratio of disbursements to commitments therefore depends largely on how fast current commitments are growing in relation to past commitments. When the growth of IDA's operations accelerated in 1969–74 and 1978–80, the ratio of disbursements to commitments fell to about 40 percent. Conversely, the slowdown in the growth of IDA's commitments in 1975–77 raised that ratio to 80 percent. Over the 1970s, disbursements rose at an annual rate of 21 percent, or slightly slower than commitments, and continued to rise at that rate in 1980–82, even as commitments were declining.

Eligibility and Allocation

In determining where to lend, IDA decided in its early years to allocate funds to countries on the basis of their characteristics, rather than on the particular features of a project or sector. It was also decided that the standards for IDA projects should be the same as those of the IBRD. Although some had argued that IDA funds should be used for non-revenue-producing projects in a wide spectrum of countries, to do so would have disregarded the large differences of need among countries and the alternatives available to them. Three principal criteria have been developed to determine eligibility for funds:

- The recipient's poverty, measured by per capita income.
- The recipient's limited creditworthiness for borrowing from conventional sources.
- The recipient's economic performance, including its ability to make effective use of resources and the availability of suitable projects.

In addition to these criteria, IDA takes account of population size when determining the allocation of funds among countries, to avoid wide disparities in per capita lending levels. Thus in distributing the resources available to it, IDA takes account of four main criteria—population size, poverty, economic performance, and creditworthiness.

Table 3.3. Status of IDA Credits at the End of Fiscal 1982 by Year of Approval
(billions of dollars)

	Year of approval			Total 1961–82
	1961–71	1972–76	1977–82	
Credits approved				
Number of credits	273	395	634	1,302
Amount	3.23	6.86	16.65	26.74
Credits fully disbursed				
Number of credits	271	291	46	608
Amount	3.12	4.93	1.18	9.23
Credits disbursing				
Number of credits	2	104	588	694
Amount disbursed	0.01	1.45	3.96	5.42
Amount undisbursed	(.)	0.38	10.86	11.24
Credits canceled				
Amount	0.10	0.10	0.09	0.29

Note: Includes joint IBRD/IDA operations. The sum of disbursed and undisbursed credits does not equal the amounts approved at commitment because of the effect of exchange-rate movements on the dollar value of credits made in SDRs.

A considerable amount of judgment has been involved in applying these criteria. They do not always point in the same direction, and some are not readily quantifiable. One country may be relatively poor, but its economy may be well managed and it may be able to borrow commercially to meet its needs. Another country with a higher GNP per capita may have export earnings that fluctuate widely and hence may be deemed a poor credit risk. Although IDA's staff has tried to quantify these criteria, it has found in weighing them that judgment must still be applied case by case.

Per Capita Income

From the beginning, though not without some controversy, IDA's Board felt that IDA should lend primarily to the poorest countries. This view was formalized in 1964, when the Board agreed to a strong presumption against lending to countries with per capita incomes above $250. Although 94 percent of IDA funds had gone to countries below that level, this decision excluded four that had previously borrowed from IDA: Chile, Colombia, Costa Rica, and Nicaragua. The income ceiling has remained largely unchanged in real terms, although inflation adjustments raised it to $730 in 1980. On occasion, credits have been made to countries after they crossed the income limit, for projects already in progress. Even though the ceiling is not absolute, it has ensured that countries graduate almost automatically from IDA. This has served to minimize the scope for political influence in determining eligibility for IDA finance.

Creditworthiness

IDA is intended to supplement, not substitute for, finance from conventional sources. Limited creditworthiness—that is, a limited ability to service debt in foreign currencies—has always been required for a country to be eligible for IDA loans. Under its Articles of Agreement, IDA is barred from providing assistance if financing is "available from private sources on terms which are reasonable for the recipient or could be provided by a loan of the type made by the Bank."

Assessments of a country's creditworthiness are necessarily judgmental and are based on long-term factors. Poverty itself places severe limits on a country's ability to service debt. But while limited creditworthiness can be a function of poverty, the two are not identical; an economy may be stronger or weaker externally than it is domestically. Lack of creditworthiness has not enabled countries above the per capita income ceiling to receive IDA credits, because in such cases there is sufficient potential to gain creditworthiness over time by other means. Countries below the ceiling that were considered creditworthy have usually received both IBRD loans and IDA credits, with the more creditworthy countries receiving a higher proportion of IBRD funds. There have also been several instances in which countries that were below the ceiling received only IBRD loans. Indonesia is a case in point: though well below the per capita income limit, as a major exporter of oil it did not receive aid from IDA after the 1973–74 oil price rise and is not currently considered eligible. It did receive credits in 1978–80, however—illustrating that judgments about creditworthiness, although based on long-term considerations, are not immutable.

Performance

IDA's Articles of Agreement require it to pay "due attention to considerations of economy, efficiency, and competitive international trade and without regard to political or other noneconomic influences or considerations." Measuring performance, though inexact, has been assisted by quantitative indicators, such as savings rates and GNP growth, as well as by qualitative assessments of administration and economic management and the extent to which economic growth is broad based. The speed and direction of change is as important as the level of performance. IDA also takes into account a government's willingness to listen to advice.

In evaluating performance, IDA has tried not to penalize a country for failings that are due to external circumstances, scarcity of resources and skills, or even weak institutions; rather, the object is to alleviate these constraints. However, lending has been cut when a country's own willingness to make serious development efforts is seen to be deteriorating. Even then some limited lending has usually been continued—to preserve existing investments, to support particular institutions, to prevent further deterioration, or to provide a basis for continuing discussions on policy reform.

Regulating lending on the basis of short-term events has not been considered feasible or desirable. IDA's projects take years to plan and carry out; its whole focus is on long-term development. However, there have been cases in which countries that might otherwise have qualified for IDA were considered ineligible on performance grounds. Past examples have included Haiti, Uganda, Guinea, Equatorial Guinea, and the Central African Republic. In extreme cases—civil unrest and warfare, for example—IDA has had to suspend even its existing operations. Afghanistan and Chad have recently been in this category.

Project Availability

IDA has always insisted on economically viable projects. In its early years, the fact that some countries were better able to present projects of the right standard affected the allocation of credits. This result was criticized because it seemed to exclude some countries in obvious need. Members therefore agreed that IDA should help in the preparation of projects. Ultimate responsibility for project preparation remains with the borrower, since IDA has wanted to preserve its discretion to turn down a project, or to require modifications before it is approved. In some cases, pilot projects have included financing for preparing other and larger projects. Project preparation has also been assisted through the establishment of resident Bank missions, particularly in Africa, and through the use of technical assistance funded by the UNDP. In addition, a project-preparation facility was established by the Bank in 1975. Nonetheless, projects have been difficult to develop in some countries, with the result that they have received fewer credits than they would have otherwise.

The Distribution of Lending

As noted in Chapter 2, IDA's lending has been concentrated in the poorest countries. On a cumulative basis, 81 percent of IDA's commitments were to countries that in 1980 had per capita incomes of $410 or less; 98 percent has gone to countries with incomes of $730 or less.

IDA's list of clients has changed considerably over the past 20 years. Some 56 countries were added to the list of recipients after the initial subscription

Table 3.4. Former IDA Recipients

Country	GNP per capita (current dollars)			Fiscal year of last IDA credit
	1964	1970	1980	
Chile[a]	450	720	2,150	1961
Colombia[a]	270	340	1,180	1962
Costa Rica[a]	360	560	1,730	1962
Nigeria	100	120	1,010	1965
Dominican Republic	210	350	1,160	1973
Ivory Coast[a]	200	310	1,150	1973
Korea, Rep. of	120	250	1,520	1973
Turkey	240	310	1,470	1973
Botswana	65	110	910	1974
Ecuador	190	290	1,270	1974
Syrian Arab Republic	180	290	1,340	1974
Mauritius	140	240	1,060	1975
Morocco	170	230	900	1975
Swaziland	80	180	680	1975
El Salvador	260	300	660	1977
Paraguay	200	260	1,300	1977
Tunisia	180	250	1,310	1977
Jordan	220	250	1,420	1978
Philippines	140	210	690	1979
Thailand	110	200	670	1979
Bolivia	140	180	570	1980
Honduras	190	280	560	1980
Indonesia	70	80	430	1980
Cameroon	110	180	670	1981
Egypt	150	210	580	1981
Nicaragua	320	430	740	1981
Congo, People's Rep.	140	300	900[b]	1982
IDA eligibilty guide-line	250	375	730	

a. Received one credit only.
b. Revised subsequent to *1981 World Bank Atlas*, which showed $730.

Table 3.5. IDA Commitments by Region, 1961–82

	Millions of dollars				Percentage			
	1961–70	1971–76	1977–82	Total	1961–70	1971–76	1977–82	Total
South Asia	1,786	3,992	9,957	15,735	63	55	60	59
India	1,271	2,855	6,341	10,467	45	39	38	39
Bangladesh	—	655	1,524	2,179	—	9	9	8
Pakistan	490	224	904	1,618	17	3	6	6
Others	25	258	1,188	1,471	1	4	7	6
East Asia	216	566	921	1,703	8	8	5	6
Africa, south of the Sahara	461	1,781	4,367	6,609	16	24	26	25
North Africa and the Middle East	214	713	1,142	2,069	8	10	7	8
Latin America	145	216	261	622	5	3	2	2
Total	2,822	7,268	16,648	26,738	100	100	100	100

period, while 27 have "graduated" from IDA (see Table 3.4), on the grounds that their prospective levels of development and creditworthiness justified a reasonable amount of debt on commercial terms.

In recent years countries have tended to graduate before they reach the income ceiling, especially when oil exports have strengthened their creditworthiness. Nine of the IDA graduates are below the $730 limit, though only four are more than 10 percent below it. These four—Bolivia, Honduras, Indonesia, and Egypt—graduated within the last two years.

During the commitment period of IDA's initial subscription (1961–64), 22 countries received credits; of these only eight—India, Pakistan, Bangladesh, Ethiopia, Niger, Sudan, Tanzania, and Haiti—are still eligible in 1982. In all, 78 countries have at one time or another received IDA credits, of which 51 are currently eligible. These 51 countries have received 87 percent of IDA's total commitments.[4]

Lending has been increasingly concentrated in South Asia and Sub-Saharan Africa (see Table 3.5 and Figure 3.1). Countries in South Asia have received nearly $16 billion in commitments, 59 percent of the total between 1961 and 1982. India, IDA's largest single borrower, obtained $10.5 billion (39 percent of the total). While the share of credits to South Asia fell to 55 percent in the early 1970s, largely to accommodate new borrowers in other regions, it rose to 60 percent in the second half of the decade. This rise reflects increased lending to countries other than India, as well as the absence

of South Asian graduates. The share of lending to African countries doubled from 10 percent in the early 1960s to 20 percent in the second half of the decade, as former colonies became independent and joined IDA. During the 1970s this share has remained at about 25 percent. Latin America accounted for 5 percent of credits during 1961–70, but thereafter fell to 2 percent. With the exception of Haiti, all Latin American borrowers from IDA have become graduates. Two large borrowers in other regions, Indonesia and Egypt, have recently graduated (see map on next page).

As noted, the size of a country's population is one of the most important determinants of IDA allocations. While an attempt is made to keep per capita IDA lending roughly equal across countries, very small countries tend to receive more. IDA recipients with populations of 2 million or less had an annual average of $6.30 per capita committed to them in 1979–81, compared with an overall average of $2.50. One reason for the higher per capita lending to these small countries is that a minimum size and number of projects are considered necessary for efficient operations. The average size of projects in these countries was $9 million, compared with $32 million for all countries (see Table 3.6).

The counterpart of this "small-country bias" is the lower-than-average per capita lending to the populous countries of South Asia. During the first four years of IDA, India received about 50 percent of commitments and Pakistan about 23 percent. In 1968, during discussions about IDA-2, many members felt that these large countries were tending to dominate IDA's operations. It was therefore agreed to limit their shares to 40 percent and 12½ percent, respectively, well below what their population size or other criteria would have indicated, particularly

4. The amounts of credits received by each country are in Annex Table 5. In addition, three countries that have recently joined IDA are eligible for credits and are expected to receive their first credit in the near future: Cape Verde, São Tomé and Principe, and Vanuatu.

in India's case. Reflecting this decision, India received an annual average of $2.00 per capita in 1979–81, compared with an average of $3.00 for all other current recipients.

In 1982, India's share in IDA's commitments fell to 34 percent, in light of the overall reduction of IDA's funds and India's stronger creditworthiness than most other IDA recipients. The reduction in lending to India by IDA was largely accommodated by increased lending by the IBRD, from which India has been a longstanding borrower. For prudential reasons, however, the IBRD limits its exposure to any one country. Disbursed loans to India by the IBRD were $1.2 billion at June 30, 1982 (4 percent of the IBRD portfolio); IDA disbursements totaled $6.0 billion. Had these IDA loans been provided by the IBRD, India's share of the portfolio would have exceeded 20 percent, which would be well beyond the prudential limit.

IDA and the IBRD

IDA is an integral part of the World Bank. In many respects—operational policies and procedures, the criteria used to appraise and approve projects, loan covenants, and staff—the IBRD and IDA are indistinguishable. Both share the work on project design and sector strategies, economic research, and the lessons learned from Bank operations. The main differences between them are the terms and patterns of their lending.

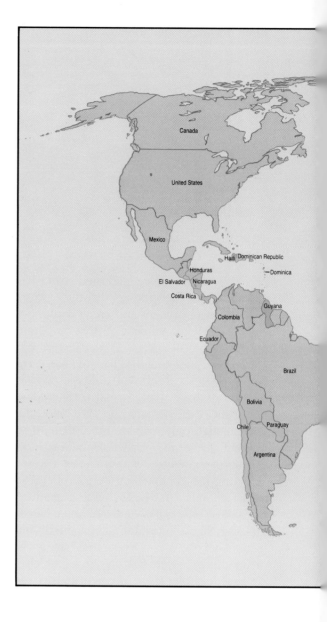

Table 3.6. IDA Commitments by Population of Recipient, 1979–81

Population of recipient	Number of countries	Population (millions)	Average annual commitments per capita (dollars)	Total commitments (millions of dollars)	Number of projects	Average size of credit (millions of dollars)[a]
Over 50 million	4	898	2.00	5,471	79	69
10.1–50.0 million	11	217	3.10	2,009	78	26
5.1–10.0 million	11	70	4.40	922	62	15
2.1–5.0 million	9	31	4.70	441	39	11
Less than 2.0 million	14	12	6.30	230	27	9
Total	49	1,228	2.50	9,073	285	32

Note: Current recipients only. This table excludes China, which received one credit of $100 million in June 1981. If China were included, the average per capita commitment would be reduced from $2.50 to $1.40.

a. Includes the IBRD component of joint IBRD/IDA projects.

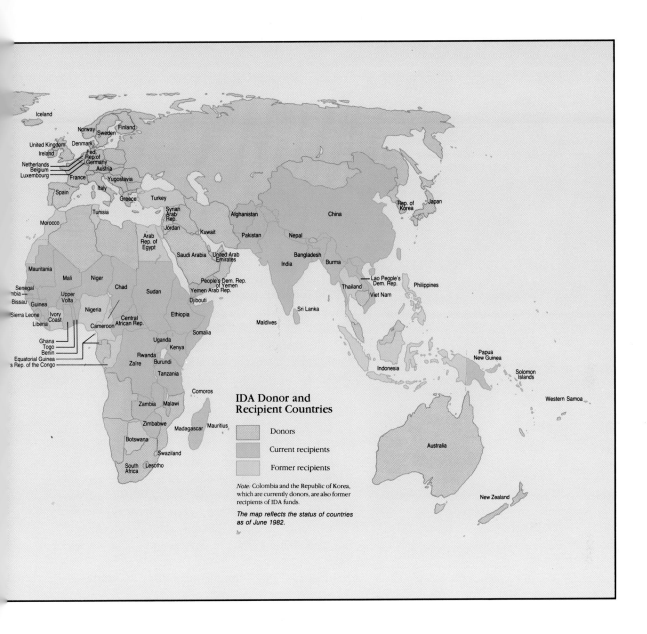

IDA Donor and Recipient Countries

Donors

Current recipients

Former recipients

Note: Colombia and the Republic of Korea, which are currently donors, are also former recipients of IDA funds.

The map reflects the status of countries as of June 1982.

Terms of Lending

The terms of IDA credits have remained essentially unchanged since 1961. Credits have a 50-year final maturity and repayments begin 10 years after the credit is signed.[5] The loans carry no interest rate, although there is a service charge of 0.75 percent a year on the disbursed balance. In January 1982, a commitment fee of 0.5 percent a year on the undisbursed balance was introduced to bring the timing of IDA's income from credits more into line with its administrative expenses, as noted above.

5. After this grace period, 1 percent of the credits is repaid in each of the next 10 years, and then 3 percent in each of the remaining 30 years.

These terms were designed to be as close as feasible to the economic equivalent of grants, while retaining the form of repayable loans (see box on measuring the concessionality of IDA credits).

For borrowers, the attractions of IDA's concessional loans are considerable. The dynamics of debt accumulation are such that, to maintain a given level of lending net of debt-service payments ("net transfer"), gross lending must grow faster than the interest rate charged. In 1982, disbursements from IBRD were $6.4 billion, more than triple the $2.1 billion disbursements from IDA. Because of the debt service on IBRD loans, however, the net transfer made by the IBRD, was only 25 percent higher than the $1.9 billion made by IDA. In terms of transfer-

done. In a number of countries, the Bank has been able to adjust the average terms of its lending by "blending" IBRD loans with IDA credits.

Patterns of Lending

Blended or not, the two institutions complement each other in their lending. Countries in the lowest income group, which received 83 percent of IDA commitments in 1977–82, obtained only 8 percent of IBRD lending; conversely, countries in the top three income groups received 66 percent of IBRD loans but only 1 percent of IDA's credits (see Table 3.8). Countries receiving a blend of IBRD loans and IDA credits have been concentrated in the $411–$730 range of per capita incomes, though six are in the lowest income group: Malawi, India, Sri Lanka, China, Pakistan, and Togo (see Figure 3.2).

The stability of the shares of each institution's lending going to particular income groups disguises changes in the membership of these groups. The 27 countries that have graduated from IDA are all now borrowers from the IBRD. Similarly, 26 countries that used to receive loans from the IBRD are no longer borrowers. While this group includes nine industrial countries that received Bank loans after World War II, it also includes some developing countries, such as Greece, Israel, Spain, and Venezuela, which are considered to have progressed far enough to make IBRD assistance unnecessary.

The shifting focus of development lending over the past 20 years has affected both IDA and the IBRD, since they share the same policies. Nevertheless,

ring resources to borrowers as a group, IDA is therefore almost as important as the IBRD, even though its commitments and disbursements are much lower. In some years, indeed, IDA's net transfer was considerably larger than the IBRD's (see Table 3.7).

Around the time IDA's terms were devised, there was considerable discussion over whether it was better to provide aid as loans or as grants. Though the intellectual debate was largely resolved in favor of grants—and most donors have moved toward grants—IDA has persisted with loans largely on practical grounds. Some donors have believed loans to be more convenient or politically acceptable. Some have thought that loans, even when they are highly concessional, are taken more seriously by recipients. Though IDA's Board has discussed the question of whether IDA's terms should be hardened or differentiated among borrowers, this has not been

Table 3.7. IDA and IBRD Gross Disbursements and Net Transfer, 1965–82
(millions of dollars)

	1965	1970	1975	1980	1982
Gross disbursements					
IBRD	606	754	1,995	4,364	6,374
IDA	222	143	1,026	1,411	2,067
Service payments[a]					
IBRD	544	813	1,375	2,984	3,960
IDA	2	12	42	101	142
Net transfer[b]					
IBRD	62	−59	620	1,380	2,414
IDA	220	131	985	1,310	1,925

a. Repayments of principal and payments of interest and other charges.

b. Gross disbursements less service payments. Figures for IBRD include transactions with former borrowers; for current borrowers, IBRD net transfer figures were 120 in 1965; 135 in 1970; 702 in 1975; 1,665 in 1980; 1,929 in 1981; and 2,774 in 1982.

Figure 3.2. Current IDA and IBRD Recipients

Per capita GNP	IDA only		IDA/IBRD blend	IBRD only	
Over $2,200				Oman Cyprus Bahamas Barbados Uruguay Yugoslavia Argentina Portugal Romania	
$1,276–2,200				Chile Mexico Brazil Algeria Fiji Seychelles Costa Rica* Panama	Malaysia Korea Rep.* Turkey* Jordan* Syrian Arab Rep.* Tunisia* Paraguay*
$731–1,275			Papua New Guinea	Ecuador* Colombia* Dominican Rep.* Ivory Coast* Guatemala Mauritius* Jamaica	Nigeria* Congo, People's Rep.
$411–730	Dominica Djibouti Solomon Islands Mauritania Yemen Arab Rep. Yemen, PDR Lesotho Ghana		Guyana Zimbabwe Zambia Liberia Senegal Kenya	Philippines* Swaziland* Thailand* Cameroon* El Salvador* Egypt* Bolivia* Honduras* Indonesia*	
$410 or less	Sudan Madagascar Niger Benin Uganda Comoros Western Samoa Equatorial Guinea Central African Rep. Guinea Tanzania Sierra Leone Haiti Maldives	Gambia Zaire Upper Volta Rwanda Burundi Mali Viet Nam Afghanistan Burma Guinea-Bissau Somalia Nepal Ethiopia Bangladesh Chad Lao PDR	Togo Pakistan China Sri Lanka India Malawi	* Former IDA recipient. Note: Reflects status of countries as of June 30, 1982. Countries are listed in desending order of 1980 per capita GNP.	

Table 3.8. Distribution of IDA and IBRD Commitments by per Capita Income of Recipient
(percentage of total commitments)

Per capita income of recipient in 1980	IDA				IBRD			
	1961–71	1972–76	1977–82	Total	1961–71	1972–76	1977–82	Total
Below $410	71	78	83	81	13	7	8	8
$411–730	16	17	16	17	9	23	26	24
$731–1,275	4	2	1	1	16	13	17	17
$1,276–2,200	9	4	0	1	32	43	36	36
Over $2,200	0	0	0	0	30	14	13	15
Total	100	100	100	100	100	100	100	100

Note: Data are based on amounts in 1982 dollars.

the sectoral distribution of their lending does vary, because each is lending to a group of very different countries. Since low-income countries tend to be heavily dependent on agriculture, IDA lending has been more concentrated in agriculture than IBRD lending (37 percent of the total compared with 22 percent). Even though resources are fungible in borrowing countries, in "blend" countries IBRD money has tended to be used for projects where revenue is going to be raised—particularly in industry and public utilities—and IDA funds used where benefits are longer term or more difficult to translate into revenue, such as projects for education and other human resources or rural development (see Table 3.9).

Aid Coordination

The World Bank has often been placed in the role of coordinating aid to particular countries. Aid consortia and consultative groups have been set up for this purpose, with the Bank serving as chair and

Table 3.9. IDA and IBRD Lending Operations by Sector, 1961–82
(percentage)

	Total commitments		Blend countries only[a]	
	IBRD	IDA	IBRD	IDA
Agriculture and rural development	22	37	14	39
Basic infrastructure	42	30	47	31
Industry	20	8	30	7
Human resource development	12	13	5	10
Other[b]	4	12	4	13

a. Countries currently eligible for resources from both the IBRD and IDA. For list, see Annex Table 4. Excludes former IDA recipients.

b. Includes program lending and technical assistance.

secretariat. Its lending through IDA has permitted the Bank to continue in this role in aid groups for the poorest countries. The first of these aid groups emerged from a series of meetings in 1958–60, convened by Eugene Black, then the Bank's President, to discuss the foreign-exchange crisis in India, and attended by that country's principal creditors and trading partners. The discussions broadened to consider India's development needs over a longer period and to find ways of ensuring that enough external finance would be available. A similar meeting was held to discuss Pakistan's request for assistance in 1960. The desire of donors to coordinate their support for these countries' development programs, along with their recognition that aid required long-term strategies, gave impetus to the establishment of IDA as well as the DAC.

During the 1960s, the number of aid groups increased, as newly independent countries wanted more aid and the principal donor countries, particularly the United States and the United Kingdom, were anxious to share the aid burden. Most of these new aid groups concentrated on a country's needs and the coordination—as opposed to commitment—of aid. By 1970, there were 14 active aid groups with 22 countries attending as donors in one or another group. All except two groups were sponsored by the Bank. The others, for Indonesia and Turkey, were sponsored by the Netherlands and the OECD—although the Bank has served as secretariat for them. Increasingly, aid groups became a forum for discussion between donors and recipients over economic policy.

There are now 21 active aid groups, of which 12 are for countries eligible for IDA assistance. The groups have tended to be confined to countries receiving relatively large amounts of aid from many sources, where the expense of meeting arrangements has seemed justified. This has meant that for a number of smaller countries, particularly in Africa,

Table 3.10. Cofinancing of IDA Projects, 1972–81

	1972–76	1977–82	Total
Number of projects with cofinancing	116	266	382
Amount of cofinancing (millions of dollars)	1,103	4,814	5,917
Cofinancing as a percentage of project cost	22	27	26
Amount of IDA contribution (millions of dollars)	1,514	6,989	8,503
IDA contribution as a percentage of project cost	31	39	38
IDA credits with cofinancing			
As a percentage of total number of IDA credits	33	46	41
As a percentage of total amount of IDA credits	23	42	36

aid has not been coordinated among donors in this fashion.

IDA also has a coordinating role through cofinancing projects with other donors, an activity that grew in importance in the 1970s. During 1972–82, 382 credits totaling $8.5 billion and accounting for 41 percent of IDA's operations went to projects that were cofinanced with other official agencies. The money provided by these agencies covered 26 percent of the total cost of these projects (see Table 3.10). Cofinancing from private sources, though important for projects financed by the IBRD, has been negligible for IDA projects because IDA countries are not as creditworthy. Cofinancing has permitted IDA to be involved in more projects than would otherwise have been possible; however, the extent to which it has brought in extra financing overall is harder to tell.

Project Finance

The Articles of Agreement of the IBRD and IDA are identical in requiring each to make loans for specific projects, except in special circumstances. Between 1961 and 1982, project finance accounted for 88 percent of all IDA's lending. The remaining 12 percent has been for nonproject or "program" loans, which are discussed in Chapter 4.

Staff Involvement. The process of choosing projects is identical for both IDA and IBRD operations. It begins with a staff analysis of a country's economy and the needs of the sectors where lending is contemplated. The country's long-term development strategy is analyzed and discussed with the government—discussions that go on regularly in countries where operations have been established.

Bank staff also draw up regular economic reports on each country. These help to determine the Bank's strategy, the scale and focus of its lending, and the extent to which a country qualifies for lending from

the IBRD or from IDA. Country and sector reviews provide the broad framework for the selection and development of the individual projects through which a lending program is implemented.

IDA's involvement with a project lasts, on average, about 10 years, much the same as the IBRD's. The project cycle has several stages (see box on the project cycle), which require varying amounts of staff time (see Table 3.11).

The amount of staff involvement also varies greatly by sector. It has been greatest in areas where the need to adapt to local conditions is greatest, such as population and urbanization projects, and lower for infrastructure projects, such as power and transport, where design tends to be more standardized (see Table 3.12). These differences are also reflected in the number of agencies involved in implementing a project. Based on a sample of projects in 1979 (including IBRD projects), 74 percent of those in agriculture and rural development, education, urbanization, and population involved more than one executing agency, and 32 percent dealt with more than four agencies; in infrastructure projects, the figures were only 18 percent and 2 percent, respectively.

Table 3.11. Time Spent on IDA Projects by Stage of the Project Cycle
(years)

	Staff time	Elapsed time
Identification, selection, preparation, and design	0.8	2.0[a]
Appraisal	1.3	0.6
Negotiation with borrower and approval by Executive Directors	0.2	0.3
Implementation and supervision	0.8	6.3
Ex post evaluation	0.1	1.1
Total	3.2	10.3[a]

Note: Data are based on experience for fiscal 1977–81.
a. Estimated.

The Project Cycle

The Articles of Agreement state that IDA financing shall be for areas of "high development priority" and "except in special circumstances, shall be for specific projects." Before the creation of IDA, the Bank had already established a procedure for the identification, preparation, and appraisal of projects. This procedure, generally labeled the "project cycle," has been applied to IDA projects as well. Indeed, in blend countries, it is often the case that initial preparation and appraisal is undertaken without a clear determination of whether the project will be financed by IDA or the IBRD.

The project cycle consists of six phases:

Identification. By collaboration between the borrower and IDA, suitable project "ideas" are selected, which support national and sectoral development strategies and agree with IDA's view of development priorities. These projects are then incorporated into the lending program of the Bank for a particular country.

Preparation. The borrowing country or agency examines the technical, institutional, economic, and financial aspects of the proposed project. IDA staff provide guidance and may offer financial assistance for preparation or help borrowers obtain assistance from other sources. Often this assistance comes from other United Nations agencies, including UNDP, FAO, or WHO. The preparation stage may take as long as two years to complete.

Appraisal. IDA staff undertake to review comprehensively and systematically all aspects of the project. This may take three to five weeks in the field and covers four major aspects: technical, institutional, economic, and financial. An appraisal report is prepared and reviewed by staff at headquarters. This report serves eventually as a basis for negotiations on outstanding issues with the borrower.

Negotiations. Representatives of the borrower come to Washington to discuss the necessary measures that must be undertaken to ensure the success of the project. Many of the measures that are reviewed and agreed at this time become covenants in the loan documents. Some covenants stipulate steps that must be taken before the credit becomes effective. The project is then presented to the Executive Directors of IDA for approval, after which the loan documents are signed.

Implementation and supervision. The borrower is responsible for implementation of the project that has been agreed. IDA is responsible, however, for supervising that implementation, through progress reports from the borrowers and periodic field visits. An annual review by the Bank of its experience in supervising all projects under way serves to improve policies and procedures. Procurement of goods and works for the project must follow World Bank guidelines for efficiency and economy. An average IDA credit takes about seven years to disburse and will require supervision during all of that time. On average, less than 20 percent of a credit is disbursed during the first two years following commitment; it takes four and a half years for half of a credit to be disbursed.

Evaluation. After the project is completed, a completion report is prepared by the operational staff of IDA. This report is reviewed by the Operations Evaluation Department, which prepares its own independent audit of the project. This evaluation emphasizes the lessons learned from the project, which can be incorporated into the project cycle of subsequent projects.

Table 3.12. Time Spent on IDA Projects by Sector
(years)

	Staff time	Elapsed time[a]
Nonproject lending	1.6	3.4
Telecommunications	1.9	7.6
Development finance companies[b]	2.1	7.7
Energy	2.4	7.5
Water supply and sewerage	2.6	11.6
Transport	2.7	8.1
Industry	2.8	8.3
Education	3.7	10.0
Agriculture and rural development	3.9	8.7
Urbanization	4.8	8.5
Population, health, and nutrition	7.5	8.7
Total IDA projects	3.2	8.3
Total IBRD projects	3.0	8.2

Note: Data are based on experience for fiscal 1977–81.
a. Excludes time prior to appraisal.
b. Includes small-scale enterprises.

Complexity increases when projects involve different components—as is the case with rural and urban development projects, for example. The difficulties of supervising and carrying out these projects have stimulated a move toward closer review of this aspect of project design. The issue is to determine when the benefits of mutually reinforcing components are outweighed by the risks of overloading the institutional capabilities both of the recipient and of IDA.

IDA's procedures for appraising and implementing projects have been intended to ensure that funds are used well (for example, see box on procurement). However, recipient countries have often been critical of the delays these procedures can entail. In addition, countries with very limited administrative resources have often found these procedures to represent a real burden. While recognizing these complaints, IDA has been unable to reduce this burden without sacrificing project quality. This problem is more acute for first credits to a country or sector before working relationships have become established.

Cost Sharing. Generally, the Bank does not finance the entire cost of a project. The financial involvement of the borrowing country itself is thought desirable to ensure a project's success. Conversely, if it is to have a real influence on a project and—through its lending—on the country, the Bank needs

Procurement Arrangements under IDA Credits

In supervising projects, IDA insists that goods and services be obtained economically and efficiently. Although the borrower is ultimately responsible for the award and administration of contracts, IDA establishes the basic rules for procurement. The procedures that have been developed for procurement, which are identical to those of the IBRD, are designed to ensure that money is used well and that qualified firms in all of its member countries have an equal opportunity to provide the goods and services needed. They are also intended to encourage the development of local manufacturers and contractors in the borrowing country. In reviewing the specifications, bidding procedures, evaluation of bids, and proposed awards, IDA ensures that procurement conforms to the agreement with the borrower.

Most procurement under IDA projects has taken place under international competitive bidding (ICB), which serves as a safeguard against waste, corruption, and discrimination in procurement. Generally, under ICB, timely notification must be provided to prospective bidders. No bidder may be disqualified for reasons unrelated to its capacity to supply the goods and works in question, and bids must be opened in public.

In order to encourage the development of local industry, a margin of preference equal to the level of import duties in the recipient country, up to a maximum of 15 percent, has been allowed for local suppliers of goods since 1965. Countries with per capita income below $370 in 1980 dollars have also been allowed a preference of 7½ percent on civil works contracts since 1974.

In a variety of circumstances, IDA has found ICB not to be the most efficient method of procurement. This is particularly true in projects such as those in rural development, which do not involve large-scale civil works or machinery and equipment that must be imported. In these situations, IDA has developed guidelines for alternative procedures to let contracts.

Because investment capital is so scarce in poor countries, some IDA money is used for local costs—buying goods and services in the recipient country itself. In this case IDA provides foreign exchange that the recipient country converts to local currency, the original IDA funds helping to boost its foreign-exchange resources. About 30 percent of IDA procurement went for local costs in 1960–80. It is impossible to tell precisely how the foreign-exchange counterpart of the local costs is ultimately used, but in general these funds support imports, mostly from industrial countries. Procurement under IDA credits is limited to member countries and Switzerland, which, though not a member, has provided funds to IDA. Procurement shares exceed commitment shares for about half the donors—apparently those with strong historical ties or proximity to IDA recipients, or those with strong exports generally (see figure).

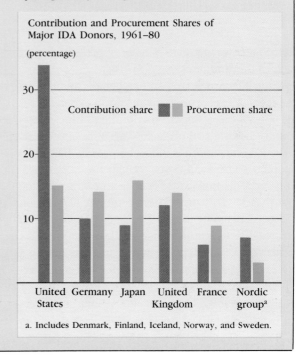

Contribution and Procurement Shares of Major IDA Donors, 1961–80

(percentage)

■ Contribution share ▨ Procurement share

a. Includes Denmark, Finland, Iceland, Norway, and Sweden.

---

to finance a significant proportion of project costs. The proportion of a project's cost that is financed varies considerably by country, being higher in the poorest countries. They face the greatest difficulties in raising domestic finance and have the smallest chance of borrowing from other foreign lenders. In the very poorest countries, IDA is often willing to finance between 60 percent and 90 percent of project costs.

Over the past decade, IDA provided an average of 44 percent of the total financial cost of projects it supported (compared with 35 percent for the IBRD). Recipient countries themselves contributed 45 percent, while other official agencies provided 11 percent through cofinancing arrangements (see Table 3.13). The degree of cost sharing also depends on the objectives IDA wishes to achieve in a country.

If there are many good projects available in sectors in which IDA wishes to concentrate, it may finance a smaller proportion of each project's cost. Doing so, however, runs the risk of overextending the government in the recipient country, which not only has to provide its share of the project cost, but also finance the recurring costs of the project after it is completed.

The degree of cost sharing for IDA projects reflects these considerations as well as the availability of other sources of funds. Thus, borrowers in Africa provided 28 percent of the total costs of the projects in which IDA was involved over the past decade, while South Asian countries contributed 48 percent from their own resources. Cofinancing met 26 percent of project costs in Africa, 6 percent in South Asia. IDA (including the IBRD in joint projects) fi-

Table 3.13. Cost Sharing of IDA Projects, 1972–81

	Foreign exchange	Local currency	Total
Total project cost (billions of dollars)	18.9	24.9	43.8
Percentage financed by:			
IDA contribution	74	21	44
Domestic contribution	5	75	45
Cofinancing	21	4	11
Total	100	100	100

Note: Data are based on estimates at appraisal.

Table 3.14. Local Currency Costs and Recipient Shares of IDA Project Costs in Selected Sectors (percentage of total project costs)

	Local-currency costs	Recipient share of total
Development finance companies	35	27
Transport	38	36
Education	46	31
Industry	55	50
Population, health, and nutrition	72	39
Water supply and sewerage	63	42
Agriculture and rural development	65	42
Energy	65	52
Telecommunications	72	73
Urbanization	76	47

Note: Data are based on experience for fiscal 1977–81.

nanced an average of 46 percent of project costs in each of these regions.

While the Articles of Agreement permit IDA to use foreign exchange to finance local expenditures in "special cases," in fact the funding of local costs has not been a real obstacle. The bulk of the borrowers' contribution is in local currency. IDA often finances some local costs, though the larger proportion of its finance is for foreign exchange (see Figure 3.3). This proportion depends, in part, on the percentage of the total project IDA wishes to finance. There is still a tendency, however, for IDA to finance a larger proportion of projects having a high foreign-exchange component. Conversely, recipients tend to finance a larger percentage of projects having a high local-cost component (see Table 3.14), although in some sectors, notably population,

agriculture, and urbanization, recipient shares are well below local currency costs.

Because many of the areas that have been at the core of IDA's attempts to reach the poorest people have tended to require relatively little foreign exchange, the financing of local costs has accounted for almost 30 percent of IDA credits in the past decade, and this share has been rising. By comparison only 7 percent of IBRD lending covered local costs, largely because its borrowers are better able to meet local expenses themselves. Overall, IDA credits financed 74 percent of the foreign-exchange costs of the projects it was involved in, but only 21 percent of the local costs.

In its first two decades, IDA has had to adapt the techniques of the Bank to the particular needs of the poorest developing countries. At the same time, the lessons learned from IDA's operations have contributed to the Bank's ability to assist middle-income countries. The concessionality of IDA's loans has enabled it to play a significant role in countries that could not have borrowed over a sustained period from the IBRD or from private financial institutions. However, many of IDA's former clients are now able to do so. By concentrating its resources in the poorest countries, IDA has become the single largest source of assistance to these countries, even though it accounts for only about 3 percent of the total official assistance to developing countries. Combining the IBRD and IDA, the World Bank has become a center of understanding about development. Its broad membership has helped it to serve as a focal point for coordination among aid donors and for communication between donors and recipients.

Figure 3.3. IDA and Borrower Contributions to Project Costs in Foreign and Local Currency

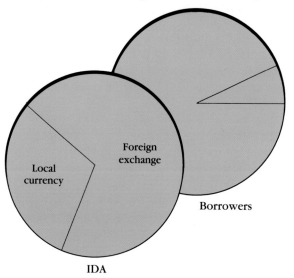

IDA

4 Sector and Country Experience

IDA's ultimate goal is not merely to ensure the success of its projects, but to improve the overall economic performance of its borrowers. Of course, no one project or series of projects can determine an economy's fortunes; however, they do provide a means of dealing with specific development constraints and a basis from which IDA and its clients can develop a long-term plan of action.

Projects are linked to broader issues by IDA's economic and sector work. In collaboration with borrowing countries, IDA staff review the performance of particular sectors and the economy as a whole, identify bottlenecks and priorities, and establish a lending program. Countries benefit from the lessons that IDA has learned in the past 20 years: the kind of technological adaptations that will work, the sectoral planning and institutions that are needed, the policies that have been associated with past successes and failures. These discussions are a two-way process, because IDA is constantly having to adapt its experience to new realities and to the circumstances of particular countries.

Reflecting changes in development thinking, IDA has become more concerned with finding ways to ensure that the benefits of growth reach the poorest people. This concern with equity has not reduced IDA's emphasis on efficiency. Indeed efficient management at every level—project, sector, and economywide—can determine how much of a contribution to progress IDA lending will make. For this reason, IDA's influence on policy, and on building up effective policy-making bodies, is critical to its achievements in particular sectors.

Although IDA operates only in the poorest countries, where institutions are weakest and risks are greatest, much has indeed been accomplished. Progress has been neither uniform nor rapid, however, largely because of differences in overall economic management, including trade and exchange-rate policy, public finance, and approaches to investment. Nevertheless, IDA has played a constructive role in advising clients on investment priorities, sector policies, and overall development strategy.

Precisely what achievements are due to that role is hard to pin down. No mechanistic relationship can capture the value of sector planning in education or policy advice in agriculture or of a well-functioning public utility or agricultural extension system. Even in terms of physical infrastructure, such as roads and power plants, quantification is misleading. Roads are not only constructed; procedures for maintaining them are established. Power stations are not merely erected; tariff charges are determined and distribution systems are planned, all

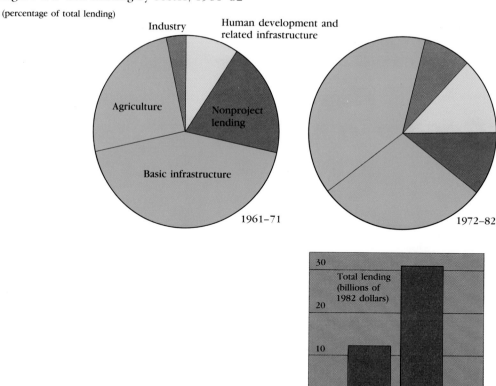

Figure 4.1. IDA Lending by Sector, 1961–82

(percentage of total lending)

Industry

Human development and related infrastructure

Agriculture

Nonproject lending

Basic infrastructure

1961–71

1972–82

Total lending (billions of 1982 dollars)

30

20

10

61–71   72–82

of which will profoundly affect the worth of the stations themselves. In the social services, it is even more difficult to measure the overall impact of changed policies. Trained workers produce more, educated mothers feed their children better, and literate individuals can absorb and then use more of the advances in technology and science.

A country's economic prospects seldom change cataclysmically. Most improvements are the result of patient endeavor and policy reforms. Few projects manage to achieve all their goals. Similarly, not all of the sectoral assistance from a body like IDA leads to sustainable progress. There are setbacks, caused by world events, domestic politics, and mistakes. But development in poor countries is a risky business, and progress can only be expected to occur slowly and incrementally.

It is within this context that the next two chapters look at IDA's impact at the national, sector, and project level. Chapter 4 attempts to trace IDA's involvement in sectors and to show how its lending and policy advice have assisted its borrowers. The first section describes the overall shifts in IDA's sectoral lending, and this is followed by a more detailed discussion of what IDA has attempted in various sectors. The last sections discuss program

lending and IDA's policy dialogue with governments, both at the sector and the national level. Finally, Chapter 5 deals with the effectiveness of IDA's projects and the reasons for success and failure in project work.

Changes in Sectoral Lending

IDA's lending pattern has changed over time in response to the needs of its clients and changes in development thinking (see Figure 4.1). In IDA's early years, accelerating growth was the main objective, and it was assumed that growth would follow once an economy's basic infrastructure was in place. Thus IDA concentrated largely on investments ranging from railways and roads to ports and power plants. It was also assumed that poverty would be reduced and income disparities narrowed in the wake of industrialization.

Both sets of assumptions proved too simplistic. Early efforts at industrialization failed to generate sufficient employment and resulted in a neglect of agriculture. As food deficits increased and payments imbalances mounted, it became clear that agricultural production was indeed a key development

Table 4.1. IDA Commitments by Sector, 1961–82

	Millions of dollars				Percentage			
	1961–70	1971–76	1977–82	Total	1961–70	1971–76	1977–82	Total
Agriculture and rural development	633	2,341	6,978	9,952	23	32	42	37
Basic infrastructure	1,164	2,167	4,855	8,186	41	30	29 -	30
Energy	167	615	2,742	3,524	6	8	16	13
Transport	861	1,218	1,594	3,673	30	17	10	13
Telecommunications	136	334	519	989	5	5	3	4
Industry[a]	107	688	1,301	2,096	4	10	8	8
Other infrastructure	80	309	1,145	1,534	3	4	7	6
Water supply and sewerage	80	211	766	1,057	3	3	5	4
Urbanization	—	98	379	477	0	1	2	2
Human resource development	179	461	1,187	1,827	6	6	7	7
Education	179	390	951	1,520	6	5	6	6
Population, health, and nutrition	—	71	236	307	—	1	1	1
Nonproject lending[b]	659	1,302	1,182	3,143	23	18	7	12
Total	2,822	7,268	16,648	26,738	100	100	100	100

a. Includes development finance companies, industry, small-scale enterprises, and tourism.
b. Includes technical assistance.

priority. In response, IDA increased its agricultural lending, which rose from 23 percent of total commitments in 1961–70 to 32 percent in 1971–76. Much of this increase reflected IDA's support for South Asian agriculture and included substantial lending for irrigation. At the same time, the share of IDA commitments devoted to transport fell from 30 percent to 17 percent (see Table 4.1).

By the early 1970s, it was recognized that the benefits of economic growth would not automatically "trickle down" to the poor. Action was necessary to prevent growth from widening income disparities. The World Bank was among the leaders in making equitable distribution of income growth an explicit objective of development. Although development strategies had been aimed at boosting employment, their focus shifted toward raising the productivity and income of the large numbers of "working poor," particularly in rural areas.

In 1973, the Bank announced a major expansion in its lending for rural development,[1] through projects that would combine to assist small farmers to increase their production and income. As a result, substantial resources were provided for small-scale irrigation, rural roads, and agricultural credit programs. This "poverty focus" was later extended to towns and cities, with special emphasis on small-scale industrial development and economical housing and infrastructure.

1. Rural development projects are those in which 50 percent or more of the project benefits go to persons below the poverty line in rural areas.

Although technical packages could be designed to increase the productivity of small farmers and entrepreneurs, these kinds of projects were less suited to the rural landless and the urban poor, who had few productive assets. Increasingly it was recognized that increases in the productivity of the poor required investments in human capital, such as primary education, basic health and nutrition, safe water, and sanitation. Thus IDA modified its approach in lending for education and water supply, for instance, to emphasize primary education and village water supply systems. Lending has also been expanded in recent years for population, health, and nutrition programs.

IDA has also increased its lending for energy projects. With rising oil prices, such projects have high priority in many IDA countries. IDA has financed feasibility studies for private-sector investment in energy, forestry projects designed to meet the fuelwood crisis, and other innovative approaches.

Finally IDA has increased its nonproject lending. Worsening economic conditions after 1973 heightened the need for assistance to facilitate broad structural changes in many IDA borrowers. In 1980, structural adjustment lending was initiated. It is available to countries that agree to a major program of long-term reforms.

IDA's sectoral emphases are borne out in the regional pattern of its lending. South Asia and Sub-Saharan Africa together account for 84 percent of IDA's total commitments, with South Asia alone taking 59 percent ($15.7 billion). During the 1970s,

Sub-Saharan Africa became the second largest borrower, commanding a quarter of IDA's resources. In both regions lending is concentrated on agriculture. In Africa IDA is also attempting to ease specific bottlenecks in transport and education, while its involvement in South Asia spans a wide range of activities, including major programs in power, telecommunications, fertilizers, and nonproject lending (see Table 4.2).

India is IDA's largest borrower, followed by Bangladesh and Pakistan. Egypt and Indonesia have also borrowed heavily, though both are now IDA graduates. In Africa, IDA's largest clients are Tanzania, Sudan, Kenya, and Ethiopia.

IDA's 10 largest borrowers have received approximately three-quarters of its lending. In only one of these countries, Bangladesh, are IDA flows a major share of gross domestic investment. In many of the least-developed countries, especially those in Africa, IDA plays a relatively larger role (although the absolute amount of lending is small). If policy influence were solely a function of the relative importance of IDA credits, that influence might be expected to have been most successful in Sub-Saharan Africa. This has not been IDA's experience, however, as will be discussed in the final section of this chapter.

Agriculture

Over the past two decades, IDA has invested almost $10 billion in agriculture, in activities ranging from the financing of irrigation pumps in Bangladesh to fertilizer distribution in Zaïre and research facilities in Pakistan. As a proportion of total IDA commitments, agricultural lending almost doubled between 1961–68 and 1977–82. Since 1974 alone, IDA has reached an estimated 100 million poor people. Most have been in South Asia, which received $5.8 billion in 1961–82, 58 percent of IDA's total agricultural credits. Of this, almost $4 billion was committed in India alone, with $2.7 billion going to irrigation and drainage.

The main shift in IDA's agricultural lending has been geared to raising the productivity and income of small farmers (those typically farming less than a few hectares). This has involved more work on water control—secondary and tertiary canals, and drainage schemes—and more training and extension services. In addition, IDA has continued to promote agricultural credit as a way of helping farmers acquire tubewells and pumps. Combined with new seeds and fertilizer, they have boosted output dramatically in South Asia.

The focus of irrigation projects has changed from dams and major canals to complete systems, including not only water sources, but distribution networks and on-farm facilities. IDA has financed tubewell irrigation to utilize groundwater. In salinated areas, such as in Egypt and Pakistan, the use of underground tile drainage has been financed.

More lending for agricultural research and extension has taken place in recent years (see Table 4.3). It reflects the need to create agencies capable of generating, adapting, and disseminating information directly to farmers, especially smallholders. IDA pioneered the "training and visit" (T&V) extension system in India. Fieldworkers keep in close contact with farmers, advising them on technological adaptations and basic farming techniques. At an

---

Fisheries

Fisheries projects have been a small part of IDA lending. Between 1964 and 1981, IDA lent $135 million to 17 projects. The basic objectives of early projects were to increase catches and boost export earnings. Approximately 60 percent of lending was for building boats and port facilities. Such capital-intensive schemes ran into difficulties, partly because their appraisal and design was poor, partly because they were badly carried out. Taking four examples between 1969 and 1973:

• In Ghana, only 10 of the 40 planned boats were built, as a result of inappropriate engine selection, delays, and higher-than-appraised costs. Catches were disappointing, and the rate of return at audit was only 10 percent.
• In Indonesia, problems included poor-quality boats, bad design and construction of shore facilities, and ineffective management (exacerbated by local cultural difficulties). After initial negative rates of return, new management is turning the project around.
• In Tunisia, the demand for new motorized boats was overestimated, so that most were sold to inexperienced fishermen.
• In the People's Democratic Republic of Yemen, project design overestimated the availability of skilled labor and local equipment. Although some local fishermen welcomed the new boats and improved their productivity, production was again overestimated.

Since these early days, IDA has learned a great deal about fisheries. Rather than relying on large, expensive boats (and ignoring ancillary industries and marketing), IDA is supporting more small projects. These aim to increase the productivity and income of fishermen and to improve nutrition. Coastal fisheries increase the benefits for rural populations, as do inland schemes—a small but expanding area of lending.

Table 4.2. IDA Commitments by Sector and Region, 1961–82

	Sub-Saharan Africa		South Asia		Other		Total	
	Millions of dollars	Percentage	Millions of dollars	Percentage	Millions of dollars	Percentage	Millions of dollars	Percentage
Agriculture and rural development	2,400	36	5,824	37	1,728	39	9,952	37
Basic infrastructure	2,228	34	4,775	30	1,183	27	8,186	30
Energy	343	5	2,631	16	550	12	3,524	13
Transport	1,761	27	1,375	9	537	12	3,673	13
Telecommunications	124	2	769	5	96	3	989	4
Industry[a]	408	6	1,335	9	353	8	2,096	8
Development finance companies	254	4	236	2	140	3	630	2
Other	154	2	1,099	7	213	5	1,466	6
Water supply, sewerage, and urbanization	273	4	932	6	329	8	1,534	6
Human resource development	776	12	339	2	712	16	1,827	7
Nonproject lending[b]	525	8	2,529	16	89	2	3,143	12
Total	6,610	100	15,734	100	4,394	100	26,738	100

a. Includes development finance companies, industry, small-scale enterprises, and tourism.
b. Includes technical assistance.

annual cost of about $1 per hectare, programs have succeeded in raising yields by as much as 50 percent in the course of a few years. To be efficient, T&V work requires strong organizations and heavy concentrations of farmers. It is therefore not immediately applicable in all IDA countries, although Burma, Nepal, and Sri Lanka have begun to adopt it.

Area development is a relatively new activity for IDA, and it accounted for 15 percent of agricultural lending in 1975–81. It combines different programs—new farming methods and extension services along with rural road building and marketing, for example—under some form of overall government administration. An integrated approach to rural development therefore has ambitious goals and involves a large number of programs. Its record has been mixed: where administrative support has been strong, it has managed to build on the benefits achieved by individual programs. In Africa, IDA has considerably expanded its area development work as an effective way of tackling several development problems simultaneously. But the integrated approach has often proved too complicated for countries to administer successfully. In Nepal, for example, an initially successful effort broke down because frequent policy changes in the role of the coordinating agency led to inadequate local supervision and execution.

Lessons have also been learned in other parts of agriculture. In fisheries, for example, IDA projects were initially beset by problems. In part these were due to inadequate appraisal and poor procedures for carrying out the schemes. Early fisheries projects concentrated too much on construction of vessels and neglected price incentives, management, and marketing aspects (see box on fisheries).

South Asia and Sub-Saharan Africa received about 83 percent of IDA's total agricultural commitments. The following sections look at those two regions in particular, but should not obscure IDA's role in other regions, such as the Middle East (see box on Egypt), East Asia, and Central America.

Table 4.3. IDA Lending within the Agricultural Sector, 1961–81
(percentage of sectoral total)

	Irrigation and drainage	Agricultural credit	Livestock and fisheries	Perennial crops	Research and extension	Agro-industry	Area development	Forestry
1961–68	61.2	17.1	4.2	2.6	—	6.3	8.7	—
1969–74	34.4	25.4	13.7	12.0	—	3.3	10.2	—
1975–81	38.0	13.7	7.2	5.3	5.9	6.9	15.4	3.9

A Drainage and Health Program in Egypt

Egypt's agriculture has for centuries been nurtured by the Nile. The antiquated flooding and drainage system has gradually raised the water table, increased salinity, and reduced productivity. In a series of credits totaling $130 million during the past decade, IDA is financing a significant part of one of

Molluscicide to control bilharzia is sprayed on a canal in the Beni Suef region of Egypt.

the world's largest drainage programs, covering 1.15 million hectares in the Nile Delta and Upper Egypt. The program includes 22 pumping stations and related power transmission lines, 6,500 kilometers of open drains, and workshops and soil laboratories. When fully completed, it will improve the productivity and income of 780,000 farming families. Sample surveys comparing "drained" and "undrained" villages show that drainage is helping to produce significantly higher yields. Increases in production of about 10 percent were achieved within two to three years, with the best results in rice and cotton.

Despite these initial achievements, the long-term benefits of the program will depend on how well the new drainage system is maintained. Effective means must be found to de-weed, desilt, and reshape open drains and to inspect and flush buried pipes. To help in this task, the government established a public drainage authority. With the assistance of the Dutch government, this drainage authority has been strengthened.

Associated with the drainage scheme is a joint effort by the Egyptian government, IDA, and other donors to control bilharzia (schistosomiasis). This debilitating disease is transmitted through water snails, which come into contact with human excreta in canals and drainage ditches, and then pass the disease back to humans who use or wade in the infected water. Bilharzia affects young children in particular; it lingers in its victims, and is difficult and expensive to treat. It exacerbates malnutrition and leads to other more severe illnesses. In the mid-1970s between 27 percent and 43 percent of the population was affected in parts of rural Egypt. Past irrigation schemes, such as the Aswan Dam, ended up spreading the disease more widely, because no attempt was made to tackle it.

To control bilharzia, those infected must be treated and the snails must be neutralized; improvements in sanitation are the ultimate solution. As part of the drainage program in Middle and Upper Egypt, where 8.5 million people live, IDA has supported bilharzia control since 1977. The effort is organized by snail control inspections in 48 districts, 104 control centers, and over 400 control units in the Ministry of Health. Village surveys show a marked reduction (often up to 50 percent) of the incidence of disease as a result of control programs. These results are encouraging; as with drainage maintenance, however, long-run success will depend on the government's ability to finance the programs and manage them effectively.

South Asia

If IDA can be said to have concentrated on a particular sector or region, it is agriculture in South Asia. And for good reason: the region includes half of the world's absolute poor,[2] and improvements in science and technology have dramatically increased yields there. In India, particularly, IDA has helped to transform agriculture. India is now able to meet its own food needs for the first time in recent history. Although IDA borrowers in South Asia have managed to reduce their dependence on agriculture from half of GDP (1960) to just over a third (1979), 720 million people in the region still rely on it for employment and income. In most countries, agricultural development has therefore become the main objective of policy.

Reliable irrigation is usually a precondition for the new methods of farming that use high-yielding seeds and fertilizers. Irrigation is expensive, however, and South Asian countries have depended in good measure on concessional aid to finance it. Since 1970, IDA-supported irrigation investments in India alone helped to expand or improve irrigation systems serving 6 million hectares of farmland, affecting 2.4 million families. The effects can be striking. Although only 32 percent of South Asian paddy fields are irrigated, for example, those fields produced 62 percent of the increase in rice output between 1961 and 1980. As for wheat (the second most important foodgrain), irrigated lands—67 per-

2. Excluding China.

cent of the total acreage—accounted for 91 percent of the increase in wheat production.

Views on irrigation have changed with experience. IDA-supported irrigation projects have increasingly concentrated on improving the performance of existing systems, making water deliveries more dependable and irrigation systems more efficient. More attention is now paid to secondary and tertiary distribution of water and to the farmer's actual use of water on the farm. IDA has also increasingly financed groundwater development schemes that give farmers better control of on-farm water supplies through the use of private tubewells.

An example demonstrates the impact of tubewell irrigation. In Bangladesh, a $10 million investment in shallow tubewells irrigates 35,000–40,000 hectares and produces about 90,000–100,000 tons of additional grain every year. In the past five years alone, with IDA assistance, the Bangladesh government financed 50,000 shallow tubewells, 7,000 deep tubewells, and 20,000 low-lift pumps. IDA has directly financed about 15 percent of all public investment in Bangladesh's agricultural sector in recent years. Improvements on irrigated lands have been impressive: for example, production since the early 1960s has increased fourfold for dry-season rice and twentyfold for wheat as a result of drainage and flood-control investments, installation of pumps and tubewells, almost complete adoption of high-yield variety seeds, and extensive use of fertilizer and pesticides.

However, 90 percent of rice growing still depends on capricious monsoons. Thus, improvements in drainage and flood control must parallel changes in cropping techniques. These are quasi-public investments, beyond the resources of individual farmers, and governments therefore need to take the lead. Subsequent improvements can effectively involve the private sector. For example, in Bangladesh pesticide distribution was turned over to the private sector two years ago, and greater reliance is being placed on private markets for the retailing of fertilizer. To allow farmers to borrow necessary capital, IDA and other donors are assisting local agricultural credit institutions. It is important that their loans be on market terms, so as not to create a permanent budgetary drain or change the behavior of farmers and suppliers.

India and the Green Revolution

In the mid-1960s, India was importing 10 million to 12 million tons of foodgrains annually, an untenable situation. The Indian cabinet debated whether to continue to import, which required both financing and improvements in the transportation system, or to assign a much higher priority to domestic agriculture.

At that time, a number of foreign experts in the India division of the Rockefeller and Ford Foundations began urging the importation of the high-yielding wheat seed that had been developed by Norman Borlaug and his team in Mexico. Many Indian agricultural scientists and planners were skeptical of transferring seeds to Indian soil and doubted whether the Mexican wheat would be acceptable to the Indian consumer. There was also some apprehension that the farmers would not wish to purchase these new inputs.

Nevertheless, the decision was made to go ahead. Under Minister C. Subramaniam's direction, the Indian Council of Agricultural Research (ICAR) was made the focus of research: it was given the task of coordinating all activities bearing on the development of crops and other agricultural products of significance to more than one state. B. P. Pal, a scientist, was brought in as ICAR's chairman.

It became clear that the introduction of high-yielding technology would eventually change the structure of Indian agriculture—from a basically subsistence system to a sector in which marketable surpluses would become important. Expansion of the agriculture sector meant that farmers would shoulder greater risks: to reduce these risks, farmers required some assurance on the price of their output. The concept of "economic price" of agricultural output was thus developed and the Agricultural Prices Commission was set up in 1964–65 to help the government determine these prices.

For a regime of incentive prices to be effective, it was necessary to develop a mechanism for buying, storing, and marketing foodgrains. Accordingly, the Food Corporation of India was set up to procure food from farmers at the "economic price" and to distribute it to deficit areas, if need be at a subsidized price.

The introduction of the new seed technology was not a one-time innovation. It demanded constant scientific work, which was carried out by the reorganized research apparatus. Although ICAR could ensure that the seed technology was gradually adapted to Indian use, it had to be helped with the task of commercial seed development and distribution. This led to the creation of national and state seed corporations. But to increase yields, major investments in irrigation and the extension of services were also needed.

In the words of Mr. Subramaniam: "These were major innovations; to be fully implemented, they needed a tremendous amount of assured resource flows. It was at that time that the World Bank's President promised India this flow of concessional resources for a number of years. It was the marriage of scientific development, institutional support, and IDA funding that contributed to the remarkable success of Indian agriculture. Consequently, the growth of Indian agriculture moved on to a different trend line: in the sixties it was widely accepted that the growth of Indian foodgrain output would never be much more than the rate of increase in India's population. Now it appears that Indian agriculture is on a higher trend line. IDA can claim credit along with Indian planners, scientists, and politicians for making possible this transition."

In most of South Asia, progress has come chiefly from cultivating existing land more intensively, not from bringing more land under the plough. Only in Nepal and Sri Lanka have virgin lands been cultivated on any significant scale, although in Nepal the output on existing cropland has declined. For the region as a whole, 12 percent of the increase in agricultural production was due to the net expansion of cultivated acreage, 19 percent to an increase in multiple cropping, and 69 percent to productivity gains.

The most spectacular gains have occurred in Indian agriculture, the largest IDA program. Between 1969 and 1980, for example, more than $3.0 billion of IDA funds were committed to improving Indian agricultural production. IDA has contributed only about 3 percent on average to total annual capital formation in the sector. Indian experts believe, however, that these aggregate figures understate IDA's real importance in financing some critical elements of their agricultural development (see box on India and the green revolution).

During the past two decades, 25 million hectares have been brought under irrigation, and between 1966 and 1979, fertilizer consumption increased more than sixfold to over 5 million tons a year. India's rapidly rising grain production, averaging gains of almost 3 percent a year during the 1970s, enabled it virtually to cease foodgrain imports, to build up stocks to unprecedented levels, and to spread these benefits throughout the economy (see supplement on South Asian agriculture).

Sub-Saharan Africa

IDA's involvement in African agriculture increased sharply during the 1970s. Commitments have totaled $2.3 billion since 1969, of which $1.1 billion has been disbursed. Most countries in Sub-Saharan Africa are among the world's poorest, and progress has been slow; in the 1970s, the region's agricultural output increased by only 1.3 percent a year, while the population grew at an average annual rate of 2.7 percent. This poor performance was influenced by many factors—sharp rises in the price of petroleum and petroleum-based products, drought in the Sahel, wars, civil strife, frequent changes in governments, and injudicious agricultural policies in many countries. Where output increased, it was due largely to expanded acreage, very little to increased yields. And parts of Sub-Saharan Africa are losing ground— they are less productive now than they were in 1961.

The challenges facing IDA in Sub-Saharan Africa are therefore enormous. The continent is more diverse than South Asia, agriculture is almost exclusively rainfed, and droughts are common. Good technical packages of seeds and fertilizers are harder to devise. Losses after harvest are considerable because of poor infrastructure and storage; inappropriate pricing policies provide few incentives for farmers to produce more. Extension services are often inadequate because of weak local institutions and a widely dispersed population.

Nonetheless, there are countries where IDA's involvement has produced encouraging results, notably Malawi and Kenya. By and large, the countries that do best are those with good management, plus the best natural advantages of weather and soil, and a national commitment to agricultural development. This is generally reflected in less control over inputs and marketing and less intervention to suppress producer prices in the hope of keeping food cheap.

Various lessons can be derived from IDA's agricultural experience in Sub-Saharan Africa. The first is that price distortions, irregular and unreliable supplies of inputs, and marketing problems are significant impediments to success. Policy reform is therefore essential. Second, greater flexibility must be exercised in project design and greater efforts made in project supervision to compensate for the continent's deficiencies, particularly in the development of human capital. Third, revenues must be increased to support agricultural development, particularly because the recurrent costs—local wages, maintenance expenses, and so on—are rising as a result of newly implemented projects, and government budgets are already strained. Finally, macroeconomic policies matter a great deal. What happens in one area of the economy affects other areas, for better or worse.

Efforts in agriculture can therefore be complemented by training and education, adapting science and technology to suit the environment, and helping to develop better management. IDA has had to design simpler projects and concentrate more on training programs. Drawing on the Bank's study of Sub-Saharan Africa,[3] IDA is paying closer heed to overall sectoral and macroeconomic policies as well as sociocultural factors. Recurrent costs, and the budgetary problems they create, are receiving greater attention. To promote overall adjustment, clearer

3. *Accelerated Development in Sub-Saharan Africa* (Washington, D.C.: World Bank, 1981).

(Text continues on page 46)

Supplement: South Asian Agriculture

One-fifth of the world's population lives in South Asia and about half of the absolute poor. Some 80 percent of the subcontinent's 900 million people live in rural areas, where there is an average of one hectare of cultivated land for every three people and average per capita incomes are below the regional norm of $230 a year. Yet South Asia popularized the term "the green revolution," and has made tremendous progress in the battle against hunger.

IDA has been closely associated with South Asia's agricultural development. It has lent $5.2 billion to support 163 agriculture and rural development projects in seven countries.[1] These credits, which constituted 58 percent of all IDA's commitments to agriculture and rural development, were spent mainly on irrigation, drainage, and flood control (41 percent) and on agricultural credit (25 percent). Other activities included area development (10 percent), food storage and processing (7 percent), and research and extension work (6 percent).

Spraying a field in India.

History

Until 1950, South Asia's agricultural production had been growing slowly. Most farmers had to rely on rainfall to water their crops, and monsoons are inherently unreliable. They start too late or end too early; they bring too much rain or too little. Floods cause serious damage, and prolonged drought can be disastrous. As population growth continued to be rapid, food supplies became increasingly unreliable and often inadequate. Malnutrition, even starvation, was common.

Once the colonial period ended, most governments in South Asia adopted development plans aimed at promoting rapid industrialization. Agriculture was seen as intrinsically backward; its main contribution to development it was felt, was to provide a continuous flow of labor and raw materials to sustain industrial growth. Nevertheless, some progress was being made. In India, agricultural output grew during the 1950s, largely because of a rapid expansion of the cropped area. Construction of irrigation works, which had slowed during the first half of this century, was expanded; the irrigated area increased at a rate of about 0.5 million hectares a year. The extension service was reorganized and expanded to cover most of the country. Certain farm supplies, particularly fertilizers, became more widely available. In Nepal, the eradication of malaria in the mid-1950s opened up the

Terai, the extension of the Gangetic Plain in southern Nepal. In Pakistan, after years of virtual stagnation, policy changes in the late 1950s and early 1960s helped to accelerate agricultural growth, from less than 1 percent a year between 1948 and 1955 to 2.7 percent a year in 1960–65.

Despite this progress, food shortages increased, and food imports placed a serious burden on the balance of payments. In the early 1960s, Pakistan imported about 1 million tons of grain a year; India's food imports averaged 5 million tons a year in the 1960s, but in bad years reached twice that level. In the early 1970s, Bangladesh found that it had to import nearly 2 million tons of grain. Even countries that were traditional food exporters were affected. Nepal's exportable surpluses declined substantially and some imports increased. Burma, which had been the largest exporter of rice in the world before World War II, saw its exports dwindle from a high of 3 million tons in the late 1930s to an all-time low of 0.2 million tons in 1974.

South Asia had the land, the labor, and the climate to feed itself. But four things were missing: schemes for water control; new farming technology and methods; adequate support services to help farmers apply these new methods; and sufficient capital. And these changes had to be nurtured and led by the right government policies.

In India as well as Pakistan, governments had deliberately depressed farm prices to provide the politically important urban population with cheap food, even though this discouraged farmers from producing more. In Sri Lanka heavy taxation held back the growth of production and exports of tree crops, particularly tea, rubber, and coconut. In Burma during the 1960s and early 1970s, the government had been restructuring the economy through widespread nationalization, industrial development, and comprehensive price controls; agriculture suffered as a result. Bangladesh faced

Harvesting radishes in Bangladesh.

1. Bangladesh, Burma, India, the Maldives, Nepal, Pakistan, and Sri Lanka. Because the Maldives joined IDA only in 1978, it is not included in this supplement.

rather different problems: its 1971 war of independence, an unprecedented cyclone, and a tidal wave combined to cause a drop of 17 percent in agricultural production between 1969 and 1971.

The Green Revolution

Changes began in 1964. A number of foreign experts working in India for the Rockefeller and Ford foundations began pressing the Indian government to import the high-yielding wheat varieties that had been developed by the International Maize and Wheat Improvement center (CIMMYT) in Mexico and the rice varieties that had followed at the International Rice Research Institute (IRRI) in the Philippines. These new strains were highly responsive to fertilizers and good water control, and offered the potential for much greater yields. The Indian government decided that the potential of this technology far outweighed its risks.

IDA was closely involved in this decision. It had carried out a massive study of Indian agriculture (and other key sectors) in close collaboration with the government of India. Although it was completed before the implications of the new high-yielding varieties were fully grasped, the report recommended the adoption of policies, programs, and institutions that became integral parts of the efforts to exploit the new technology. To underline its own commitment to these recommendations, IDA offered very significant levels of assistance.

As a result of this study, an Agricultural Prices Commission was established to set prices at which the government would purchase crops from farmers; the favorable mixture of grain and fertilizer prices it set encouraged farmers to produce more. The Food Corporation of India was created to buy up grain in the good years to store for the lean; largely as a result of this organizational effort, India now maintains comfortable stocks of rice and wheat. The Agricultural Refinance and Development Corporation (ARDC) was reorganized and expanded; IDA supported large-scale training programs for ARDC staff and massive credit schemes later on to help farmers finance groundwater investments and mechanization. The Indian Council for Agricultural Research was strengthened; it has been very successful in adapting the imported seed technology for Indian use. National and state seed corporations were set up. And irrigation works and fertilizer factories were expanded.

IDA was similarly involved in Pakistan. After partition, the headwaters of three of Pakistan's important eastern rivers were in India, and India had plans to divert this water for its own use. The Bank took a major role in the formulation of the Indus Water Treaty in 1960, whereby India agreed to delay diversion of water from these rivers until a system of replacement works could be constructed that would feed water through canals from Pakistan's three western rivers to the eastern ones. These works were financed by contributions from many donors, including the IBRD and IDA, through the Indus Basin Development Fund and later the Tarbela Development Fund. Total contributions amounted to about $2.4 billion, and the result was the conversion of the Indus Basin into the largest continuous irrigation system in the world, covering some 13 million hectares. With the installation of thousands of pumps and tubewells, irrigation was extended to about 70 percent of the country's cultivated area.

The joint effort with Bangladesh was smaller but no less thorough. After Bangladesh's independence in 1971, IDA and

the government carried out a land and water resources sector study, food policy reviews, and joint reviews of the Bangladesh's Water Development Board, minor irrigation program, and integrated rural development program. With IDA assistance, the government recently drew up a medium-term foodgrain production plan, which, if successfully implemented, could lead the country to self-sufficiency in food by 1985. Most of the $5.4 billion earmarked for investment under the plan will go to improve water control, supply farmers with more materials, and improve their access to markets. Current financial difficulties are expected to force some reductions in the plan, but the flexibility of its 57 projects, as well as the high priority given to it by the government, should limit the effects of the reductions.

Irrigation and Drainage Lending

IDA lending for irrigation and drainage in South Asia has totaled $2.15 billion. India and Pakistan have been the two largest borrowers. Two big projects have been supported in Burma, six in Nepal, and seven in Sri Lanka, involving commitments of $350 million. Bangladesh has been supported with 12 projects, worth $220 million. The projects cover the whole spectrum: large-scale infrastructure; deep, shallow, and hand tubewells; drainage and flood control; and low-lift pumps.

Since the late 1970s, there have been intense discussions on the longer-term strategy to be followed. In Bangladesh, IDA wanted to promote small-scale, short-maturity pump irrigation works; the government tended to favor large-scale, long-gestation gravity projects. The strategy that is now being followed involves a combination of both approaches. In Pakistan, IDA lending has moved away from the capital-intensive projects of the earlier decade. More emphasis is being placed on complementing, rather than expanding, existing irrigation facilities by augmenting the supply of essential inputs, such as fertilizer, seeds, and credit, and by improving water management and reclaiming land that is subject to salinity and waterlogging.

The results of irrigation investments have been impressive. In India, the area irrigated by surface water, which was growing between 1 percent and 2 percent a year during the 1950s and 1960s, accelerated to 3 percent a year in the 1970s. In Bangladesh, it grew 4 percent a year during the 1970s. In Pakistan, the amount of water supplied by irrigation schemes increased 3.4 percent a year in both the 1960s and the 1970s, and the net irrigated area grew 1.5 percent a year.

As irrigation has expanded, so it has had more impact on foodgrain production. About half of the value of all agricultural output in South Asia comes from irrigated areas. One-third of the cereal land is irrigated; it produces half of the region's cereal output and has been responsible for two-thirds of the increased cereal production between 1961 and 1980. In India, between fiscal 1951 and 1978, about one-third of the increase in foodgrain output was generated by the expansion of the irrigated area, and another third by the higher yields and productivity achieved on already irrigated land.[2]

In Pakistan, the emphasis on irrigation during the 1960s diverted attention away from problems downstream where inadequate drainage had created severe waterlogging and salinity problems on millions of hectares of land. In the 1970s,

2. The remaining increase was in rainfed areas and was due mostly to technical innovations.

IDA provided credits totaling $162 million for four projects to control salinity, improve drainage, and provide irrigation. Subsequent studies provoked IDA to lend more to rehabilitate canals and improve watercourses and drainages, as well as support services like research, extension, and water management.

IDA's Agricultural Credit Program

IDA opened a second line of operations in South Asia in 1965 in the form of support to Pakistan for agricultural credit. This was followed by three more projects in Pakistan, and 14 in India, involving a total of almost $1 billion. Agricultural credit operations have proved very successful in expanding production. Of the 14 Indian operations, 12 have already been completed and evaluated; their rate of return has averaged 37 percent. The only Pakistan project completed and evaluated is likely to yield a rate of return of 40 percent.

In India, IDA faced a unique opportunity to increase agricultural production by following up a scientific breakthrough and encouraging internal policy reforms. Its credits, which primarily supported on-farm irrigation investments, brought an additional 2 million hectares under irrigation, more than one-quarter of the total land affected by groundwater development in the 1970s. Aided by effective institutions—the Agricultural Refinance and Development Corporation, commercial banks, and cooperative land banks—IDA was able to support the purchase by farmers of wells and pumpsets, which, when combined with new seeds and fertilizer, completed the highly successful package known as green-revolution technology. The result was a rapid and dramatic improvement in productivity.

Some questions have been raised about the overall impact of these agriculture credit projects. There was a tendency for credit to go mainly to the larger farmers, while small farmers are unwilling or unable to borrow to invest in new technologies. Recent operations, however, have earmarked a substantial portion of lending for small farmers. In addition, it has proved difficult to identify and support agricultural credit projects in the smaller South Asian countries. There are two possible reasons for this. First, successful credit schemes require established and effective agencies to act as intermediaries in the borrowing countries. And second, the green revolution's high-yielding varieties, which make the credit projects so profitable in both India and Pakistan, have not been easily adapted to local conditions in other countries. Only now is progress being made in Sri Lanka and Burma.

Extension and Other Lending

One important ingredient of the success of the green revolution is the training and support that farmers receive from extension workers. In 1975, IDA started building up research and extension services, particularly in India where $227 million was earmarked for this kind of work. A stronger extension service, using the training-and-visit approach pioneered by IDA in India, is more effective in informing farmers of the latest technical developments. And more research will be required to produce a continuous stream of new techniques that will eventually improve on the current generation of high-yielding varieties, and achieve similar technical breakthroughs in other crops. The IDA-assisted National Agricultural Research project, which supports the development of regional research capacity in each state, is expected to meet this need.

Some of IDA's other projects in South Asia have benefited people who have not been affected by the green revolution. In 1974, IDA started lending for both area development and livestock farming. The livestock projects have mainly covered dairy production and have been designed to help small farmers and landless farm workers. IDA started lending for forestry in 1975, with the main emphasis on projects that would increase the supply of firewood in villages. IDA supported fisheries developments in 1977, and one large, innovative credit for sericulture (silk production) was granted to India in 1980.

Progress and Prospects

South Asia has made encouraging progress. Between 1961 and 1980, while its population grew 2.3 percent a year, South Asia's agricultural production grew 2.6 percent a year (see table on individual country performance). In most countries, it has speeded up recently. After a series of calamities in the early 1970s, Bangladesh's agriculture is now growing slightly over 3 percent a year. Since 1976, Burma has had five record harvests in a row. In spite of significant regional disparities, India's agricultural output is now outpacing the 2 percent a year rise in population. Pakistan expanded its agricultural

South Asian Agriculture

	GNP per person (1980 dollars)		Share of agriculture in GDP (%)		Average annual growth rate of agricultural value added (%)	
	1960	1980	1960	1980	1961–70	1971–80
Bangladesh	100	130	58.0	54.0	2.7	2.2
Burma	140	170	33.0	46.0	4.1	4.3
India	180	240	50.0	37.0	1.7	2.2[a]
Nepal	140	140	69.0[b]	57.0	—	0.5
Pakistan	170	300	46.0	31.0	4.9	2.3
Sri Lanka	160	270	32.0	28.0	3.0	2.8

a. 1966.
b. Revised.

production by 6.3 percent a year in the second half of the 1960s, a performance matched by few other developing countries. In the early 1970s the rise in production slowed to less than 1 percent a year as a result of floods, three severe droughts, a war, and increased oil and fertilizer prices. But growth picked up again during the second half of the 1970s, to almost 5 percent a year. Sri Lanka's food production grew at an annual rate of 4.4 percent during the 1970s, including five successive years of record food production between 1976 and 1980. The decline in tree-crop production, however, reduced the overall growth rate for agriculture to 2.6 percent a year.

For Bangladesh, India, and Pakistan—the three most populous countries in the region—self-sufficiency in foodgrains has been a major national goal. Pakistan has not only achieved this objective since the mid-1970s, it has also been exporting over 1 million tons of grain a year since 1979. India, which was the world's second largest cereal importer in 1966 and 1967, reached basic self-sufficiency toward the end of the 1970s. Although Bangladesh continues to import food, it is also on the road to achieving self-sufficiency during the 1980s. Even if self-sufficiency is attained, it is likely that serious problems of malnutrition will remain.

Nepal is the only exception to this impressive record. In spite of large immigration to the Terai, population density has remained extremely high in the hilly northern part of the country—almost twice the average of neighboring Bangladesh. As a result, more and more marginal land has been brought under cultivation, there has been widespread deforestation and erosion, and the average yield for most crops has gradually declined. Since the early 1960s, both food and other agricultural production have failed to keep pace with population growth.

Nepal's difficulties embody the challenges that still lie ahead. Although much has been achieved in South Asia, malnutrition continues to affect about 250 million people, 28 percent of the region's population. That in itself shows the critical need to speed up the rate of progress. There is no doubt that South Asia has the wherewithal to provide all its people with a decent diet. For example, if India's rice and wheat belts were to match the productivity of Punjab, they could produce some 350 million tons of grain by the year 2000. After allowing for increases in population and improved diets, that would still leave a surplus of some 60 million tons. Likewise, if Pakistan fully exploits the potential of the Indus Basin, it should be able to double its present yields and produce grain surpluses by 1990. For Bangladesh, too, it is technically feasible to raise production from 13.5 million tons in 1978 to at least 20 million tons by 1990. The potential is there; the task is to realize it.

conditions are being attached to IDA's project and nonproject lending.

Infrastructure

The second largest area of IDA lending has been basic infrastructure. In the past 22 years, almost $8.19 billion (one-third of IDA's portfolio) has been committed to transport, energy, and telecommunications. Including contributions from other donors and local finance, these investments exceed $20 billion. IDA has financed the construction and improvement of between 15,000 and 20,000 kilometers of highways and roads and more than 10,000 megawatts of electricity generating capacity.

Even though infrastructure projects exhibit generally high rates of return, these measures do not adequately reflect their importance. Once countries have acquired basic infrastructure, their prospects for agricultural and industrial development and for attracting foreign investment are greatly improved. IDA has played a central role in many of today's middle-income countries, particularly in the energy sector, and it has helped to establish autonomous agencies in many countries to operate railways, roads, and public utilities. Increasingly, it has been drawn both into the problems of road transport in Sub-Saharan Africa and into the search for new supplies of energy.

Transport

IDA has put 45 percent of its infrastructure lending into transport projects, spending $3.67 billion over the past two decades. The main recipients have been India, in particular Indian Railways, and highway and road programs in Sub-Saharan Africa.

IDA's overall approach to transport policy has been to concentrate first on sector studies to determine investment priorities and then to assist countries with planning and institutional support as a complement to capital assistance. During the 1970s, in particular, IDA introduced project innovations, stressing, for example, road maintenance and more labor-intensive construction methods. It has invested very little in big, capital-intensive projects, such as airports; rather, it has preferred to help mobilize support from other donors. In Cameroon, for example, $10 million from IDA and $15 million from the IBRD were combined with $100 million from eight bilateral and multilateral donors to finance the deepening of the port of Douala and related infrastructure investments.

In Sub-Saharan Africa, IDA has lent about $1.8 billion for transport projects in 36 countries, accounting for as much as 10 percent of the region's total investment in surface transport (see box on African highways). As with irrigation, IDA's strategy has moved from large but necessary capital-intensive programs (be they dams or trunk highways) to smaller programs whose benefits can be directed more easily to target groups like the rural poor. It has promoted highway maintenance and safety and the construction, rehabilitation, and maintenance of secondary and feeder roads.

Road maintenance in particular involves considerable recurrent expenditure. Although IDA does finance local project costs, governments are essentially responsible for running costs. Eager for new investments, they are often faced with the difficult choice between letting existing infrastructure deteriorate or increasing their budget deficits. To try to overcome this constraint, IDA has helped set up bodies to organize self-help efforts. In Kenya and Rwanda, for example, local communities are paying for the cost of road maintenance.

A second principal constraint in African transport lending is the dearth of adequately trained staff. IDA has expanded its work in training and institutional development; even so, after a series of projects, most countries are not yet in a position to undertake strong management and planning of their transport sectors. Many countries are also in the early stages of reforming their policies on such issues as setting road user charges and enforcing limits on axle load. In a few countries, such as Kenya and Ethiopia, IDA has approved sector credits because they provide for closer liaison on transport policy, and because the implementing agencies can handle these fairly demanding lending operations.

The bulk of IDA's lending for railway projects has gone to Indian Railways (IR), which operates a system vital to the Indian economy. IR runs over 150,000 kilometers of track; every year it carries 240 million tons of freight and 3.5 billion passengers. During the last decade, IDA financed about 10 percent of IR's annual investment. Without that support, IR would have found it very difficult to finance its expansion and replacement programs. IDA has also provided technical assistance in accounting, evaluation, management, planning, and maintenance.

In addition to its emphasis on the maintenance and management problems of railroads, IDA has tried to encourage countries to undertake some difficult reforms. In some cases, results have been slow or disappointing because reforms include difficult policy decisions—like service closings and reduced rail subsidies. Nonetheless, some of the Bank's main achievements have been in IDA countries, including Senegal, Mali, Pakistan, and India. Experience suggests the need to reach agreement on required reforms before a credit is approved. This is a principle that applies to areas besides railways.

African Highways

In recent years, about 40 percent of IDA lending to Africa has been for transport. Since 1961, IDA has financed 59 highway projects in East Africa, and 66 in West Africa. Commitments have totaled approximately $1.2 billion. Adding in contributions from other donors and the governments themselves, IDA-supported investments probably exceeded $3.5 billion, with the bulk of lending occurring in the 1970s. In most countries, IDA has been the major source of external financing for highway and rural road construction. In some, it accounted for a sizable portion of total gross domestic investment in roads: examples include Niger, Malawi, Mali, Upper Volta, Rwanda, Ethiopia, Benin, Cameroon, and Madagascar.

IDA's association with transport in Niger dates back to 1963 when only 132 kilometers of roadway were paved. With the help of seven IDA credits totaling $30 million, big improvements have been made. Today 2,700 kilometers of roads are paved, and over 5,000 kilometers receive regular maintenance—a record that owes much to Niger's Ministry of Public Works. Using a 1968 IDA credit for highway maintenance, it set up a road maintenance organization, which (by special arrangement with the Ministry of Finance) had its own budget to stock spare parts for road equipment. A 1976 IDA credit included training for regraveling brigades to maintain roads, and a 1979 credit will finance part of an 800 kilometer network of agricultural feeder roads, administered by a new Feeder Roads Unit.

In Malawi, IDA first got involved in transport in 1966, when less than 500 kilometers of roads were paved. Assisted by four IDA credits totaling $65 million, another 550 kilometers of paved roads have been built. IDA's main impact has been in helping to bring about a shift of emphasis from main road construction to (1) improving and maintaining the country's 5,500 kilometer district (feeder) roads network and (2) greatly increasing budgetary support for road maintenance. A special District Roads Improvement and Maintenance Program, which started in 1974, has improved and maintained over 1,500 kilometers of minimum-access, all-weather roads, and the program is being expanded. Moreover, labor-intensive methods are increasingly being used (over 5,000 laborers are presently employed) because they have proved to be a cost-effective way of building and maintaining district roads. This program is considered a model for neighboring countries.

Energy

IDA credits for power generation, transmission, and distribution have totaled $3.2 billion over the past 22 years, some 12 percent of its lending. Until 1975, energy lending was confined to electric power projects; since the sharp rise in oil prices, however, IDA has begun to deal with energy in a broader context. A separate program for oil and gas exploration has absorbed approximately $300 million of IDA money. The program emphasizes the financing of pre-development activities to promote exploration for oil and gas, especially in Africa. IDA also lends for renewable-resource development, such as fuelwood projects to help meet rural energy needs.

In traditional electric power projects, IDA's major objectives have been efficient resource mobilization and institution building as well as long-term sector planning. About half of IDA's lending has been for electric power generation; the other half has financed transmission and distribution facilities, since these areas often constrain the sector's performance. Rural electrification, principally for irrigation pumping, has been a significant component of IDA programs in India, Pakistan, and Egypt. Rural electricity can encourage agroindustries and increase employment as well as improve the delivery of health services and education.

IDA's experience in power investments has led it to set conditions in its lending agreements covering revenue targets, borrowing limits, and tariffs. It encourages power authorities to set tariffs so as to cover their long-run marginal costs—essential if they are to generate enough revenues to act autonomously. IDA has assisted the establishment of such authorities in Jordan, Ghana, Sri Lanka, Turkey, and Indonesia and has tried to improve managerial efficiency.

Most recently, the Bank has participated with the United Nations Development Programme in undertaking energy-sector assessments. This program, already completed in Sri Lanka, Zambia, and Zimbabwe, among others, provides IDA clients with an assessment of their energy resources and current and projected demand, a review of the efficiency and pricing policies of their energy sectors, and a judgment on prospects, constraints, and priorities.

India, IDA's largest client for power-sector investment, has borrowed approximately $2.1 billion for 15 projects since 1961. About 73 percent of these funds have been earmarked for generation projects and the remainder for transmission and distribution and for rural electrification.

The Indian electricity-supply industry is large and complex. It faces many difficult and politically sensitive problems. The Indian states, through their Electricity Boards (SEBs), operate and develop most of the country's power facilities. However, the responsibility for supplying electricity is shared between the central government and the state governments, requiring full agreement between them before action can be taken. Despite many difficulties, important steps have been taken toward the establishment of an improved organizational structure. To facilitate planning and coordination, IDA encouraged the reorganization of the Central Electricity Authority in 1976. Regional Electricity Boards were established to further improve coordination among the states in matters of power development and operations. During 1979 and 1980, SEBs developed and implemented plans to improve their financial performance so as to achieve a rate of return of 9.5 percent on net fixed assets, as agreed under previous IDA projects. These plans include substantial tariff increases, rationalization of labor requirements, improved maintenance practices, and other related measures.

Another significant borrower has been Indonesia. Between 1969 and 1975, IDA committed a total of $100 million, almost all within a program of technical assistance for the Indonesia power agency, PLN. Consultants were brought in to establish a system of uniform accounts, provide training in management and planning, and initiate a review of tariffs. A financial recovery program was established in 1971 to make the system self-supporting. Efficiency was improved and tariffs were increased (by 145 percent between 1973 and 1976); by 1976, operating expenses were fully covered by revenues. PLN's installed capacity has increased fourfold since 1968. It now provides about 70 percent of Indonesia's electricity requirements. The power agency's remarkable financial recovery is one of the most significant examples of institutional improvement in recent Bank lending. Moreover, since 1975, Indonesia has borrowed more than $1 billion from the IBRD for subsequent power projects.

Telecommunications

IDA's telecommunications lending aims to solve problems in communications and to increase a country's capacity to attract and generate investments. Since financing for telecommunications is often available directly from suppliers, IDA has acted only as a lender of last resort. Between 1961 and 1980, $600 million was invested, though a further $390 million was committed in fiscal 1981 and 1982, mostly for India. This program will finance a large expansion of telecommunications and telex facilities in major cities, extend the telephone service to about 40 million people in rural areas, and expand domestic manufacturing of telecommunications equipment and cables.

IDA's objectives are to provide borrowers with technical advice and financial planning. To ensure the suitability of equipment, it also supervises procurement through competitive bidding. IDA concentrates on sectorwide planning studies to anticipate future problems and help develop the institutional capacity to deal with them. It also provides assistance in areas such as pricing policy, operations and maintenance, and investment planning.

Major institutional overhauls are sometimes needed. In Upper Volta, for example, IDA credits between 1969 and 1973 helped rehabilitate a deteriorating system and aided the transformation of the Office des Postes et Télécommunications into an autonomous entity. With IDA's help, a basic service was established in the six main cities, and long-distance connections between them and the outside world were initiated. In other remote countries, such as Nepal and Burma, IDA has brought in modern technology and methods. With the UNDP, IDA established a telecommunications corporation in Nepal in the early 1970s. In Burma, which had a poor telecommunications network, major improvements followed IDA's lending; 14,000 new telephone extensions, 4,000 automatic exchanges, and some limited telex facilities were installed.

Water and Sewerage

There is a strong relationship between clean water, sanitation, and health. Water-borne diseases are the leading cause of infant mortality worldwide and are among the most serious in the developing world. Although IDA has only recently begun lending to the health sector, per se, its water and sewerage projects have indirectly had major effects on health standards. Those projects have represented just in excess of $1 billion, 4 percent of IDA's commitments

during the past 22 years. However, more than 65 percent of that lending has occurred since 1978— a reflection of the World Bank's increasing focus on 400 million urban dwellers and 1.2 billion rural people[4] who still lack access to safe water and to sanitation.

In the 1960s, IDA usually supported large projects in urban water supply and sewerage, and it also helped to build up local water authorities. Beginning in the 1970s, IDA broadened its lending objectives to provide clean and affordable water for the poor in rural areas and to ensure that services reached the poor in urban fringes and, increasingly, in slums. In addition, IDA invested in new types of sewerage systems, since the standard systems, used in the industrial countries, were generally unsuitable and too expensive in IDA countries. IDA now provides a range of low-cost technical options, ranging from pit latrines to pour-flush toilets, all of which, if properly used, bring substantial benefits to public health. IDA has concentrated on improving water systems and adapting them to its borrowers' climatic and cultural conditions. It has built public standpipes in urban areas and systems for collecting rain water in the countryside. Finally, IDA has helped develop workable institutions, ranging from municipal water authorities to rural organizations that help maintain water systems.

As with other public services, the long-term constraint on water and sewerage development is usually financial. Water authorities frequently charge too little, perhaps because governments view water as a quasipublic good. Governments can themselves be the greatest financial offenders, not paying for the water they use. If pricing and revenue collection are inadequate, the ensuing deficits become a national budgetary problem. Therefore, technical and financing solutions need to proceed in tandem, and IDA has been involved in both.

Urban Development

Even in low-income, predominantly rural countries, urban populations are being swollen by migration. They are growing two or three times faster than the population as a whole, and up to four times faster in capital cities. Uncontrolled urbanization brings with it wider income disparities and greater need

4. Excluding China.

for services, especially in housing, transport, water, and sanitation. To help address these needs, IDA has spent $477 million on urban development projects since 1972 and has committed $350 million of that amount since 1978. Furthermore, it has tried to help its clients design urbanization schemes that are economical, replicable, and financially viable.

The traditional approach to urban slum and housing problems has been to clear slums and resettle the inhabitants in costly public housing. These developments have been out of the reach of low-income groups—or they have required large subsidies, typically ranging from 50 percent to 90 percent of cost. Limits on public funds have prevented such programs from being implemented on any big scale.

IDA's approach has been to concentrate on slum upgrading as opposed to clearance, with emphasis on providing security of tenure to slum dwellers. It has also aimed for economical improvements in infrastructure, such as roads, and for health-related investments in water supply and sanitation. IDA has been successful in helping countries provide this kind of basic upgrading at a cost of between $30 and $50 per person.

A similar approach is being taken in new area development. Known as "sites and services," it provides small plots of land with some basic services, such as roads and drains. The houses are then built by the owners themselves. These programs aim to recover all their costs from individual households

IDA and India's Cities

Urban population growth in India has been accelerating over the past three decades, from 2.3 percent a year in the 1950s to 3.9 percent a year in the 1970s. This growth, which is now

Water supply has been improved through an urban development program in Calcutta, India.

more than twice the rate at which the rural population is increasing, adds some 7 million people to India's towns and

cities each year. India was not prepared for such rapid growth, and conditions reached a critical state by the late 1960s and early 1970s. In most cities, between a third and a half of the population was living in slum or squatter conditions, without a secure right to the land they occupied and very limited access to urban services.

IDA has helped to build up the main institutions coping with urban growth, particularly the planning, development and financing agencies. For example, the Calcutta Metropolitan Development Authority (CMDA) was established in the early 1970s, and IDA was asked for assistance. Its first urban development credit to India followed, a $35 million credit to support a program of investments in five areas: water supply, sewerage and drainage, solid-waste collection and disposal, transport, and housing and area development. More than 2 million people have been affected by this program.

This was followed by a second multipronged program in 1978 and a transport project in 1980. IDA also supported programs in other big cities, principally Madras and Bombay, and has started trying to extend the experience it has gained to rapidly growing medium-size cities. One of the main lessons IDA has learned was the priority of strengthening institutions. Policy adjustments, changes in planning and design, and improved cost recovery need to be accompanied (even preceded) by improved organization and financial management, program monitoring and evaluation, and training. In recent projects, institutional programs have been initiated much earlier and are usually well under way by the time an IDA credit is approved.

A second lesson is the value of planning and design changes. In transport, where the traditional response to traffic congestion and delays has been to widen roads and build new ones, IDA projects have shown that existing facilities can be adapted through improved traffic management and engineering—at a fraction of the cost of constructing new facilities. Similarly, better use of existing facilities is possible in water and sewerage schemes. After the initial investment, changes can often be made to pay for themselves. In Bombay and Madras, for example, periodic increases in bus fares have brought their public-transport undertakings close to the point of financial self-sufficiency, an achievement that has often eluded public transport systems worldwide.

and businesses. The experience so far is encouraging (see box on India's cities).

Despite some successes, IDA's work has shown that urban transport and, more critically, urban employment pose significant obstacles. Without jobs in the modern sector, poor urban dwellers cannot afford to pay for public utilities and social services; nor can they maintain or upgrade housing. And without adequate transportation to those jobs, they are forced to fall back on low-pay employment in the informal sector.

Industry

The industrial sector has been looked to as a source of employment and income generation; however, industrial-led growth strategies have only been successful in a few countries, which possessed either a large resource base or a highly skilled work force. IDA's lending to traditional industrial projects has totaled $2.1 billion since 1961. The bulk of activity concentrated on South Asia, a good deal of it being support for fertilizer production in India—which has the size, population, and agricultural demand to sustain this form of import substitution. Other industrial projects IDA has financed include textile plants in Egypt, paper and pulp production in Tanzania, and jute rehabilitation in Bangladesh.

Despite the scope for labor-intensive technologies and the potential for export expansion, large-scale industrial lending is risky. Much depends on local efficiency and international competitiveness. And even successful ventures do not usually provide sufficient employment generation. To promote non-

traditional exports and local manufacturing, IDA has turned to the development of local financial institutions. The development finance companies (DFCs) relend money lent by IDA (on-lend) to eligible business concerns at market-related interest rates.

DFCs have been supported by about $530 million in commitments as of 1982. Lending has been concentrated in Sub-Saharan Africa, where IDA has funded 23 DFCs. It is not unusual for DFCs to suffer losses as ventures fail or borrowers are simply unable to repay. Therefore, they may have to fall back on local government guarantees,[5] and at times they have benefited from subsequent IDA assistance. Although DFCs can also on-lend to public enterprises, they generally help develop the local private sector (see box on the private sector).

In recent years, IDA has begun separate programs supporting small- and medium-scale industries. Lending to these businesses, to which IDA has committed at least $248 million since 1978, tends to create more jobs than does investment in large industrial projects. In Bangladesh, for example, there are 50,000 small enterprises and 500,000 cottage industries, which account for 35 percent of industrial value added and 80 percent of industrial employment. There is potential for expansion in areas such as fish drying, fruit processing, and rice milling. IDA credits for industrial development have been used to finance over 3,000 local projects in South Asia and helped to create 100,000 new jobs.

In Mauritania, IDA assistance helped turn a deteriorating system of state-owned workshops into a

---

5. In some cases, the DFCs themselves are public entities.

privately operated enterprise in which artisans are paid according to output. By providing training, working capital, and marketing advice, IDA assistance has enabled weavers to regain employment. In West Africa, recent IDA credits have created 150 new enterprises, employing 5,000 workers. While this may be a slow and possibly expensive way of creating jobs, it is one of the few means at IDA's disposal of trying to boost industrial employment directly.

In order to increase industrial efficiency and employment, IDA has sometimes advocated specific government policy reforms. In assisting Sri Lanka's effort to liberalize its trade regime and stimulate industrial production, IDA has created and assisted private small- and medium-scale industries. It has lent to commercial banks for on-lending to firms in agroprocessing, building materials, light engineering, and wood products. In Indonesia, IDA supported the rebuilding of public estates, the main producers of rubber, palm oil, and coconut oil, which together account for about 50 percent of nonpetroleum export earnings. By providing new management plans, teaching improved husbandry techniques, and supporting imports of equipment, IDA has helped to turn production and earnings around and to resettle and reemploy agricultural workers.

Social Sectors

Investments in social services—education, health, nutrition, and family planning—are in some respects different from IDA's other activities. Their benefits take longer to realize and are difficult to measure; their ultimate impact is seen mostly in aggregate indicators of literacy, infant mortality, fertility, and the like. Social investments can require more staff time because their design needs to take account of complex social and cultural factors. Even when success is achieved, it can be difficult to reproduce. Services have to be wanted, and part of that demand will depend on how they are priced, presented, and delivered.

In the social sectors, governments are responsible for continuing to provide services after the credit has ceased, and over time these recurrent costs can far exceed the initial investment. Before expanding its social lending, therefore, IDA undertakes a serious assessment of the country's fiscal ability to maintain its projects. Some imprecision is inevitable, though, and decisions have sometimes been

based on an unrealistic view of revenues and the demands that are put on them. In the difficult past few years, budgetary crises have often meant that social services were cut back, in the process unraveling carefully designed programs. Hence IDA has realized the importance of viable macroeconomic policies, as discussed in the last section.

Education

Among social sectors, IDA's longest track record is in education. It has committed $1.52 billion since 1961, of which $460 million was in 1981 and 1982 alone. In recent years, about half of IDA's educational lending has been in East and West Africa, where literacy gains have been fastest but absolute levels are still significantly below those of other regions.

IDA's initial involvement in education can best be described as the "bricks and mortar" approach. The World Bank has been involved in the construction or improvement of 10,000 educational facilities in the developing world. This emphasis has gradually been broadened into a greater concern for overall policies, including education planning, curricula reform, textbook production, and teacher training. Swaziland provides a good example of IDA's work (see box on education in Swaziland).

Although its initial support was for higher education, IDA has increasingly financed primary education, especially in rural areas. Difficulties abound: children who go to school have to be released from some of their work on farms, and teachers who will work in rural areas are difficult to recruit. In a series of credits to Senegal, IDA has supported rural youth training centers, primary-school teacher training, and technical training programs in applied and vocational subjects. In Indonesia, technical training centers established through IDA credits annually graduate 4,500 students, and support for local polytechnics has substantially increased the number of engineering technicians. IDA loans helped to produce 170 million schoolbooks during the 1970s, half Indonesia's total. IDA projects also helped to broaden curricula in Uganda, diversify secondary education in Morocco and Sierra Leone, and create new institutions (such as local advisory boards and ministerial units) in Lesotho, Malawi, and the People's Republic of the Congo. In Pakistan and Bangladesh, IDA is supporting a significant effort to raise the quality of primary education through projects that integrate efforts to provide better administration,

Education in Swaziland

Swaziland's National Development Plan, introduced in 1973, included the following objectives: (1) universal primary education; (2) expansion of junior secondary education; (3) reorientation of both primary and secondary education toward practical, technical, and scientific subjects; (4) establishment of adult education programs; and (5) improvement in the overall quality of education. The government of Swaziland turned to IDA for assistance.

IDA's first project financed the building of rural education centers, the expansion of the Swaziland College of Technology (the country's only technical training institution), and more teacher-training facilities. In 1977, a second project provided for the expansion and improvement of 13 existing junior secondary schools, the establishment of four new ones, and the expansion of facilities for training agricultural teachers. By this time, Swaziland had achieved the status of a middle-income country and could afford IBRD loans rather than IDA credits. A further loan in 1980 continued to emphasize secondary education, but also built 31 new primary schools and expanded 12 others. In conjunction with other bilateral and multilateral donors, the project provided technical assistance in a wide range of areas (for example, textbooks and curricula).

These credits and loans—$19 million since 1973—are the equivalent of $35 per capita, one of the highest levels of education lending by the Bank. When completed, 42 of Swaziland's 70 secondary schools, accounting for two-thirds of enrollment since 1974, will have been assisted by either IDA or the IBRD. The Bank has financed 6,100 new places in secondary schools, plus 11,000 primary school places and 350 technical and vocational places. Swaziland's literacy is already among the highest in Africa, and the percentage enrolled in secondary school has risen sharply. Swaziland traditionally has employed 40 percent of its work force in service industries where the benefits of secondary education are high.

improved teaching facilities, and better trained teachers.

The long-term success of IDA's educational lending depends on the development of effective, country-specific education strategies and on the ability of countries to manage their public expenditure. Since spending on education involves primarily local costs—often accounting for anywhere from 10 percent to 30 percent of public expenditure—and since these costs recur every year, IDA has become more aware that education projects have to fit into a country's overall budgetary plan if they are to be maintained after the IDA credit has ceased.

Population and Family Planning

Population programs are a small and comparatively recent area of IDA lending: some $110 million was actually lent between 1975 and 1982. The importance of supplying safe, cheap, and effective family-planning services, especially in rural areas, is now well recognized; family planning is no longer seen as a mere adjunct of medical care. Like other institutions, IDA has also had to learn that family-planning programs require strong government support and a credible strategy for providing information and services. Acceptance of family planning is not a one-time event. Reductions in fertility require a sustained demand for family planning. Parents often want many children for practical economic reasons: because of high mortality, high fertility is seen to

be a way of ensuring the survival of a certain number of offspring. Improvements in maternal and child health care to combat infant mortality are therefore essential; so are better educational opportunities for women.

IDA has been associated with a successful program in Indonesia, where the National Family Planning Coordinating Board (NFPCB) was set up in 1970 to oversee family-planning services. IDA and the UN Fund for Population Activities financed much of the NFPCB's establishment, including provincial training centers, midwifery schools, and mobile information units. These have been combined with an effective system for reaching villages and towns, initially involving fieldworkers but shifting to community-based distribution centers, and assisted by other donors such as the U.S. Agency for International Development. The government of Indonesia is now running a successful nationwide population program, the results of which are seen in significantly lower birth rates.

IDA also offered technical assistance to Bangladesh to build a family-planning program into its first five-year plan. With strong political support, a $15 million IDA credit, and $25 million from other donors, the project was begun. It funded a staff of 4,000, increased the distribution of contraceptives, and boosted education and information efforts. Among married women, use of contraception rose from 10 percent in 1975 to 20 percent in 1981. Despite changes in governments, political support has remained firm. The importance of government

IDA and the Kenyan Population Program

Kenya's population growth rate is among the highest in the world. While the number of births per 1,000 has remained fairly constant, the number of child deaths has fallen by almost 50 percent since 1960. The net result is a population growth rate of 4 percent a year. In part, parents want children for economic reasons; they will eventually have fewer as they realize that offsprings' chances of survival have improved. In part, however, there are cultural reasons for large families—Kenya's fertility rate is the highest in Africa.

By 1971, the pressure on arable land was severe, with 80 percent of the population living on 18 percent of the land. Spending on social services accounted for 43 percent of the government budget (compared with 24 percent in 1964), and 25 percent of the labor force was unemployed. Only 45 percent of the population was supporting the 55 percent who were below 15 or above 60 years of age. These disturbing trends prompted the government into action.

From late 1969 to 1973, IDA participated in negotiations with the government and seven international donors to develop a five-year program, costing $39 million (of which IDA contributed $12 million). The program was very ambitious, calling for:

- The introduction of maternal and child health care, combined with family-planning services, in over 400 government health centers.
- An extension of those services, through the use of 17 mobile teams, to 190 other facilities where staff had not been formally trained in family planning.
- The establishment of eight community nursing schools, 30 associated rural health centers, and the training of a new class of supervisors for 600 nurses.
- The introduction and training of a new class of fieldworkers, family-health field educators, and their supervisors.
- A provision for the Ministry of Health to produce more health education material.
- The establishment of a new organization, the National Family Welfare Center, to plan and support the activities of the program.

The idea of combining family planning with health care was deliberate, to provide people easy access to family-planning information and services. When the $39 million program got started, however, it was realized that the level of support for family planning varied among the principal interest groups. The government was interested primarily in rural health care and saw family planning as only a small part of that effort. The people themselves have traditionally favored many children—eight per family, according to one survey. Health workers, reflecting the mood in the country, were unwilling to give family planning any priority.

Lacking coherent support, the five-year program had only limited demographic impact. The population growth rate did not fall as expected; indeed, it actually increased by the end of the program in 1979. Only 5 percent of the reproductive age group is estimated to be using contraceptives regularly. The project aimed for 650,000 new acceptors, but only 310,000 adults visited family-planning centers during the period, and the actual number of long-run acceptors is not known. In contrast, maternal and child health, which had stronger support from the government, did much better: between 65 percent and 75 percent of all pregnant women were reached by this part of the program.

The Kenyan government has given IDA good marks for the quality of its technical assistance and for closely supervising the progress of the project. Others have faulted IDA for paying too much attention to the technical and quantifiable elements of the project; putting too little emphasis on its institutional limitations and management problems; concentrating more on supplying family-planning services and less on disseminating information; and agreeing to an expensive health program under the guise of family planning.

The Bank's project staff came to the view that the family-planning program was far too ambitious considering existing cultural norms and the weak political support the program enjoyed. Some of the lessons learned from the program—the first population project in Sub-Saharan Africa—have been incorporated into the second population project now under way. Key government ministries and private organizations are now involved. A clearer distinction between family planning and health has been drawn. And more is being done to educate people about family-planning services. Perhaps most important of all, the establishment of the National Council of Population Development in the Vice President's Office has sent out a clear signal of political commitment to family planning.

---

commitment can be seen in Kenya, a country where encouraging GNP growth is being eroded by extremely rapid population growth (see box on the Kenyan population program).

IDA's long-run success in promoting economic development, especially in Africa, will in large measure be affected by progress made in social sectors. Population growth rates above 2.5 percent a year are offsetting GNP growth and creating food and nutrition problems. Combined with a dearth of human skills and suitable institutions, population growth is therefore hindering the task of development in Sub-Saharan Africa.

Program Lending

About $2.9 billion—or more than a tenth of IDA's lending in 1961–81—was not tied to particular projects.[6] These "program credits" can be disbursed rapidly and are intended to ease severe foreign-exchange constraints. They have generally been accompanied by policy advice aimed at improving a country's overall performance. In some cases, program lending has been used for major reconstruc-

6. This does not include small amounts of nonproject technical assistance.

tion. During the past two decades, program lending went largely to countries in South Asia. India received 50 percent of the total ($1.3 billion) between 1964 and 1976, in the form of 11 industrial import programs (IIP). Another $715 million was used to finance imports of agricultural inputs and industrial raw materials for Bangladesh (see box on Bangladesh import credits).

In the case of India, credits were initially provided with the objective of making capital available to the private sector; subsequently, in the late 1960s, the primary purpose was to help bridge chronic current account deficits.[7] In the early 1970s, this approach was altered to allow more imports for industry; in the final two IIP credits, in 1975 and 1976, foreign exchange was earmarked for certain vital capital-goods industries, where a shortage of imports was curtailing production. These two credits accounted for almost 20 percent of total nonproject assistance

---

7. IMF programs were also in place during this period.

Bangladesh Import Credits

When Bangladesh became independent in 1971, the newly formed government inherited a shattered economy. The country had lost many skilled individuals in the process of partition, and a good deal of physical infrastructure had been demolished. Agricultural and industrial production were at a standstill. Attempts to revive the economy were complicated by the need to fashion a national government out of a provincial administration, to establish new development institutions, and to reorient the economy after the loss of the key West Pakistan market. Pervasive poverty in the country made these tasks more difficult and more urgent. It was vital for the government to obtain substantial and sustained external assistance to prevent further deterioration and to begin rehabilitation and reconstruction.

Given the gross inadequacy of the country's domestic savings and foreign-exchange earnings to finance its development program, IDA agreed to provide program assistance. Thus between 1972 and 1981 IDA provided Bangladesh with $715 million through 10 import program credits, with the focus of each credit reflecting the economic conditions prevailing at the time. The primary rationale for the first three program credits was to rehabilitate the economy, hard hit by the cyclone of 1970 and the war of 1971. These credits provided rapidly disbursable funds for critical raw materials and spare parts. The first credit covered all the major sectors of the economy. The second and third import programs focused on priority exports, such as jute, and import substitution industries, such as cotton textiles, pulp and paper, fertilizer, and cement.

The fourth import credit introduced a new detailed action program aimed at improving the efficiency of the two largest industries—jute and cotton textiles—through the upgrading of management and operational systems. The fifth credit expanded these programs and initiated studies to determine the development needs of the pulp and paper industry. The sixth credit strengthened the ongoing programs and reviewed pricing policies, industry investment requirements (including possible mill closures), and sectoral performance targets.

Improvements to the jute and textile industries were expected to be gradual. By 1979 sufficient progress had been made to allow the policy focus of subsequent credits to be directed to other key areas of the economy, such as export development and agricultural policy reform. Thus the seventh and eighth import programs were aimed at strengthening export infrastructure and institutional capabilities and identifying nontraditional export lines.

While rehabilitation and development of the industrial sector were urgently needed, agriculture and population growth were also areas of concern. Subjected to the vagaries of extreme weather, the country faced fluctuating supplies of food-grains and chronic food deficits. Because agriculture represents over half of GDP and provides 70 percent of total employment, the latest two credits have been directed at agricultural and food policies. These credits support a new medium-term food production plan, involving a core of projects in the annual development plan, the removal of restrictions on private-sector involvement in the irrigation sector, and a review of fertilizer subsidies. Greater emphasis is being placed on government pricing and expenditure policies.

The fundamental case for program assistance to Bangladesh was the gross inadequacy of domestic savings and foreign-exchange earnings to finance development programs and ongoing operations. Without program aid, the supply of agriculture imports (such as fertilizer) and nonagricultural inputs would have been severely compressed. Since 1972, IDA program credits have been a significant source of aid, accounting for 4.4 percent of total imports and 19.3 percent of commodity aid.

Considering the desperate situation in 1972, program credits have given the country a major boost and have furthered important reforms, but many problems in the industrial and agricultural sectors remain unresolved, as do issues relating to overall efficiency and management. Industry, in particular, faces major difficulties in eliminating operating losses, competing against imports, and improving production efficiency. Still, industrial output has grown at about 3.5 percent annually, and without commodity aid, this improvement would not have been possible. As a result of the action programs, jute production has been restored, and textile productivity slides have been halted. The government has accepted the principle of free-market pricing, divestiture of mills to the private sector, and private investment in new mills. Rehabilitation programs are now under way in the jute, cotton textile, and fertilizer industries, and the government has requested IDA assistance for the rehabilitation of the pulp and paper industry. IDA for its part has indicated its willingness to work with the government in augmenting the country's resources and improving its policy environment.

and financed approximately 18 percent of India's imports (other than oil) at the time.

All IIPs involved policy discussions as well as money, to ensure that the credits were used to the best possible effect. During the period of the 1975 and 1976 credits, the government of India embarked on a series of policy reforms aimed at easing import restrictions and expanding exports. A succession of good harvests, increased remittances, and improved exports helped India out of its balance-of-payments difficulties. By providing a sizable portion of the foreign-exchange requirements of Indian industry, IDA is credited for its role in maintaining production levels. The IIPs did not become a vehicle for reforms in specific industries, despite attempts to improve the dialogue on industrial policy. But they did help support some broader policy shifts, including import-licensing reform, improved export promotion policies, and general antiinflationary macroeconomic policies.

As for other program loans, in 1975 IDA took the view that further program assistance to Sri Lanka would not be justified, since the government's policy reforms fell far short of what was required. In Pakistan, a good deal of the intended reform measures were carried out, but Pakistan's external deficit was not significantly narrowed as a result of the IDA credit. The results of program lending have therefore been mixed, in part because it was expected to provide both urgently needed finance and a basis for basic sectoral reforms. It is difficult to do both. To improve the effectiveness of program lending, the Bank therefore decided to deal more explicitly with macroeconomic reforms.

It has done so, since 1980, by offering some members structural adjustment credits. IDA funds were used for such credits to Kenya and Senegal as complements to formal adjustment programs, with drawings made conditional on actual reforms. Kenya's quantitative restrictions on imports have been reduced as a first step toward improving its trade regime; in Malawi, the government has begun to review agricultural prices and to take steps to improve the position of key public-sector enterprises. However, budgetary problems have remained intractable. Malawi is an important case because its excellent overall development performance—real GDP growth exceeded 6 percent a year in the 1970s— is being threatened by adjustment problems (see box on Malawi). Where policy measures are considered inadequate, IDA has blocked the release of

tranches until it is confident that satisfactory progress is made.

Nonproject lending—including program aid and general technical assistance—is a valuable instrument in dealing with overall policy reform and economic management. A strong argument can be made for this kind of lending before countries reach an economic crisis. Too often, however, necessary reforms are delayed too long and a serious compression ensues. IDA has at times been associated with successful recovery efforts (see box on Indonesia).

While program lending had been relatively modest in the late 1970s, it is now seen as a more important sector of lending for IDA in view of the difficulties that low-income developing countries have had adjusting to higher oil prices and slower world growth. Program lending provides a more direct focus for macroeconomic reforms, but it is only one of the approaches that IDA takes to these issues.

Policy Dialogue

Quite apart from its role in project financing, some of IDA's most important contributions to development have been made through the discussions it has with governments on a broad range of policy issues. Considerable time is spent on general economic and sector work before any actual project lending takes place. Economic reports survey macroeconomic conditions and the main sectors— agriculture, industry, and energy. They tend to study the key issues of investment and savings; public finances; the balance of payments, particularly the performance of exports; and overall prospects for growth. They act as the starting point for discussions with governments on the nature and severity of their development constraints, and on the policies and resources needed to overcome them. Sector reports go into more detail on sectoral developments— specific bottlenecks, investment programs, and government policies—and set the stage for project identification. These reports are valued not only by the borrowing country but also by other donors and institutions, since they are usually the most comprehensive and up-to-date assessment of the country's economic prospects and development strategy. The fact that detailed reports are produced periodically for each country underlines IDA's belief that each economy is unique and changing. While IDA recognizes that every government has its own

IDA and Malawi

Malawi has been one of the most successful African economies in the past 15 years. IDA has accounted for roughly 50 percent of Malawi's total external assistance and has played a catalytic role in strengthening key development institutions

A unit supervisor explains the boundaries of family plots to extension workers on the Lilongue rural development project in Malawi.

and in launching programs that were critical for Malawi's success. Three areas of development deserve particular mention:

- *Agriculture.* Between 1969–71 and 1977–79 Malawi's agricultural output rose by 4 percent a year, the fastest in Sub-Saharan Africa. However, while estate production has expanded rapidly, the output of small farmers, especially of export crops, has lagged. With substantial IDA support, the government has tackled this problem through rural development projects covering several sectors. Intensive in terms of staffing and investment, most of these projects had good records. But they were expensive. By 1981, it became apparent that they could not be replicated throughout the country. A joint IDA-government review in 1982 recommended that future rural development investment should concentrate on directly productive activities (such as extension services, credit, training, and marketing). This less capital-intensive approach, together with increased producer prices,

is expected to lead to increased production by small farmers in the 1980s.
- *Transport.* Land-locked Malawi badly needed more roads. In 1966 IDA financed the engineering design of the Zomba-Lilongwe road linking the old capital with the new. It also funded studies on road transport licensing and road–rail coordination. Subsequent investments financed the major north–south highway linking Lilongwe with Karonga. The projects have helped Malawi achieve its initial transport objectives. However, IDA's main impact has been in helping to extend and maintain the district feeder-road network to handle a larger volume of agricultural output.
- *Education.* IDA has provided assistance for a program that will result in self-help construction of 1,000 primary-school classrooms. Each classroom is estimated to cost less than a third what it would if it had been built by conventional methods. The program has galvanized community support and forged links with several government ministries.

IDA's impact has frequently extended beyond its projects. It has helped to coordinate aid from other donors, and its technical assistance has enabled it to assist Malawi to develop programs responsive to national priorities. IDA has also strongly supported the government's outward-looking development strategy, based upon agricultural exports. Tariffs in general have been kept low, quantitative restrictions on imports have been largely avoided, and price and wage restraints have been used to moderate inflation.

Although Malawi's achievements have been considerable, the recent deterioration in its balance of payments and fiscal position have revealed several structural weaknesses in the economy. IDA has helped Malawi to identify those problems—the narrowness of the export base, the worsening financial position of public and private enterprises, a growing budgetary deficit due to high recurrent expenditures, and rigidities in the system of administered tariffs, prices, and wages. IDA staff helped the government to formulate a recovery program, and supported it with a structural adjustment credit of $45 million.

The program was designed to accomplish many (perhaps too many) objectives: diversify the export base, encourage efficient import substitution, adjust incentives, improve public- and private-sector performance, and strengthen the government's economic planning and monitoring capability. Its record so far has been mixed. Although substantial progress had been achieved in a number of important areas (appropriating additional funds for agriculture, increasing tariffs for several public utilities, creating an Investment Coordinating Committee, and ameliorating the institutional problems of enterprises in the public and private sectors), the credit's second $20 million tranche was delayed until various prerequisites were met. It was released in April 1982 after the government took corrective measures to put its adjustment program back on track. After 15 years of successful performance, Malawi is now at a critical stage in its development. And IDA, after a fruitful 15-year partnership, is adjusting its lending program accordingly.

economic philosophy and is free to choose its own development goals, it does point out distortions and inefficiencies that hinder resource mobilization.

Macroeconomic and sectoral policies are naturally interrelated, and they often have a direct bearing on the success or failure of individual projects. It is difficult to sustain a good project in an unfavorable environment. Furthermore, fruitful policy dialogue can do more to influence a country's development than even a series of good projects. Some critics maintain, however, that IDA devotes too much effort to promoting projects and too little effort to changing the policies that hinder development. But there is a limit to how much influence IDA actually has in any country. Governments respond best when they are convinced that policy advice is correct and

will work. They will not be persuaded by threats to reduce lending, for example. And IDA is not always right. Its solutions may not suit the political or social conditions of particular countries, and it has learned many lessons from recipient governments. Knowing this, IDA prefers to make governments aware of problems, then to suggest solutions, listen to alternatives, and support government policies that seem headed in the right direction.

Even when policies have become a serious impediment to operations, IDA has sometimes chosen to maintain a residual influence rather than to cut off lending altogether. That is viewed as the last resort in circumstances that have become untenable. Precisely because the Bank attempts to work with governments, despite imperfections in poli-

---

IDA and Indonesia

IDA assistance to Indonesia began in the mid-1960s, at a time of severe economic disruption, institutional fragmentation, and disorder in the wake of the Sukarno era. The country was struggling to launch a rehabilitation program that required a large amount of external resources. Inflation ran at 650 percent in 1965, and foreign reserves were dwindling rapidly. By the late 1960s, Indonesia's external debt amounted to $2.1 billion, 20 percent of GDP. After three partial moratoriums in 1966–68, the Paris Club agreed in 1970 to a long-term rescheduling of Indonesia's external public debt.

IDA assumed a leading role in mobilizing and coordinating aid through the Intergovernmental Group on Indonesia (IGGI), established in 1966. IGGI is chaired by the Dutch government and consists of all major donor countries; the Bank serves as its secretariat. In 1970, half of Indonesia's development spending was financed by foreign aid, all on concessional terms.

In the early years of IDA involvement, special attention was given to meeting Indonesia's shortage of skilled labor and its rehabilitation requirements. In addition to five technical assistance credits amounting to $25 million, IDA provided advice and financed training activities. Recognizing the urgent need for institutional reforms, most IDA projects took steps to reorganize project authorities, including drafting charters, assisting in preparing legislation, and financing substantial organizational analyses and managerial and technical upgrading.

To develop skilled workers, IDA aimed at strengthening and creating new educational and training institutions, assisting the Ministry of Education in its planning and educational management. Two IDA credits and two IBRD loans helped the government to upgrade senior secondary agricultural schools and service centers. They also established a new agency for coordinating and administering middle-level agricultural training, and a successful national agricultural extension program.

Given agriculture's key role, its rehabilitation was a priority. IDA has assisted the water authority to design and execute its irrigation program, with four IDA credits (followed by eight IBRD loans). Between 1968 and 1978, 5.3 million hectares came under cultivation. Irrigation investments have had a substantial impact on rice production. Whereas in 1968 Indonesia was producing only 12 million tons of rice and was the world's largest rice importer, by 1978 Indonesia was producing 17.5 million tons, almost enough to meet its steadily expanding demand.

IDA has also played a leading role in electrical power. Since 1969, it has helped to reform the Indonesian power authority, provided credits for rehabilitating Jakarta's electricity distribution system, and begun the development of the Java grid (to be completed with the help of IBRD power projects). Power generation has increased by 150 percent since 1974; supply is reliable, and the power authority is generating enough money to continue its program.

From 1968 until 1974, all lending to Indonesia was made through IDA. The country's creditworthiness then improved as a result of the commodity and oil price boom. Virtually all of the Bank's lending since 1974 has been through IBRD loans. A modest amount of lending continued to come from IDA, as Indonesia's per capita GNP was well below the IDA ceiling. Given Indonesia's much improved balance of payments, however, IDA lending was discontinued in 1980.

Indonesia has received 48 IDA credits totaling $932 million, and 59 IBRD loans amounting to $3.8 billion. IFC investments have totaled $133 million. By 1980, only 24 percent of the development budget was externally financed.

IDA has been only one element in Indonesia's rapid development. After a disastrous phase in the 1960s, the country has benefited from good macroeconomic management and a rapidly expanding corps of qualified people. However, in the absence of IDA assistance—financing, technical assistance, and institutional support for key sectors—it is hard to see how such development efforts would have progressed as rapidly as they did. Moreover, when Indonesia's oil revenues emerged in the mid-1970s, it could use these funds effectively because it had the institutions and management capacities already in place.

IDA and Sudan

In the 1970s, Sudan's investment rate was stagnating at about 10 percent of GDP. The government launched an ambitious public investment program, to be financed by domestic resources and a substantial increase in external assistance, particulary from the oil exporting countries. At the time, IDA thought the investment program of needed infrastructure and irrigation projects was well conceived, and approved credits totaling $400 million between 1975 and 1980.

But IDA and other donors financed only half of project costs; the government bore the cost of the balance. Subsidies to consumers for wheat, sugar, and gasoline and to parastatals further dissipated government revenues. As a result, the government's budget deficit rose to 25 percent of expenditure in 1977 and 35 percent in 1979. And the large increase in concessional external resources did not materialize, leading the government to resort to commercial borrowings.

Project implementation in agriculture, transport, and power was slow and often problematic. Skilled labor was lacking because many workers had migrated to jobs in neighboring OPEC countires. With the push into large public-sector projects, existing infrastructure deteriorated, making the implementation of new projects even more difficult. In addition, the agricultural sector was not well managed. Cotton farmers worked for public agricultural enterprises, beset by inefficiences and price distortions. As a result, cotton output fell by more than 50 percent in the 1970s, and total exports fell from 17 percent of GDP in 1972 to 8 percent in 1977.

IDA had clearly overestimated Sudan's absorptive capacity, management capabilities, and ability to attract foreign assistance. However, some of Sudan's problems were externally rooted. In addition to the exodus of skilled labor, Sudan suffered from falling prices for its exports and rising prices for imported petroleum. As as result, Sudan now finds itself in an economic crisis. Its import bill is running at twice the level of exports, and its debt-service obligations, despite recent reschedulings, are still more than half its export earnings. Sudan has been in arrears several times to official and private creditors, and further reschedulings of its debt appear likely.

Since the late 1970s, the government has been trying to undertake necessary reforms. It has been working with the IMF to improve its exchange rate and budgetary situation through devaluation and reductions in subsidies. In 1979, the government agreed with IDA to abandon its ambitious six-year plan and to adopt a more cautious three-year public investment program aimed at restoring productive output, particularly in agriculture and for export. IDA has supported this policy change through several tranched credits directed toward agricultural rehabilitation. A joint IDA-Sudan study of parastatal organizations led to several constructive reforms, and several of these organizations have been turned over to the private sector.

The macroeconomic policy dialogue continues to stress the need for futher reductions in subsidies, better debt management, and improved government resource mobilization and expenditure policies. Some improvement in agricultural output waas achieved in 1981–82, and there are prospects for petroleum development. But the country's heavy debt burden, continued shortage of foreign exchange, and depressed export prices mean that restoring economic stability and growth will be a long-term process.

---

cies, it is often the most influential external agency. Were IDA only to operate in those countries where policies were best and prospects were brightest, it would be missing important opportunities to be of real assistance and would also be abrogating a role the international community expects it to perform. In Sudan, for example, IDA is working with the government to seek solutions to a complex set of problems (see box on Sudan). In a few cases where IDA cannot establish the basis of a policy dialogue, it has withdrawn the bulk of its support.

IDA's influence is often disproportionate to the funds it provides; it has not financed a dominant share of investment in most of its major clients (see Table 2.2). However, IDA's constituency has changed over the past decade; its lending makes up a significant proportion of gross domestic investment in an increasing number of borrowers.[8] Whereas in 1970 IDA's contribution was large in only three countries (Malawi, Somalia, and Mauritania), by 1980 it was comparably important in seven (the Central African Republic, Bangladesh, Burundi, Nepal, Mali, Ethiopia, and the Gambia), all of which are least-developed countries. Although IDA might be expected to exert more policy influence in these countries, their policy environment is generally less favorable (and at times the political direction is less clear). Ministries may change their policies by directive; but carrying them into effect requires strong institutions, and these are often lacking. This is one reason why IDA has put major efforts into institution building (see Chapter 5).

There are many more countries where IDA's financial contribution has loomed large in particular sectors. It is a matter of independent judgment as to just how much sectoral influence IDA has and whether it uses it to full effect. As with macroeconomic matters, most reforms are undertaken slowly and incrementally, and usually not in response to overt external pressure. Experience has shown that IDA has established a particularly close rapport with

---

8. An arbitrary 7 percent figure is used to gauge "significance." IDA flows (measured as an average of two fiscal years' disbursements) also exceeded 5 percent of gross domestic investment (1980) in Rwanda, Benin, Senegal, and Guinea. See Annex Table 4 for further details.

Senegal's Agriculture

Since independence in 1960, per capita income in Senegal has hardly changed. A single commodity, groundnuts, still accounts for 30 percent of export earnings. Growth of agriculture as a whole barely kept pace with population, because prices were kept artificially low to maintain the purchasing power of the urban work force. Added to this was a series of droughts and rapid increases in inport prices. Farmers suffered from inefficient extension services, mismanaged government support agencies, and poorly maintained irrigation facilities. Until recently, groundnut farmers tended to receive less than world prices for their crops. Foreign groundnut traders were replaced by a state cooperative system; later, the processing industry was brought under state control.

Overambitious infrastructure investments and increased government participation in industry strained public finances. The government was unable to put up counterpart funds for projects, causing delays in execution. In the absence of agricultural reforms, overall macroeconomic problems became so serious in the late 1970s that some major public enterprises collapsed, and eventually Senegal was forced to ask for debt rescheduling.

In conjunction with an IMF program, the Bank offered Senegal a structural adjustment loan/credit (SAL) to support a serious program of reforms. This included a revised investment program, concentrating on productive activities; a price incentive scheme for industrial production, particularly for exports; a strategy to reduce the weight of the parastatal sector in the economy and to eliminate losses in the remaining public enterprises; and basic changes in agricultural policies. The agricultural program involved a reorientation from a centralized, state-controlled system to a system based on autonomous farmers' groups at the village level, and included liquidation of the state marketing organization, direct supply of inputs to farmers' organizations, a reform of the agricultural credit system, and a move toward economic prices.

Political changes and a poor harvest hindered the introduction of some crucial reforms, including the reduction of the subsidy on imported rice. This measure was delayed by more than a year. Because of the slow pace of agricultural reforms, the Bank did not release the second tranche of its SAL.

India and Bangladesh in agriculture, for example. In India, common goals were easily identified and a general strategy put in place. These successful links helped in other areas, such as urban development. In Bangladesh, a country that faced enormous problems at the time of independence, substantial progress has also been made.

Sector dialogues have improved the policy environment not only for IDA projects but more broadly. Adopted reforms, based on demonstrably better policies, are replicated in other regions of the country and in other sectors. But improvements have been uneven and have often been reversed by external events or internal political developments. In some environments, fairly basic reforms are needed in areas such as agricultural pricing policies and sector management. These difficulties merely exacerbate the overall macroeconomic situation (see box on Senegal). IDA is often in the unenviable situation of implicitly aiding and abetting inappropriate policies that waste precious resources, while trying to use consistent and constructive liaison with sovereign countries to reform those policies.

IDA has been most effective when it can work with strong government support, basing its lending program on a viable, sectorwide development plan. This requires a certain amount of political stability and continuous IDA involvement, often with a series of credits. IDA has promoted tariff reductions and devaluations, higher charges for electricity and water, agricultural reforms favoring smallholders, better road maintenance procedures, and urban planning. IDA's expertise and advice is often sought, but not always followed. IDA's clients at times see it as too rigid in its economic orientation and insufficiently sensitive to political factors. Some donors, however, have suggested that the IBRD and IDA could make greater use of their influence in promoting economic reforms, particularly in countries with serious economic problems. But without IDA credits, desirable policy reforms would have been even less likely to have taken place.

5   Issues in Project Effectiveness

Judgments on the effectiveness of IDA's investments are difficult to make with any precision. Projects are affected by a variety of factors, some of which are unpredictable and beyond IDA's control. The impact of a particular project can be measured in several ways—by comparing its results with what was there before, for example, or with what might have happened had it not been undertaken. Except in straightforward physical terms—the amount of megawatts added to a country's electric power capacity, for instance—such comparisons are difficult to quantify.

Bearing these qualifications in mind, this chapter explores some of the factors that help in deciding just how effective IDA has been. It begins by examining the rates of return on projects, and goes on to discuss some of the reasons why they vary. It then considers those of IDA's contributions that cannot easily be quantified but are no less important for that. The chapter draws heavily on IDA's project experience.

Rates of Return

The majority of projects undertaken by IDA include estimates of their prospective rates of return. These returns measure the potential benefit to the country from undertaking the project and permit comparisons to be made between alternative projects. Although rates of return have certain deficiencies, they are the single most convenient indicator of project effectiveness (see box on the rate of return).

When IDA projects are completed, they are audited by the Bank's Operations Evaluation Department (OED).[1] The auditors reestimate the rates of return and compare these with the returns anticipated at the time of project appraisal. It should be remembered, though, that these audit returns are not the actual rate of return of the project over its entire life. That cannot be measured until the investment has completely worn out and the final results have been added up.

Overall, 273 audits of completed IBRD projects, and 183 of IDA projects, contained a quantified rate of return. On the IBRD loans, the average rate of return was 17 percent; on IDA credits it was 18 percent (see Table 5.1). These averages are not weighted to account for the size of projects. Innovative and experimental projects often have low rates

---

1. Technically, these are government projects that are assisted by IDA. They will be referred to as "IDA projects" for convenience.

61

Project Analysis and the Rate of Return

Project analysis assesses the benefits and costs of a project with a common yardstick. If benefits exceed or equal costs, the project is acceptable; if not, the project should be rejected. Costs are defined relative to their opportunity costs, which is the benefit forgone by not using these resources in the best available alternative.

Economic analysis of projects is similar to financial analysis in that both assess the profitability of an investment in money terms. However, financial analysis identifies the money profit accruing to the entity undertaking the project and is concerned with the entity's ability to meet its financial obligations and to finance future investments. Economic analysis, by contrast, measures the effect of the project on the fundamental objectives of the whole economy. Thus, while wages are clearly a financial cost for a project, they will be an economic cost only if the use of labor causes reduced output elsewhere in the economy; if labor is normally unemployed, there will be no sacrifice. Conversely, a project may entail an economic cost that does not involve a money cost. Environmental damage is a cost to society that often does not appear as a monetary cost to the project itself. Economic costs and benefits, therefore, may be larger or smaller than financial costs and benefits, and are derived using "shadow" or efficiency prices rather than market prices in order to reflect true resource constraints.

Inputs and outputs are generally valued at "border" or international prices, plus some adjustment for domestic transport and handling costs. Those that are actually traded internationally will be converted to domestic equivalents using existing exchange rates. Where these exchange rates do not reflect the true scarcity of foreign exchange, a shadow exchange rate will be employed. Outputs expected to occur in the future are valued at prices likely to prevail in those years, adjusted for inflation in order to keep the analysis in real terms.

As the Bank has become more directly concerned with the effect of its projects on the alleviation of poverty, it has begun experimenting with an expanded system of analysis that can accommodate multiple policy objectives, including better provision of services or more equal distribution of income, in contrast to the single objective of efficiency underlying the traditional approach. For example, a social wage rate would reflect, in addition to the effect on output, both the benefit of that increased income in its impact on the poor and the cost in reduced savings and reinvestment. Such shadow prices differ in concept from those relating to efficiency objectives alone, and are referred to as "social" prices. The determination of social prices, however, is difficult because it requires explicit judgments about the relative value of consumption by different income groups.

Future costs and benefits of a project can be discounted to present values using an agreed-upon discount rate. According to this approach, projects with positive net present values would be viable undertakings. An alternative approach, which is more common in the Bank, is to calculate an internal rate of return. This rate of return is the discount rate that equalizes the present value of project benefits and costs. The larger the benefits, the higher the discount rate must be to bring benefits down to the level of project costs, and hence the higher will be the internal rate of return.

Since benefits and costs can be measured using financial, economic, and social approaches, there are corresponding financial, economic, and social rates of return. Most rates of return calculated by the Bank are economic or financial rates of return; social rates of return are still rarely used. Where project benefits cannot be quantified, such as in education lending, it is not possible to calculate any rate of return. In many cases, economic costs and benefits are difficult to estimate. This is the case for many public utility projects to improve water supply or sanitation, where the benefits are based on the financial returns of the utility and do not reflect their true economic or social value. Low rates of return may then reflect inadequate cost recovery and tariff policies, rather than lack of real economic benefits.

---

of return, but are generally small; successful projects are then replicated on a larger scale. If the average were weighted, the rate of return on all audited IDA projects would be about 21 percent.[2]

Of course, rates of return vary from one project to another. On one hand, some 20 percent of IDA's projects managed rates of return below 10 percent; close to half of these registered negative rates of return (where the projects' benefits failed to equal their costs). On the other hand, 15 percent of IDA's projects had rates of return in excess of 30 percent (see Table 5.2).

The difference between the rate anticipated at appraisal and the rate estimated at audit is often taken to demonstrate the gap between intention and achievement. The average IDA project had a 21 percent rate of return at appraisal; at the time of audit the average rate was 18 percent. A comparison of average rates of return between appraisal and audit conceals a wide range of variation, since the averaging process merges good performance with bad. Looking at the absolute difference between appraisal and audit for each project, however, reveals an average difference of nine percentage points (see Table 5.3). In other words, an average IDA project with a 21 percent estimated rate of return at appraisal was likely to have a reestimated rate of return of between 12 percent and 30 percent. While this

2. The high rates of return on IDA projects raise the possibility of their being financed by the IBRD or some other nonconcessional source. These returns are long-term in nature, however, and often produce benefits, such as public-utility services and human capital improvements, which cannot be turned directly into foreign exchange to meet debt-service requirements. More broadly, the need for concessional resources is based on country creditworthiness and level of development, and is not related to the productivity of individual projects.

Table 5.1. Rates of Return for IBRD Loans and IDA Credits by Sector

	IBRD loans		IDA credits	
	Number of projects[a]	Average rate of return (%)	Number of projects[a]	Average rate of return (%)
Agriculture	74	14.2	95	19.5
Infrastructure	89	14.1	24	15.2
Energy	54	14.2	11	10.3
Water supply	17	8.0	5	16.6
Telecommunications	18	19.6	8	21.1
Transport	97	22.0	59	16.4
Industry	13	15.4	5	15.0
Total	273	17.0	183	17.9

Note: Data do not include 28 projects that had a blend of IBRD and IDA financing.

a. Total number of projects for which there is a quantified rate of return available. For IDA, this represents 74 percent of the audited projects.

Source: Compiled from reports of the World Bank Operations Evaluation Department.

range attests to the uncertainties of undertaking projects in developing countries, it also suggests that they can work both for and against project success. Variations are considerably higher in agriculture than in transport and infrastructure, but the average returns expected in agriculture are also higher.

IDA's rates of return also vary widely between regions. They are decidedly lower in Africa than anywhere else: the average rate of return on 88 IDA projects in Africa was about 14 percent, compared with about 22 percent on 40 projects in South Asia (see Table 5.2). This contrast underscores the difficulties of operating in Africa, which is relatively less developed and where IDA's involvement and experience has been less extensive. In many cases, these are first-generation projects, which could be expected to have lower returns. In African countries, IDA's work in providing technical assistance

and supporting institutional development takes on added significance.

The generally high rates of return on IDA projects can give a misleading impression, however, of the projects' impact on development. If IDA chooses the best projects, it may be leaving the others for funding by governments or other donors. Its true impact is the rate of return on the marginal project that would go unfunded if IDA resources were unavailable. It is impossible to tell, however, whether these projects differ from those actually funded by IDA and whether their rates of return are significantly different.

Reasons for Project Variations

There are three sets of reasons why rates of return can vary so widely, making some projects exceed

Table 5.2. Rates of Return for IDA Projects by Region

Rate of return	Number of projects				Percentage of all projects
	East Africa	West Africa	South Asia	Total[a]	
Negative	5	7	0	16	8.7
0–9 percent	6	8	3	20	10.9
10–19 percent	24	16	20	82	44.8
20–29 percent	6	10	7	37	20.2
30–39 percent	2	2	6	16	8.8
40 percent and over	0	2	4	12	6.6
Total	43	45	40	183	100.0
Average rate of return	13.2	14.7	22.5	17.9	

a. Includes projects in North Africa, Middle East, East Asia, and Latin America.

Table 5.3. Audit and Appraisal Rates of Return for IDA Projects
(percentage)

	Average rate of return		Mean absolute difference
	Appraisal	Audit	
Agriculture	23.6	19.5	12.0
Infrastructure	14.8	15.2	5.0
Transport	18.4	16.4	6.6
Total[a]	20.6	17.9	9.1

a. Includes projects in industry.

expectations while others fall well short. First are external factors, which neither IDA nor the recipient country can control. Second are country-related factors, such as the institutional and policy environment. Third are factors connected with the projects themselves, including project design and execution.

External Factors

Changes in international prices and exchange rates, variations in climate, and unforeseen political events can all have a powerful effect on projects.

Prices. Fluctuating commodity prices can overshadow a project's inherent good qualities, or undermine its goals. An example is a tea project in Mauritius, in part designed to train prospective tea smallholders. While it was being implemented, international tea prices declined, tea wages increased, and international sugar prices increased. As a result the smallholders lost interest in producing tea. By the time the project was audited, tea production was only 24 percent of the level originally forecast. The opposite effect occurred in a project in Papua New Guinea (see box on Papua New Guinea), where higher palm-oil prices increased project benefits. IDA attempts to deal with this issue through the use of "sensitivity analysis" in the project appraisal stage. This assesses how sensitive the outcomes of projects might be to variations in prices and other factors deemed important for the attainment of project goals. Also, IDA attempts to project what future prices will be under varying assumptions.

Climate. Adverse weather affected 29 percent of the projects with returns below 10 percent. Projects in the Sahelian region of Africa were particularly affected by the devastating drought that struck the region after 1972. The weather was also mainly responsible for difficulties in a livestock scheme in

Mauritania. Floods in 1973 seriously affected a power project in Pakistan, requiring the Water and Power Development Authority to give repair work priority over the new construction that had been planned. A severe flood likewise delayed progress on the Mahaweli Ganga power project in Sri Lanka. The climatic effect can also work in a positive direction. Several agricultural projects have experienced climatic benefits, principally from favorable patterns of rainfall.

Politics. When projects are being appraised by Bank analysts, political events are impossible to anticipate, except in a very general way. Yet their effects can be profound. Recent examples include the revolution in Ethiopia and the civil war in Chad.

The revolution in Ethiopia affected virtually all IDA projects under way there, particularly those in agriculture and rural development. Its impact was mixed. In one agricultural program, IDA had been distributing fertilizer to small peasant farmers, with poor results initially. Then revolution and far-reaching land reform intervened. IDA's audit of the completed project concluded that the success of the program "was due as much, if not more, to land reform and the subsequent increase in the prices of foodgrains as to any improvement in extension." In another project in Ethiopia, however, revolution led to a virtual standstill in 1973. The road that was the key to the project's success could not be completed because of recurring fighting in the area.

Similarly, the civil war in Chad caused great problems for a livestock project. One of its central features was the construction of new wells as watering holes for cattle, but political turbulence and the resulting lack of security around the wells consistently bedeviled their use.

A final example comes from Pakistan. An IDA credit to support the Industrial Development Bank of Pakistan (IDBP) was one of the Bank's first credits to a publicly owned development finance company. Troubles began with the split-up of Pakistan. This cost the Industrial Development Bank its head office in Dacca, half of its professional staff, and 42 percent of its portfolio. The political upheaval and aftereffects of the war caused substantial difficulty for IDBP. IDA assisted the government in formulating a solution to the problem of assets lost in Bangladesh and devoted a great deal of effort to solving a serious problem of arrears that had accumulated among IDBP's borrowers. As a result, little progress could be made in finding solutions to the longer-

How to Build on Success? The Problem in Papua New Guinea

When IDA helped some 1,500 rural families move to the undeveloped, but fertile, forested areas of New Britain, it was hoped the resettlement efforts would succeed in establishing many small farms that could produce oil palm. But little did the planners know that the problem would not be one of achieving success, but rather, one of maintaining it.

In 1980, four years after $6.5 million in credits had been fully spent, a team of experts evaluating the impact of the two palm-oil projects came in for some surprises. Family incomes of settlers had risen more than six times what had been anticipated ($900 in 1979 dollars) because of higher-than-expected yields, earlier fruition of palm trees, and a worldwide boom in the price of palm oil. Export earnings from the crop helped diversify the economy (an important objective). At the same time, the settlement rallied the many diverse language groups together (not an explicit goal of the projects). There were fewer ethnic conflicts in the settlement than in other parts of the country. Buoyed by these successes, the government began to sponsor similar schemes elsewhere in Papua New Guinea.

But the new prosperity did not drastically change the living style of the settlers. They continued to maintain their traditional food habits. Much of the increase in incomes—60 percent, in fact—went to meet such social obligations as remitting money (some $1.5 million a year) and flying back to visit relatives in villages the settlers left behind. A modest $150 per person has been saved in the banks so far, but very little has been reinvested in palm-oil production. Some settlers have preferred to pool their money to invest in retail stores and transportation, which some observers feel divert time and resources away from the project.

No matter how economically unproductive these social expenditures may seem, they have helped settlers keep in contact with their kinsmen and maintain continuity with crucial aspects of their cultures, and they have spread the benefits of the palm-oil projects beyond the new settlements.

Weighing oil palm fruit before transfer to the mill in the Dagi Valley, Papua New Guinea.

But there is concern that the initial successes of the New Britain projects will not be maintained in the years to come. Already, settlers' interest in the palm-oil crop is reported to be diminishing as prices have dropped from the peak 1974 level. By 1979, just 57 percent of the trees scheduled for replacement had been replanted. Some observers contend that the quick repayment of loans during the boom period was counterproductive in the long run. An OED evaluation noted "repayment terms actively encouraged production during the early years of the project rather than creating conditions for sustained production over the life of the project."

After a decade of development, the smallholder projects seem to stand at the crossroads.

---

term industrial development issues raised at the time of project appraisal.

Government Policies

Of necessity, projects are undertaken in an environment that is not always (or even often) conducive to their success. The government concerned may not heed IDA's advice on the need to charge adequate interest rates for agricultural credit, for example, thereby jeopardizing the financial viability of a credit agency. Counterpart funding can also present difficulties: because IDA finances only a portion of total project costs, recipient governments must provide the rest at appropriate intervals while the project is being executed. If they fail to do so, there will be obvious consequences for the projects.

Labor shortages, poor management, and inadequate infrastructure will also affect the projects adversely. These kinds of country-related weaknesses were found in 58 percent of the IDA projects having rates of return of less than 10 percent.

A common cause of difficulty in agricultural projects is the government's pricing policy. Thirteen projects evaluated in 1981 were implemented under favorable price conditions; of these, 11 achieved or surpassed their production targets. Five projects were implemented when prices were being artificially suppressed by the government; of these, all five failed to reach their targets.

Such difficulties marked a number of African projects. In the Zou-Borgou project in Benin, the low official price for cotton acted as a serious disincentive to its production; farmers opted to grow maize instead, because its price was more attractive. In an agricultural credit project in Niger, farmers preferred to sell their products outside the country to avoid the low domestic prices fixed by the government. In the Casamance rice project in Senegal, the official price was a major deterrent to the development of rice as a cash crop.

IDA is naturally limited in its ability to oblige borrowers to change their pricing policies, although it is an issue frequently raised in discussions with governments on agricultural strategy. In order to minimize the dangers of price controls, IDA has moved away from single-commodity projects toward more diversified farming schemes. These allow farmers to adjust their production to the relative price movements of various commodities. The evidence shows that farmers, even those with very small farms, do respond to market incentives and alter their crops accordingly.

Irrigation projects also demonstrate the vital importance of the institutional and policy environment. Once built, irrigation schemes can be frustrated by deficiencies in the national system of water management. In irrigation projects appraised between 1961 and 1973 and completed between 1974 and 1980, the one clearcut factor associated with success was the existence of experienced, nationwide irrigation agencies. Where these were lacking, water management was almost uniformly poor.

The value of positive government policies has also been demonstrated in urban development projects. Some governments prefer expensive housing and urban renewal schemes to the more modest strategies favored by IDA. In the absence of government support, it is difficult for IDA's projects to be effective. One example concerns IDA's projects to provide "sites and services"—tracts with water supply and other basic services on which poor urban dwellers can build their own homes. If there are delays in the acquisition of land, the whole project will obviously be delayed. Moreover, the financial and managerial capacity of many urban development agencies leaves a great deal to be desired.

It must be recognized, however, that the failure of recipient governments to adjust policies so as to favor IDA projects often reflects difficult tradeoffs in economic management. As in industrial countries, budgetary constraints often limit the amount of financial support developing countries can provide. A desire to help the urban poor may result in low agricultural producer prices or low tariffs for public services. Within these constraints, however, IDA can provide technical assistance, help create or strengthen government institutions, and provide other nonfinancial contributions that improve the chances of success for its projects.

Project Design

Projects sometimes run into difficulties because they have been improperly designed. In agriculture, IDA has promoted some technical packages that had demonstrated their worth on agricultural research stations but had not been properly tested on farms. Some projects used modern cultivation techniques that may have hastened soil erosion, leading IDA to conclude that traditional farm methods were better than it had once thought. And feasibility studies during the preparation of projects sometimes have proved inadequate.

As IDA has moved into projects that are aimed at helping poor people directly, the designs of its projects have become more complex. It has needed to pay more attention to some social and cultural considerations, as well as technical ones. In the past some IDA projects may have underestimated the importance of these factors, concentrating narrowly on economic and financial criteria. One example is the Lake Alaotra scheme in Madagascar (see box on Lake Alaotra).

Some projects have neglected the role of women as producers. The impact of several agriculture and rural development schemes in West Africa, for example, was reduced because they failed to distinguish between the roles of men and women in growing cash crops and food crops. An emphasis on cash crops—traditionally grown by men—might have exacerbated economic inequalities between the sexes, if most of the extra income went to men. Women participating in the Semry rice project in Cameroon complained that men kept the money from selling rice although they, the women, had done the critical work of preparing seedbeds and transplanting. In the Terres Neuves settlement scheme in Senegal, women were given inadequate support in operating water and millet mills, and extension workers spent little, if any, time in the fields assigned to women.

Local customs also play a big role in determining a project's outcome. In one irrigation scheme in Indonesia, a group of small farmers had traditionally been discriminated against by larger farmers upstream, who paid district and village officials to protect them. The downstream farmers therefore found

Lake Alaotra: A Failure in the Paddy Fields

In 1970, Madagascar signed an agreement for a $5 million IDA credit for the irrigation of 12,000 hectares around Lake Alaotra. An IDA team calculated that rice production on this area could possibly triple in 10 years. Production, it was felt, could also be increased by double cropping rice or encouraging farmers to plant fodder and other crops after the rice harvest.

In 1980, five years after the project was completed, an independent evaluation team from the Bank concluded that few of the original objectives were accomplished. Rice production was up only 14 percent; farm incomes had barely increased, while inequities in wealth had grown, adding to social tensions. The project's rate of return, calculated initially at 11 percent, and estimated at completion at 22 percent as the price of rice boomed worldwide, actually may prove to be negative.

The project, in short, made "no significant contribution" to the economy of Madagascar and its 9 million people. Too much focus was placed on irrigation development, and broader responsibilities for the development of the Lake Alaotra region were neglected. The project suffered from severe technical problems in managing difficult peat soils. Most seriously, the project increased tension and disrupted traditional ties and disciplines, at a time of countrywide political and social turmoil. The area's traditional inhabitants resented the distribution of land to outsiders. Traditional values of sharing and village cooperation have been eroded, and dependence on the government increased. The evaluation report listed other detailed factors contributing to the failure of the project, among them:

- *Wrong Assumptions.* The appraisal report overestimated the supply of labor available in the area. Migrant labor had to be used during critical peak periods of rice cultivation, namely at transplanting and harvest time. But this labor supply proved unreliable. Some of these problems have been eased by permanent immigration into the project area, but this had added to social tensions and other problems.
- *Unrealistic Goals.* Cultivation of an off-season crop never succeeded because poor management of the irrigation

system did not produce the water required to plant secondary crops. Double cropping of rice turned out to be technically impossible, as no suitable short-cycle varieties could be developed. Farmers preferred to graze cattle on rice stubble, rather than raising fodder crops, so that the pilot cattle-fattening component of the project did not work either.
- *Faulty Design and Execution.* Canals were dug lower than the fields they were meant to irrigate; in peat soils they sank even deeper. In rainfed areas, some marshy land was reclaimed but excessive drainage destroyed the peat soils and accelerated weed growth. When peasants attempted to eradicate weeds by burning, the peat soils often caught fire, further reducing productivity. Farmers complained of receiving less water than before, and yields in many areas have actually dropped.
- *Institutional Weakness.* The project's executing agency did not possess the technical and managerial resources required to implement a major project. Furthermore, because of low yields, farmers were unwilling to repay land recovery charges. Their arrears rose from 41 percent of their annual charges to 91 percent in five years. Without these revenues, the project agency was unable to maintain the irrigation works and provide the needed extension services.
- *Inadequate Supervision.* With more frequent and intensive supervision as an input to the management process, the project might have avoided some of the pitfalls. More supervision expertise by IDA, for instance, might have led to a resolution of the peat soil issues.
- *Factors beyond Human Control.* Longstanding erosion in the hills near the lake resulted in flooding during the monsoon, but the soils retained very little moisture in the dry season. Rivers and canals silted up, making irrigation ineffective.

While the project may achieve some increase in rice production, it will not be because of good project design. Rather, other unintended consequences—immigration, population growth, and intensive cultivation for subsistence rather than cash—will be responsible. However, there are plans to rehabilitate the scheme and strengthen the project agency as a part of a general effort to increase production in the region.

---

it hard to secure rights of way for their water.

A project's chances of success are reduced if it fails to involve the intended beneficiaries in its design and execution. IDA has sometimes suffered from not knowing enough about farming systems, labor availability, and farmer's motivation. In several projects, farmers unexpectedly gave greater priority to having sufficient food supplies for their families than to growing cash crops for market, a view that might have been ascertained while the projects were being designed. An OED audit of one rural development project in Mali noted that "the concept of farmers' participation was totally lacking." The project "was basically designed as a one-way, top-to-

bottom approach" with "implicit distrust of farmers' capabilities." This approach, combined with poor price incentives and other factors, resulted in the farmers' declining interest in recommended farming methods and the slowdown in their use of fertilizer. Another audit, on an agricultural credit project in Niger, identified the project's lack of attention to the structure of local farmer organizations as the cause of the farmers' lack of commitment to the project. As a result, the project's rate of return was negative.

IDA has learned much from these and other projects. It now pays more attention to sociological and other noneconomic aspects of project design. In several cases, it has worked through community organizations and has even helped to set some of them up. In one project in northern Haiti, groups of up to a dozen farmers began pooling their savings for small joint ventures. In the Casamance rice project in Senegal, village committees were created to channel credits and inputs to farmers. One of the unanticipated consequences of IDA's Kigoma scheme in Tanzania was the success it had in encouraging self-help efforts, like building village roads and schools. In the Maradi rural development project in Niger, farmer cooperatives were encouraged to extend credit to their members and to set up village markets. In the Hinvi area of southern Benin, the project cooperatives are becoming efficient farmer organizations.

The overall conclusion is clear: projects should contain a blend of "top-down" and "bottom-up" approaches. All projects require guidance and supervision by IDA and the borrower. They cannot be expected to do exactly what each intended beneficiary might want. But this does not imply ignoring local norms and institutions. Increasingly, IDA sees its task as harnessing these local forces in the service of development.

While external factors, government policies and institutions, and specific project designs all contribute to the variations in project outcomes, it is virtually impossible to measure their relative importance. A project will generally "fail" because of some combination of all three factors. Even in these instances of "failure," however, it is apparent that some aspects of the project may be successful while the narrowly defined rate of return is disappointing. Likewise, of course, projects "succeed" when the external environment nurtures them, when government policies and the institutional context broadly support them, and when design work has been sensitive to the intricate array of factors likely to affect them. One of the most important factors in project success continues to be a strong commitment by the government and participants to the concept and objectives of the project.

The Wider Impact of IDA

Many of the benefits of IDA projects defy quantification and thus do not affect the rates of return. That does not mean they do not exist. As Chapter 4 makes clear, IDA aims to influence policies so as to maximize the benefits of its projects. It does so informally through its close contact with recipient governments. An incalculable benefit in rural development projects, for example, might be IDA's ability to urge ceilings on the incomes of those eligible to benefit from irrigation works, certain regulations on interest rates, limits on the installation costs of rural electrification, and so on.

These policy efforts are most important in assessing IDA's influence. Beyond them lie other non-quantifiable contributions that are closely linked to IDA's project work. This section discusses three of them: IDA's insistence on ensuring that project costs are recovered; its role in institutional development and technical assistance; and the way in which IDA projects aim to tackle poverty.

Cost Recovery

If a project is genuinely productive, beneficiaries should be able to pay for the costs of goods and services it provides and still increase their real incomes. To the maximum extent feasible, therefore, IDA wants the costs of its projects to be recovered. This is not because IDA is concerned about having its loans repaid; they are repaid by the recipient government no matter what rate of return or degree of cost recovery is achieved on the project. More important issues are involved when projects fail to pay for themselves:

- The recipient may not be able to maintain the project and will be unwilling to repeat it elsewhere.
- The project beneficiaries will be receiving an income subsidy, not enjoyed by others.
- Materials and services received for free or at prices below their true cost may be wasted or used inefficiently.

In agricultural credit projects, IDA strives to ensure that "sub-borrowers," that is, those who borrow from IDA-financed banks, repay their loans and are charged market rates of interest, to avoid providing them with subsidies. In IDA-financed urban development projects, mortgage payments are required from those buying housing, tenants are charged rent, and interest is charged on materials that are lent for house improvements. In water, sewerage, and electricity schemes, charges are levied on those who use services provided by the projects.

User charges raise controversial questions about equity and are often difficult to levy, even in industrial countries. One IDA credit to Jordan, approved in May 1973, required the Amman Municipal Area Water and Sewerage Authority (AWSA) to maintain existing average tariffs until 1976 and thereafter to fix the tariff so as to achieve prescribed rates of return on assets. But the existing tariff became totally inadequate to cover the authority's rising costs, and by 1977 the financial rate-of-return requirement necessitated raising the tariff by 50 percent. This was immediately overtaken by rises in salaries and other costs, and a further increase of 63 percent was made in 1978.

IDA concluded that the financial targets established at the outset of the project were not realistic, since they made almost no provision for inflation. Politically, though, AWSA found it awkward to raise tariffs until the water supply service had been substantially improved. The result was that, although water revenues from 1973 to 1976 turned out approximately as estimated, AWSA incurred losses every year after 1973. IDA persisted in its efforts to bring tariffs more into line with costs, and the result was two sharp tariff increases. These increases, however, were not across the board. At IDA's suggestion, the new tariff was higher for wealthier consumers; their consumption was curbed, while the poorest people were protected. Lessons learned from this experience were incorporated into a later project. There, financial projections contained an appropriate allowance for inflation, and the tariff goals set for the water authority were based on cash flow rather than a return on assets.

The Amman project illustrates the tradeoffs between equity and financial viability. As a practical matter, it may not always be possible to have viable water companies, cost recovery from the poor, and safe water all together. Reconciling these goals is probably IDA's most difficult challenge in its water projects.

Cost recovery is also difficult in housing schemes. Nonetheless, if governments have the political will and administrative capacity, they can recover the costs. IDA-financed projects in El Salvador and India (Madras) showed cost recovery rates of 78 percent and 95 percent, respectively, for the sites-and-services work. This approach—the Bank's providing land and the basic services, while individuals build their own houses—facilitates the recovery of costs more expeditiously than schemes that upgrade existing settlements. In sites-and-services projects, agreements on mortgages and service charges are much more explicit and are entered into voluntar-

ily; in an upgraded area, people may not necessarily want improvements if they have to pay for them.

The chief obstacle to cost recovery has usually been the difficulties of increasing user charges for essential services, such as irrigation water and electric power, or raising taxes. One example was the Mahaweli Ganga hydro project in Sri Lanka (see box on cost recovery in Sri Lanka). Another involved the second IDA credit for the Chandpur irrigation scheme in Bangladesh, approved in 1972 and completed in 1980. The government failed to abide by provisions in the credit agreement; rather than introduce water charges, it financed the scheme's operation and maintenance out of the annual budget. IDA missions eventually encouraged the Bangladesh Water Development Board to prepare a cost-recovery plan in 1977, but the government has yet to approve it. Discussions are continuing.

In a review of its experience with agriculture and rural development projects, the Bank's West African regional department commented on the apparently growing inability of some governments to finance recurrent costs. The department's conclusion was that effective cost-recovery systems would be essential if the projects were to have a lasting impact on the rural economies of West African countries—but this would, it admitted, require an "unpalatable political decision" on the part of the governments concerned.

Institutional Development and Technical Assistance

Economic development requires effective organization and the institutions to carry it out. In a number of countries IDA has been a prime institution-building force. The Yemen Arab Republic is a good example. There IDA has assisted in the creation and strengthening of a wide array of institutions. These in turn have played a key role in the country's economic progress over the past decade (see box on the Yemen Arab Republic). IDA has contributed to the creation of some institutions from scratch (such as a port authority in Madagascar); to the establishment of new project units in existing ministries (in virtually all its education projects, for example); to the reorganization of existing institutions (such as in the first North Sumatra Estates project in Indonesia); and to the strengthening of existing institutions by emphasizing the functions of financial management and training (such as in highway projects in Indonesia).

Cost Recovery Difficulties in Sri Lanka

The first of three Mahaweli Ganga projects to date was assisted with a blend of IBRD loan and IDA credit. During negotiations, the government of Sri Lanka and the Bank agreed that water charges would be collected upon completion of the project. Shortly after loan/credit agreements were signed, however, there was a change in government and the new administration requested renegotiations. The most contentious issue was the requirement for water charges, since the new government had promised during the election campaign that all water provided under public projects would be free of such charges. The renegotiated agreement stipulated that before completion of the project the government would carry out a comprehensive study of water charges and, based on this study, would take appropriate steps to recover operating and maintenance (O & M) costs and capital costs over a reasonable number of years. In fact no water charges were collected during 1970–77. With another change in government, water-charge collection resumed in 1978, but at completion of the Mahaweli I project in 1979, collections averaged less than 9 percent of potential revenues and less than 1 percent of O & M costs.

Under the Mahaweli II and III projects, part of capital costs of irrigation and settlement are to be recovered through sale of developed land to settlers. Attempts under Mahaweli II to effect more rigorous collection of water charges and enhancement to nationwide rates, however, have had minimal success, despite the use of a different approach. This new

The main diversion dam at Mahaweli Ganga, Sri Lanka.

approach consists, first, of limiting water-charge covenants to areas directly under the purview of the Mahaweli development program, and second, a phasing of adjustments with rates starting in 1982 at a level equivalent to about 22 percent of expected O & M costs and would rise to cover 100 percent of such costs by 1991.

Despite limited success in the past, most government officials now perceive the need for an adequate cost-recovery system and a good collection rate, and they now recognize the inadequacy of the existing collection procedure for water charges. Moreover, many farmers expressed their willingness to participate in water management at the field level and to pay a reasonable fee now that they can sell paddy on the free market.

IDA and the Yemen Arab Republic

When the Yemen Arab Republic (YAR) became a member of IDA in 1970, it had been completely isolated from the world for many centuries. It had virtually none of the basic social or economic infrastructure that many developing countries had inherited. In a country of about 6 million people, less than 5 percent of the school-age children were in school and, of them, only 800 were in secondary schools. There was no central bank, no national budget, no agricultural services of any kind, and no plans for the development of the economy. The information needed to identify investment possibilities and to assess financial requirements was lacking. GDP per capita was estimated to be around $50 in 1970.

The first IDA economic report of 1970 formed the basis of a project financed by the Kuwait Fund and IDA to assist in the establishment of a Central Planning Organization. This was the first national planning and statistical agency; it has played a central role in guiding the country's development since then.

Many of the other institutions that today are responsible for development efforts were also created under the auspices of IDA-financed projects in the early 1970s. Examples include the Highway Authority, established in mid-1972; the Tihama Development Authority, a new department in the Central Bank to provide agricultural credit to farmers, set up in 1973; the Industrial Estate Development Authority (1974); and the Yemen General Grain Corporation, which plans, constructs, and operates grain silos (1975). The Yemen General Electricity Corporation (1975); the Industrial Bank of Yemen (1976); and the Ministry of Municipalities and Housing, established in 1980 with responsibility for towns and cities, all benefited from institutional assistance through IDA credits soon after they were created.

The National Water and Sewerage Authority (NWSA) was established in 1974 as part of the first IDA-assisted water-supply project for the capital, Sanaa. Since then, it has received three further IDA credits and is developing into a body able to handle complex programs, primarily as a result of technical assistance and training. Other donors, such as the U.S. Agency for International Development, the Saudi Fund for Development, the Arab Fund, the Federal Republic of Germany, and the Netherlands have been able to use NWSA as the implementing agency for their projects.

From the outset, IDA has worked to stimulate that kind of collaboration, by helping to prepare investment proposals that are technically and economically viable. IDA has contributed $270 million to its 29 projects; cofinancing from other donors, mainly regional Arab funds, has totaled about $300 million, with local contributions amounting to well over $400 million. Between 1976 and 1981, IDA disbursements represented around 6 percent of all loans and grants received by YAR. Thus, for what has been a relatively small financial contribution, IDA has been able to be of significant assistance to the government in devising its economic and sector policies, developing national institutions, and preparing projects for other donors.

In many of IDA's early projects, it tended to employ expatriates instead of nationals to oversee projects. In part this was because of a shortage of qualified nationals, but there was probably an institutional bias as well. IDA also tended to use autonomous units to implement its projects, instead of the established government agencies. This, it was assumed, would avoid bureaucratic inefficiency.

Gradually, however, IDA came to appreciate the importance of working through nationals and established official agencies. What evidence there was seemed to suggest that using expatriates and special units did not improve project performance as dramatically as was once thought. Moreover, it was clear that the long-term maintenance and supervision of projects would almost certainly have to rest with regular bureaucratic agencies.

A Bank review conducted in the late 1970s revealed that very few countries had had institutional failures in all their projects; but in most countries, certain activities consistently had better or worse results. The most successful institutions tended to be found in industrial projects, telecommunications, large-scale agriculture (that is, plantations and tree-crop estates), development finance companies, and some utility projects (mainly power). Also the technical and financial aspects of projects generally made good progress, while training, maintenance, and interagency coordination were often deficient.

IDA has been able to apply these findings to institutional development and technical assistance in its projects in a variety of sectors.

Agriculture. The Kenya Tea Development Authority (KTDA) was supported by two IDA credits, which included assistance for project management, organization, and training. Staffed entirely by Kenyans, KTDA grew into a body controlling tea operations in many parts of the country, owning and managing 22 tea factories. In Indonesia, extensive technical assistance was provided to strengthen estate management, with encouraging results (see box on the tree-crop estates in Indonesia).

IDA's Role in Rehabilitating Public Tree-crop Production in Indonesia

IDA financing and provision of technical assistance during the past 15 years have been pivotal in assisting the government of Indonesia to rehabilitate its public tree-crop estates, the main producers of rubber, coconut, and palm oil. These now generate about 50 percent of the country's total nonoil export revenue, or about the equivalent of $3 billion to $4 billion in foreign exchange annually.

Before the Second World War, Indonesia had the largest and in some ways the most advanced tree-crop estate system in the tropics, comprising 1.2 million hectares and providing 60 percent of total exports. The estates, which were largely European-owned and managed, were expropriated in the early 1950s after Indonesia gained its independence. Thereafter their condition deteriorated because of irregular procedures, low labor discipline, heavy taxation, and lack of local managerial talent and experience. Productivity and production fell until 1965, when the present government took steps to improve the estates. Since the government's financial and technical resources could not meet the vast needs of the long-neglected estates, the government approached IDA for financing rehabilitation.

The Bank has assisted the government in 14 projects for the development of rubber, oil palm, and coconut, which together account for about 70 percent of the total production of the public estates. Support for new planting, replanting, and rehabilitation of tree crops reached about 130,000 private smallholder families and covered some 280,000 hectares of rubber, 156,000 hectares of oil palm, and 103,000 hectares of coconut.

IDA was involved in the first six of these 14 projects. The IDA-financed Fourth Agricultural Estates project typifies the role played by the Association in helping Indonesia to improve its public tree-crop estates during a difficult period for the country's economy. The project, approved in 1972, was designed to rehabilitate 14 rubber and oil-palm plantations in one of the large public estates in South Sumatra, covering more than 36,000 hectares and employing some 9,000 workers. Management of the estate was poor, and organization of maintenance and production inadequate. About 12,000 hectares of rubber had been abandoned. Factories were obsolete and in disrepair, and processing facilities had very limited capacity. An ongoing rehabilitation program was hampered by the estate's lack of funds and discouraging cash-flow prospects, and the government was in no financial position to help.

Consultants financed by IDA surveyed the estate and found it still suitable for rubber and oil-palm production. At the government's request, IDA staff prepared a project which, when implemented, enabled the government to successfully rehabilitate the estate through extensive new plantings, better husbandry standards for existing plantings, construction of a palm mill and rubber factory, and the improvement of existing processing facilities. Management was reorganized and strengthened, with technical assistance provided for a wide range of specializations. The estate is now highly productive, with sound management and organization. Financial results have exceeded expectations. Net real income from rubber expressed in 1981 prices rose from a loss of $80,000 in 1971 to a profit of $4.8 million in 1981, and net income from palm oil increased from a loss of $18,000 in 1971 to a profit of $3.0 million in 1981. Considering the estates' situation when IDA began its work, there is little doubt about its critical role in assisting tree-crop rehabilitation in Indonesia.

Education. Initially, IDA restricted its loans to the construction of buildings. By the mid-1970s, it had expanded into many other aspects of education—helping to finance textbook production, educational planning and administration, and teacher training. In Lesotho, IDA's first education credit provided for extensive technical assistance to introduce more practical curricula in secondary schools, to conduct training programs for teachers, to undertake a study on the country's rural education needs, and to develop within the Ministry of Education a capacity for implementing projects. Similarly, the first IDA credit for education in Jordan assisted the improvement of general and agricultural teacher training. The project stimulated Jordan's Ministry of Education to carry these schemes along and develop its own programs.

Railways. Geographically dispersed, employing large numbers of workers, and coordinating many small activities, railways are inherently difficult to manage. IDA has made some real progress, nonetheless. Credits totaling $707.5 million have contributed to the remarkable institutional development of the Indian railways. A credit to Bolivia in 1972 led to the near-total revamping of railway organization, and a project in Mali did the same.

Roads. In rural schemes, IDA has learned the value of building up the domestic private contracting industry. This helps to reduce the burden on public agencies, which are usually overstretched and disinclined to give rural roads priority. Coordinating the work of several agencies has also been a fruitful area of emphasis. Well-coordinated rural road-building projects tend to be labor-intensive in their construction methods and to make use of local contractors.

Three highway projects in Niger all aimed at strengthening of the Ministry of Public Works by providing mechanical and administrative experts, introducing new administrative procedures, and assisting in surveying traffic patterns. Consultants and the government were charged with drawing up a detailed training program for national staff who would replace French civil servants in the maintenance organization. Maintenance is now performed with only minimal help from outside.

Irrigation. Maintenance is a key to the success of irrigation schemes, but poor countries often cannot afford it. A Bank review found that those schemes where maintenance was satisfactory were all sup-

ported by IBRD loans, while nine of the 13 projects that were poorly maintained were in the low-income countries supported by IDA credits. For example, in Senegal the agency in charge of the river polders project had practically no maintenance facilities until 1978. Maintenance difficulties also caused problems in the Roseires Dam project in Sudan and in the lift irrigation project in Sri Lanka.

IDA is keen to develop organizational intermediaries in developing countries which can in effect function like "mini-IDAs." Such bodies can "retail" the funds that IDA supplies, allowing IDA itself to act as a "wholesaler," providing credits for entire sectoral programs instead of lending for numerous small projects. For example, IDA has long supported agricultural credit agencies. In India, it began its agricultural credit work by supporting state-level projects throughout the country. It then helped to build up a central body, the Indian Agricultural Refinance and Development Corporation (ARDC), which began as a refinancing agency of the Reserve Bank of India. Supported by four large IDA credits, ARDC has become the main financial intermediary for agricultural credit in India. IDA has worked closely with it to develop its capacity for project appraisal, supervision, and control. ARDC disbursements of IDA funds now run above $100 million a year.

In irrigation, too, the same principle can apply. In Indonesia, with the help of an IDA credit, the government established a special agency (PROSIDA) within its Directorate General of Water Resources Development. This new organization was given the responsibility for all future IDA-financed irrigation projects. PROSIDA has attracted a group of experienced engineers and coordinated water supply with other agricultural efforts. It has executed all IDA-financed irrigation projects in Indonesia and six IBRD projects as well.

The same organizational efforts have been made in urban development. Several IDA credits have strengthened the Calcutta Metropolitan Development Authority (CMDA). IDA has encouraged the CMDA to adopt new financial management methods and to develop systems for monitoring and controlling projects and for evaluating their impact. It assisted the CMDA in bringing its audits up to date after having been seven years in arrears.

A similar example from another country comes from IDA's work with the Jordan Electricity Authority (JEA). At the time of the first IDA credit for the Hussein thermal power project (mid-1973), the

JEA was still in its formative stage with a very small staff. The JEA was reorganized on the basis of recommendations of management consultants funded by IDA, and subsequently it developed from a small entity with virtually no project implementation capacity into a well-managed public utility. Its staff now play a large part in the planning and supervision of new power projects, and JEA has gone on to execute other IBRD-funded projects as well.

In common with other organizations, IDA is a long way from an integrated theory of institutional development. A number of points are clear, though. Institutions can develop if borrowers are committed to them and are involved in the design and implementation of plans. But good intentions are not enough. Where institutional objectives are included in projects as clearly defined goals, with their own funding, the chances of progress are much increased. It seems, too, that IDA has helped to raise institutional standards by its own example. Valuable advice and expertise are themselves a recommendation for improving the quality of agencies at home.

Approaches to Alleviating Poverty

A question increasingly asked about all development projects is, Who benefits from them? Although IDA projects by definition benefit the world's poorest countries (since no country with a per capita income over $730 is eligible to receive IDA credits), they are also concerned to reach the poorer people within those countries. This has led IDA to reassess its lending and the design of its projects. Thus, in agriculture and rural development projects, more attention is being paid to the needs of small and subsistence farmers. Agricultural credit schemes have had specific allocations for small farmers. The first ARDC project in India established a target of 50 percent of its loans to small farmers; the second was even more ambitious, aiming to channel credit to landless laborers as well as small farmers.

Road projects increasingly concentrate on farm-to-market and rural feeder roads. Irrigation projects have placed greater stress on secondary and tertiary canals reaching the smaller, more isolated, and poorer farmers. Water supply projects are being designed to reach beyond the modern city to the slums. Housing projects aim to be affordable by low-income families, in contrast to an earlier governmental preference for middle-income dwellings. Educational lending has increasingly been channeled for basic and nonformal schooling in rural areas—less for secondary and university education.

It is still too early to say whether these newer IDA projects will indeed reach the poor people for whom they are intended. Nevertheless, the limited evidence available from completed IDA "poverty projects," as well as from those now under way, suggests some general conclusions.

Agriculture. Five points stand out: First, projects designed mainly for small farmers tend to achieve rates of return as high as or higher than those shown by IDA's more traditional agricultural projects. For example, nine projects audited in 1981 were tilted toward small farmers; their rate of return averaged 26 percent, higher than the average for the entire agricultural group audited that year.

Second, as a corollary, there is no necessary trade-off between assisting small farmers and increasing agricultural production. On the contrary, in most countries the potential contribution of small farmers to total agricultural output is considerable.

Third, as the focus on smaller farmers sharpens, the cost per beneficiary declines. The nine small-farmer projects audited in 1981 reached an average of 200,000 farmers per project, at a cost of only $38 per farmer.

Fourth, in virtually all projects, incomes of the small-farmer beneficiaries have been higher at the time of project audits than before the projects were undertaken; in many, incomes exceeded appraisal estimates by a wide margin. In the Semry rice project in Cameroon, for example, the average farm family income was estimated in 1978 (at the time of project audit) to have reached $900—almost three times that envisaged at appraisal, and almost six times the income that could have been expected without the project. Compared with conditions before the projects began, income increases were reported in the Shire Valley agricultural development project in Malawi (50 percent), an agricultural development project in the Gambia (80 percent), and the Wolamo rural development project in Ethiopia (130 percent).

Fifth, the provision of an appropriate technical package is crucial. Equally important are arrangements to provide farmers with the supplies they need to make the package work (see box on rural development in Mali).

Urban Development. Analysis indicates that, where the relevant data exist, 70 percent of the Bank's urban projects have a high "urban poverty con-

Rural Development in Mali

Located south of Bamako in a zone of 800 to 1,200 millimeters annual rainfall, the Mali-Sud project is one of the best examples of successful rural development. Financed by IDA, the African Development Fund, and the French and Arab funds, the project is executed by CMDT (Compagnie Malienne pour le Développement des Textiles), in which the government holds an equity of 60 percent in participation with a foreign parastatal enterprise. The project provides extension, input supply, and marketing services to about 100,000 farm families on small farms of 4 to 5 hectares each. Building on several years of earlier development efforts, the project started in 1976 and had spectacular results in its initial year. Cotton production went up by 40 percent, and farmers' revenue from cotton increased by 30 percent in real terms. The production of cereals, particularly maize, also increased. The project reached its three main objectives: improving food security, farmers' incomes, and foreign-exchange earnings for the government. Much of its success is attributable to CMDT's efficient extension system, coupled with a timely supply of agricultural inputs, guaranteed producer prices, and a secure marketing system. Fertilizer and agricultural equipment are mostly sold on credit. The credit recovery rate of 95 percent and over is among the highest in the region.

Although originally only interested in cotton production, CMDT services have gradually included the promotion of cereals (maize, millet, sorghum, and rice) and even fodder crops (cowpeas) in their extension recommendations. The remarkable success of this approach clearly shows that, under conditions in the project area, both industrial and food crops can be successfully promoted at the same time. The area produced food in excess of its own needs.

The Mali-Sud area has reached the highest level of farm mechanization with animal traction of all the Sahelian countries. Again, this was only possible through the increase of farmers' income because of good extension and input supply services. Also, CMDT found a solution to one of the greatest problems for on-farm mechanization—maintenance and repair—through a successful blacksmith training program. At present, over 40 percent of the plows and cultivators are manufactured by some 150 independent local blacksmiths working in the area.

Part of this success story is due to mutual guarantee groups

Literacy classes are part of the rural development effort in Mali.

in villages. These groups, which are promoted by CMDT, are formed on a voluntary basis and are autonomous. They derive their income from marketing of cotton and distribution and recovery of credit at the village level. The money thus generated is used for productive and social investments, such as improved wells, marketing equipment, small mills, maternity facilities, and shea butter processing equipment. This approach has proved to be viable and a real incentive to self-management. CMDT's assistance in this movement consists of functional literacy training aimed at the village group leaders and health training. The longer-term advantage of this unique experiment is the reduction of CMDT's recurrent cost burden through the transfer of responsibilities to the farmers.

The lessons to be learned from this success are that, generally speaking, African farmers are quick to take any technically viable opportunity offered to them to develop their production potential. But they must have access to farm inputs and receive remunerative prices for their production so that they can modernize their farms to increase productivity and revenues. An adequate balance between the cost of inputs and the value of production has to be maintained over the years to allow on-farm investments necessary to further develop productivity. The main risk in such situations is that government intervention through overtaxation of export crops or subsidization of food inputs could disrupt this long development process.

tent"—that is, more than 40 percent of their total costs were destined for the poor. IDA projects in Tanzania have demonstrated that it is possible to design slum-upgrading projects to reach the poorest 10 percent of urban dwellers. The Tanzanian Housing Bank, supported by IDA, has made about 60 percent of its loans to households with monthly incomes below $120, of which 75 percent are to those below $85. A detailed evaluation of IDA projects in El Salvador and Senegal concluded that they were "remarkably successful" in reaching the poor. The change to self-help methods for building houses, a feature of these projects, appeared to raise the

production of low-cost housing by as much as 50 percent in some instances (see box on urban development in Senegal).

Water Supply. IDA lending to improve water supplies has traditionally benefited entire communities rather than the poor alone. Nevertheless, the tendency now is to do everything possible to provide water and sewerage to the poorest 40 percent of the population in project areas. If lower service standards (such as standpipes) are adopted, this can often be done for less than a tenth of the cost required by conventional standards. IDA has also en-

Urban Development in Senegal

The story of the Senegal sites-and-services project is one of experiment, growing understanding between IDA and the government, and nearly a decade of controversy. The project, financed by an IDA credit amounting to $8 million, was designed during 1970–71, at a time when the pressures of mushrooming urbanization were just being recognized by developing countries. This project was the first "urban project" to be financed by IDA and marked the development of a new policy of urban lending.

The project emphasized the sites-and-services concept, which shifted the financial burden for shelter from the public to the private sector. Government provided essential services, such as water, streets, drainage, and electricity, to the sites while families and small-scale artisans were to construct the houses. This new approach to urban development was characterized by its focus on affordable services, its attention to the urban poor, and an emphasis on cost recovery to make the urban sector begin to pay for itself.

From the start the project encountered delays because of the late submission of the engineering design, disagreements on standards, and multiple changes at the ministerial and administrative levels—many officials were unfamiliar with the innovative nature of the project. A fledgling project unit with no experience, although supported by technical assistance, was obliged to design and execute a full complement of civil works, and to coordinate the inputs of long-established ministries and agencies. Procedures for registering, interviewing, and selecting 15,000 beneficiaries had to be developed from scratch. The most critical problem—that of late counterpart funding from the Senegal government—plagued the project throughout the implementation period. The decade of the 1970s was one of economic decline caused by the drought of 1973–74, the spiraling oil bill of the mid-1970s, and the plummeting groundnut prices toward the end of the decade. By 1978 only 48 houses were completed and only seven were occupied.

Developments then took a favorable turn. When the local banking sector proved reluctant to assist because so many of the beneficiaries were unsalaried, the project unit started a small credit line, fed by down payments on plot purchase and monthly mortgage payments. This revolving fund was an important and successful modification in project design, which permitted about 2,500 households to begin construction.

Today, civil works are nearing completion on the main site in Dakar and in Thies, the secondary center. On the Dakar site, 10,000 plots have been allocated and over 4,500 houses are under construction; the resident population is 20,000 and is growing rapidly. The project unit has some 40,000 requests for sites-and-services plots, and the government has requested IDA assistance for a second project. Mayors and governors from cities and regions outside the capital have requested similar programs. Senegal's Sixth Plan provides for both sites and services and slum upgrading as integral parts of the country's housing policy, a very significant achievement in terms of IDA's impact on policy. By 1986, when it is estimated that 11,500 households will have completed construction, each IDA dollar invested in the project will have generated $2.00 of government and foreign investment and about $8.00 of private savings for the construction of houses.

---

couraged water authorities to set tariff schedules that permit the poor to buy the water they need with as little as 5 percent of their incomes. These and related efforts are beginning to produce results. For example, water projects in Dacca and Chittagong (Bangladesh) provided a large number of standpipes for the urban poor. In Tunisia, with IDA assistance, the water distribution system was extended more rapidly than originally planned in low-income areas.

Education. A broader social and geographic spread of educational and training opportunities is gradually being achieved in projects in Tanzania, Tunisia, Lesotho, and other countries. Poorer, rural children are finding it easier to get into IDA-supported schools; in particular, girls face fewer barriers.

Family Planning. IDA's lending to family-planning projects has a decided antipoverty slant, since poverty and high fertility are mutually reinforcing. Very poor families typically contain many small children, and they suffer high infant and child mortality.

Such families feel they need many births to make up for high death rates, but having many small children drains savings and income, damages family health, and thus perpetuates high death rates and poverty. In addition, poor parents have many children in order to improve their chances of support in old age; yet each additional child means more competition for limited jobs. The link between poverty and high rates of child bearing is reinforced by the limited access most poor people have to modern means of contraception. Some IDA population projects have sought to assist the poor to escape from this plight.

This brief review, it should be repeated, is still provisional. Clearly, there are still "leakages" away from intended beneficiaries toward unintended ones, and benefits can be deflected away from the poor. Nonetheless, it can be said with confidence that IDA projects have increasingly benefited poor people in poor countries.

To evaluate its general approach to poverty, the World Bank recently set up a task force to survey the experience of projects that had tried to focus on needs of the poor. The task force concluded that the poverty focus initiated in the 1970s should remain a key feature of the Bank's overall development and lending strategy in the 1980s. Indeed, the report suggested expanding the poverty focus in project work: in rural development projects, more needs to be done to reach the landless and near-landless; in urban projects, more to increase the productivity of poor urban workers; in water supply and sewerage work, more to reach rural areas; in population projects, much more to assist both rural and urban families. In summing up, the report emphasized that "there is no other sensible way to proceed but to pursue the twin goals of economic growth and poverty alleviation."

6 Conclusions & Outstanding Issues

Over the years, IDA has emerged as a remarkable example of international collaboration. The fact that more than 30 donors have provided the Association with a significant volume of resources for economic development in poor countries indicates their belief that IDA is an effective multilateral enterprise.

Conclusions

This retrospective study has attempted to describe the circumstances that led to the creation and development of IDA, to explain its operations, and to gauge its effectiveness. The study also deals with some of the criticisms that have been raised by donors and recipients. At least four conclusions emerge from this study.

First, the evidence clearly suggests that IDA has been an effective development institution, even though quantitative measures that would clearly establish its degree of effectiveness cannot be devised. This study has focused on the different ways by which IDA's effectiveness can be measured or judged: the rate of return on the projects it finances, the sectoral policies it pursues, and the overall impact it has on the policies of the recipient countries. The

average (economic) rate of return on projects financed by IDA has remained around 18 percent—and that includes rural development projects and others aimed at the poorest people. Few projects have been found to have rates of return below 10 percent.

Rates of return on specific projects are not, however, sufficient measures of the quality or success of an institution's development effort. IDA has also had an impact on policy reform and the development of institutions—vitally important for long-term progress. But IDA's contributions to institution building and reform in development policy are hard to isolate or quantify. As the project and country vignettes in this report suggest, substantial reforms were often achieved, but they cannot be attributed to the influence of IDA alone, even when the reforms were supported by structural adjustment lending.

In evaluating IDA's effectiveness, it is difficult to escape comparisons between its record in South Asia and that in Sub-Saharan Africa. For a period, IDA pursued the same approach in the two regions—it financed the same kinds of projects and advocated the same kinds of economic and financial policies. But projects in Asia have been more successful than those in Africa, in part because IDA has been involved in Asia longer than in Africa, and the levels of human resource and institutional development in Africa are comparatively lower. As indicated in the recent study on Sub-Saharan Africa,[1] the problems faced cannot be approached in a traditional way, and lessons learned elsewhere cannot be applied to Africa without adaptation. Consequently, IDA has now taken a new approach toward Africa, which puts greater emphasis on improving human-resource development, on building a sound institutional infrastructure, and improving domestic economic management.

The second major finding is that IDA has evolved and adapted. The perception that poor countries would need a concessional source of funds for their development led to the creation of IDA. Initially, IDA financed mostly large physical infrastructure projects, which were thought to be fundamental to further development. As more was learned about the development process, IDA recognized that transfers of resources and economic growth would not automatically improve living standards of the poor and that the distribution of the benefits of growth required explicit attention. Thus, the second decade of IDA operations emphasized agriculture, rural and urban development, and improvement in human resources. By the end of the 1970s, the share in annual commitments of those projects had risen to 53 percent compared with 32 percent in the 1960s. Also, IDA increased the proportion of its lending for the poorest countries and for poor people within recipient countries. Greater efforts were also made to bring poverty issues into macroeconomic discussions and sectoral work.

The third major finding concerns the financing of IDA. Despite an adverse aid climate in many countries, IDA has consistently been able to expand its financing. However, there is some question whether this can continue, perhaps because some donors view the needs and problems that developing countries presently face somewhat differently from the way they viewed them when IDA was founded. In addition, as IDA has expanded and become a larger part of overall aid budgets, it has been subjected to closer examination and evaluation. Each replenishment of IDA's resources has been more difficult than the previous one.

The final conclusion of this study is that the needs of the low-income developing countries remain as great as ever. If anything, their needs have grown and their burdens are greater. The universe of IDA's recipients has changed over time; of the original borrowers, only eight countries continue to receive IDA funds. But the situation of IDA's current borrowers is not very different from the situation its original recipients faced two decades ago. They still have to break out of the cycle of extreme poverty, which results in a desperate need for external resources, but also limits their creditworthiness and their ability to draw on private capital.

In sum, IDA has been a very successful and very effective development institution. Its impact is difficult to judge because its accomplishments, while very real, are the outcome of processes and efforts of which IDA is only a part, often a small one. What can be said, however, is that in the face of the extremely difficult task entrusted to IDA, it has channeled its money prudently, for very useful and often vital purposes.

Outstanding Issues

This review of IDA's past reveals a large number of issues that are yet to be resolved. Some of these issues, indeed, go back to the founding of IDA in 1960; others are of more recent vintage. Without attempting to suggest how these issues might be resolved in the future, this section attempts to describe the nature of the remaining important questions concerning IDA.

Capital Needs in IDA Countries

IDA was established to help meet the needs of low-income countries—in particular those in South Asia—for concessional capital assistance, but how much of this need should be borne by IDA has remained an open question. Over the years, a number of countries have graduated, but the requirements for development assistance have remained large. In part, they reflect the deteriorating economic conditions of the past decade; rising prices for oil and manufactured imports, slow growth in exports, and falling prices of many primary-product exports. Without IDA, the situation in these countries would have been even worse, and the needs today even greater.

It is hard, if not impossible, to project how much low-income countries will "need" in the next decade. Although larger volumes of aid will help accelerate progress, the relationship between aid and

---

1. *Accelerated Development in Sub-Saharan Africa* (Washington, D.C.: World Bank, 1981).

growth is inexact, and the impact of aid occurs over a long period. Overall, the growth prospects of the low-income oil-importing developing countries, which constitute the bulk of IDA's recipients, are not very favorable. As projected in the *World Development Report 1981*, the per capita income growth of these countries is likely to be less than 2 percent a year, even under the best of circumstances (see Table 6.1). Most of this growth, furthermore, will occur in the populous countries of South Asia. The low-income countries of Sub-Saharan Africa are likely to have little growth in per capita income during this decade; indeed, their incomes could actually decline if events prove adverse.

Even to achieve these low growth rates, the low-income countries will need sound development policies and considerable amounts of concessional resources. Projected annual current account deficits are on the order of $11 billion to $18 billion (1980 prices) by the year 1990 for these countries, with ODA flows of about the same magnitude. But these projections are constrained by estimates of what level of capital flows are likely to be available; larger flows could result in more rapid growth. It is impossible to say what level of IDA is appropriate, but it is clear that a real growth of IDA will be required if it is to continue to do its share.

Political Support

IDA was founded because the industrial countries were concerned about the development prospects of the developing world, particularly South Asia. Recently, attention has shifted toward problems in Africa, but most industrial countries continue to be concerned about the development problems throughout the world. There remains a strong humanitarian concern for the alleviation of hunger, disease, and poverty worldwide. There are many

Table 6.1. Growth in per Capita Income, Actual and Projected

	1970–80	Low projection 1980–90	High projection 1980–90
All developing countries[a]	2.7	2.2	3.3
Low-income oil importers	0.8	0.7	1.8
Sub-Saharan Africa	−0.4	−1.0	0.1
Asia	1.1	1.0	2.1

a. Excludes China.
Source: *World Development Report 1981.*

important ties between industrial and developing countries, which derive from similarities of political and economic philosophy or from contacts related to history, culture, or tradition. Many developing countries are strategically located, or supply essential raw materials to the more advanced countries, or are important markets for their exports. Furthermore, the social and political stability likely to result from development is a common interest.

In times of economic stagnation and tight budgetary situations, however, aid programs generally have come in for a reevaluation. While aid programs remain a small part of total government budgets, support for these programs varies widely. Support for helping the poor is evidenced by the significant public support for private charitable agencies in assisting the victims of famine, war, disease, and other problems in developing countries. Many people, particularly in the United States, the United Kingdom, and Germany, question the effectiveness of aid programs in really promoting development in a way that reduces poverty. While IDA and other aid programs more often go to the roots of these problems, they are often not perceived as being as effective as the private programs.

Another part of the issue for government officials is the distribution of their aid between their own bilateral programs and the various multilateral programs, of which IDA is only one of the largest. The proliferation of multilateral agencies during the 1970s reflected the view that there were certain things multilaterals could do better than countries acting alone. Multilaterals are still seen as being more effective in influencing economic policies in developing countries, perhaps because their advice is seen as being disinterested and apolitical. They have become specialists in preparing and financing sound, long-term development projects having clear economic benefits. Bilateral programs, however, allow donors greater flexibility and greater control. The funds can be tied to procurement in the donor country and can be a visible sign of political support. Thus donors, in addition to determining the overall amount of their aid, have to balance these two broad means of giving aid.

Allocation

A continuing issue has been the question of how IDA should allocate its resources among various recipient countries. While allocation procedures have been worked out, there has to be room for flexibility, particularly since subjective judgments about performance and creditworthiness must be made as part of the allocation decision. India is a particularly good example in this regard. Its per capita income level ($240 in 1980) and large population would warrant substantially more than its historic 40 percent share. India's economic performance has been impressive in recent years, making it creditworthy for private capital borrowings. However, the current adverse international environment has led to a widening of current account deficits and a decline in foreign-exchange reserves. There is, therefore, no easy answer to the question of how much IDA lending it should receive. Too great a reliance on private capital markets could undermine the creditworthiness it now enjoys.

The reentry of China in the World Bank adds another dimension to the allocation problem, as does the desire to accelerate lending to Sub-Saharan Africa. While the needs of Sub-Saharan Africa are enormous, the absorptive capacity of these countries is limited. There may be a need for IDA to make assistance available in different forms; more technical assistance and training, for instance, and

more emphasis on human capital development. China, by contrast, has much larger absorptive capacity, a large population, and a low per capita income. Maintaining the proper balance between the competing claims of India, China, and Sub-Saharan Africa will be a major issue during the next decade.

Terms

The issue of the terms of IDA credits is one that has appeared regularly in the course of IDA replenishments. Some donors question whether all countries should receive credits on the same terms, and whether they should not be varied by sector. The issue is highlighted by the fact that several former recipients still enjoy the benefits of IDA credits, which were extended with the standard 50-year maturity. Some have suggested that maturities be shortened for countries likely to graduate in the next several years. Shorter maturities would allow IDA to become more of a revolving fund, using repayments on past credits to finance new lending.

It has also been suggested that interest rates be

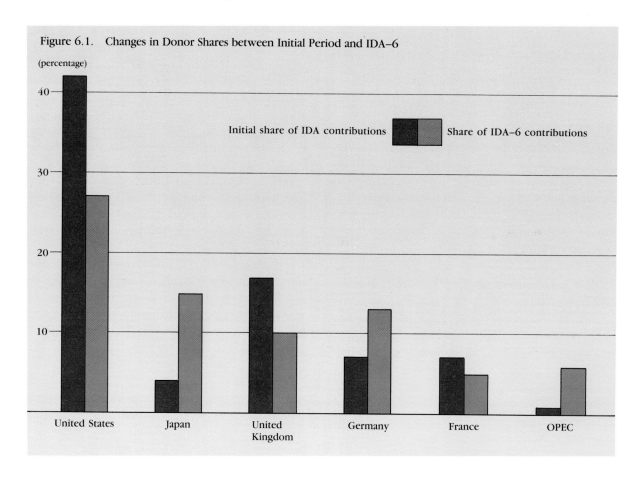

Figure 6.1.   Changes in Donor Shares between Initial Period and IDA–6

Table 6.2. Country Shares in IDA Replenishments and Combined GNP, 1961–80

	Contribution as a percentage of IDA			GNP as a percentage of DAC GNP			GNP per capita 1980 (dollars)
	Initial (1961–64)	IDA–3 (1972–74)	IDA–6 (1981–83)	1960	1970	1980	
United States	42	39	27	42	37	36	11,360
United Kingdom	17	13	10	9	7	6	7,920
France	7	6	5	8	8	9	11,730
Fed. Rep. of Germany	7	10	13	12	12	12	13,590
Japan	4	6	15	7	13	16	9,890
Canada	5	6	4	3	3	3	10,130
Italy	2	4	4	5	5	5	6,480
Others[a]	16	16	22	14	15	13	—
Total	100	100	100	100	100	100	10,620[b]

a. Includes OPEC and developing countries.
b. DAC countries only.

raised to reduce concessionality and to allow for the rise in alternative interest rates in the past 22 years. Another issue is whether credits for sectors that have high financial and foreign-exchange earnings, such as in industry, should have harder terms, since such credits directly improve the borrower's ability to make repayments. It would appear that the initial choice of IDA's terms itself was a compromise, intended to produce an arrangement with the appearance of an IBRD-type loan, but having the actual impact of a grant. The blending of IBRD and IDA, furthermore, allows the Bank to tailor its lending to the needs of particular countries.

Burden Sharing

The problem of determining the share of each donor country's contribution to IDA has been a continuing issue. The United States and the United Kingdom sharply reduced their share of IDA contributions over the past 22 years, while Germany, Japan, and more recently the OPEC countries were responsible for the largest increases (see Figure 6.1). Many of these changes reflect shifts in relative GNP. For example, Japan initially had a 4 percent share in IDA and a 7 percent share of the donor countries' combined GNP; now its share in IDA is 15 percent, and its share in GNP is 16 percent. The decline in the

United States' share broadly parallels the decline in its relative share of GNP (see Table 6.2).

Even though changes in IDA shares have roughly reflected relative changes in GNPs, there has never been any agreement that GNP should determine the allocation of IDA contributions. Consequently, absolute shares in IDA and in GNP differ widely. In 1980, the United Kingdom had a 10 percent share in IDA-6 and a 6 percent share in GNP; France had a 5 percent share in IDA, but a 9 percent share in GNP. These variations also reflect differences in living standards, attitudes toward multilateral assistance, and many other factors.

These issues, which have been with IDA during its first two decades, are also apt to be with IDA in the future. It is doubtful that they will ever be completely resolved to the satisfaction of all of the members of IDA, both donors and recipients. In the past, IDA has been successful because it has managed to meld the differing interests of members, particularly the donor countries, into a consensus on policy matters.

Today IDA represents a successful effort in economic cooperation between countries. It has evolved and adapted to meet the needs of both donors and recipients. Continuing cooperation between both sides will be required if a real commitment to worldwide development is to be maintained.

Statistical Annex

Contents

IDA Financial and Economic Data

Table 1. Voting Rights of IDA Member Countries

	(A) Voting rights under initial subscriptions as provided in Articles of Agreement		(B) Actual voting rights as of June 30, 1982		(C) Voting rights reflecting all authorized voting power adjustments	
	Number of votes	Percentage of total	Number of votes	Percentage of total	Number of votes	Percentage of total
Part I countries						
Australia	4,536	1.94	64,494	1.46	69,115	1.32
Austria	1,508	0.64	27,912	0.63	29,657	0.57
Belgium	5,040	2.15	53,716	1.22	58,076	1.11
Canada	8,066	3.45	157,028	3.56	165,730	3.17
Denmark	2,248	0.96	42,936	0.97	45,928	0.88
Finland	1,266	0.54	24,294	0.55	25,939	0.50
France	11,092	4.74	166,855	3.79	179,648	3.43
Germany	11,092	4.74	308,201	6.99	342,586	6.54
Iceland	520	0.22	10,573	0.24	10,658	0.20
Ireland	1,106	0.47	13,466	0.31	13,702	0.26
Italy	4,132	1.77	113,934	2.58	123,671	2.36
Japan	7,218	3.08	293,863	6.67	338,756	6.47
Kuwait	—	—	49,418	1.12	54,021	1.03
Luxembourg	703	0.30	11,269	0.26	11,397	0.22
Netherlands	6,048	2.58	88,326	2.00	96,098	1.84
New Zealand	—	—	13,278	0.30	13,410	0.26
Norway	1,844	0.79	39,527	0.90	42,759	0.82
South Africa	2,518	1.08	15,058	0.34	15,065	0.29
Sweden	2,518	1.08	108,610	2.46	114,958	2.20
United Arab Emirates	—	—	15,942	0.36	22,512	0.43
United Kingdom	26,728	11.42	313,019	7.10	336,440	6.43
United States	64,558	27.59	836,056	18.97	945,395	18.06
Total Part I	161,115	68.85	2,767,775	62.79	3,055,521	58.37
Part II countries						
Part II donors						
Argentina	4,266	1.82	74,787	1.70	81,053	1.55
Brazil	4,266	1.82	75,082	1.70	81,496	1.56
Colombia	1,206	0.52	21,787	0.49	23,824	0.46
Greece	1,004	0.43	18,733	0.42	19,656	0.38
Korea, Rep. of	752	0.32	14,483	0.33	14,959	0.29
Mexico	2,248	0.96	18,212	0.41	43,738	0.84
Saudi Arabia	1,240	0.53	88,413	2.01	118,838	2.27
Spain	2,518	1.08	40,084	0.91	57,788	1.11
Yugoslavia	1,308	0.56	27,401	0.62	29,446	0.56
Other Part II countries	54,077	23.11	1,261,551	28.62	1,708,571	32.64
Total Part II	72,885	31.15	1,640,533	37.21	2,179,369	41.63
Grand total	*234,000*	*100.00*	*4,408,308*	*100.00*	*5,234,890*	*100.00*

Note: Percentage totals may differ from the sum of the individual percentages due to rounding.

Table 2. IDA Procurement by Supplying Country

	Fiscal 1972		Fiscal 1975		Fiscal 1978		Fiscal 1981		Cumulative through June 30, 1981	
	Millions of dollars	Percent-age of total	Millions of dollars	Percent-age of total	Millions of dollars	Percent-age of total	Millions of dollars	Percent-age of total	Millions of dollars	Percent-age of total
Foreign procurement from Part I countries										
Australia	7.0	3.1	12.9	1.6	11.6	1.9	10.2	1.3	147.5	1.8
Austria	3.6	1.6	2.5	0.3	10.9	1.8	4.2	0.5	63.3	0.8
Belgium	7.5	3.3	20.6	2.6	17.7	2.9	18.8	2.4	193.4	2.4
Canada	2.0	0.9	13.1	1.6	5.0	0.8	11.6	1.5	129.1	1.6
Denmark	1.3	0.6	2.7	0.4	4.8	0.8	5.2	0.7	48.2	0.6
Finland	0.7	0.3	0.9	0.1	0.5	0.1	5.0	0.6	17.0	0.2
France	25.4	11.3	71.2	8.8	63.4	10.6	99.7	12.6	750.2	9.3
Germany, Fed. Rep.	27.2	12.1	110.2	13.6	72.0	12.0	59.1	7.4	1,062.6	13.2
Iceland	—	—	—	—	(.)	(.)	—	—	(.)	(.)
Ireland	(.)	(.)	0.2	(.)	1.2	0.2	0.6	0.1	4.4	0.1
Italy	11.6	5.2	32.2	4.0	42.0	7.0	58.2	7.3	398.9	5.0
Japan	44.0	19.6	140.0	17.3	93.8	15.6	97.2	12.2	1,250.1	15.5
Kuwait	0.4	0.2	8.4	1.0	—	—	—	—	14.6	0.2
Luxembourg	0.7	0.3	0.4	0.1	0.2	(.)	0.1	(.)	8.3	0.1
Netherlands	2.7	1.2	13.0	1.6	16.3	2.7	19.7	2.5	145.6	1.8
New Zealand	(.)	(.)	0.3	(.)	0.6	0.1	1.8	0.2	8.1	0.1
Norway	0.2	0.1	0.9	0.1	0.7	0.1	0.6	0.1	12.0	0.1
South Africa	0.8	0.4	1.7	0.2	1.1	0.2	5.9	0.7	30.9	0.4
Sweden	2.7	1.2	9.1	1.1	13.2	2.2	14.6	1.8	149.2	1.8
Switzerland	1.8	0.8	20.8	2.6	22.0	3.7	26.7	3.4	189.2	2.3
United Kingdom[a]	35.5	15.8	75.7	9.4	69.2	11.5	149.2	18.8	1,163.7	14.4
United States	34.8	15.5	118.4	14.7	71.5	11.9	89.1	11.2	1,188.1	14.7
Subtotal Part I countries	209.9	93.5	655.2	81.1	517.7	86.1	677.5	85.3	6,974.4	86.4
Subtotal all other countries	14.4	6.5	152.8	18.9	83.1	13.9	116.6	14.7	1,098.1	13.6
Total all supplying countries	*224.3*	*100.0*	*808.0*	*100.0*	*600.8*	*100.0*	*794.1*	*100.0*	*8,072.5*	*100.0*

a. Includes Hong Kong.

Table 3. Contributions to IDA by Country and by Replenishment

	Initial subscription		First replenishment		Second replenishment		Special contributions		Third replenishment	
	Millions of dollars	Percentage of total	Millions of dollars	Percentage of total	Millions of dollars	Percentage of total	Millions of dollars	Percentage of total	Millions of dollars	Percentage of total
Argentina	—	—	—	—	—	—	—	—	—	—
Australia	20.18	2.67	19.80	2.66	24.00	2.00	—	1.89	48.00	1.97
Austria	5.04	0.67	5.04	0.68	8.16	0.68	—	0.64	16.32	0.67
Belgium	8.25	1.09	8.25	1.11	20.40	1.70	—	1.60	40.80	1.67
Brazil	—	—	—	—	—	—	—	—	—	—
Canada	37.83	5.00	41.70	5.60	75.00	6.25	—	5.90	150.00	6.15
Colombia	—	—	—	—	—	—	—	—	—	—
Denmark	8.74	1.16	7.50	1.01	13.20	1.10	15.00	2.22	26.40	1.08
Finland	3.83	0.51	2.30	0.31	4.08	0.34	—	0.32	12.24	0.50
France	52.96	7.00	61.87	8.31	97.20	8.10	—	7.64	150.00	6.15
Germany, Fed. Rep.	52.96	7.00	72.60	9.75	117.00	9.75	—	9.20	234.00	9.59
Greece	—	—	—	—	—	—	—	—	—	—
Iceland	0.10	0.01	—	—	—	—	—	—	0.45	0.02
Ireland	3.03	0.40	—	—	—	—	—	—	4.00	0.16
Israel	0.17	0.02	—	—	—	—	—	—	—	—
Italy	18.16	2.40	30.00	4.03	48.36	4.03	—	3.80	96.72	3.96
Japan	33.59	4.44	41.25	5.54	66.48	5.54	—	5.23	144.00	5.90
Korea, Rep.	0.13	0.02	—	—	—	—	—	—	—	—
Kuwait	3.36	0.44	3.36	0.45	5.40	0.45	—	0.42	10.80	0.44
Luxembourg	0.38	0.05	0.37	0.05	0.60	0.05	—	0.05	1.20	0.05
Mexico	—	—	—	—	—	—	—	—	—	—
Netherlands	27.74	3.67	16.50	2.22	29.28	2.44	—	2.30	67.56	2.77
New Zealand	—	—	—	—	—	—	5.60	0.44	—	—
Norway	6.72	0.89	6.60	0.89	10.68	0.89	1.32	0.94	24.00	0.98
Portugal	—	—	—	—	—	—	—	—	—	—
Saudi Arabia	0.37	0.05	—	—	—	—	—	—	—	—
South Africa	10.09	1.33	3.99	0.54	3.00	0.25	—	0.24	3.00	0.12
Spain	1.01	0.13	—	—	—	—	—	—	2.50	0.10
Sweden	10.09	1.33	15.00	2.01	29.64	2.47	49.50	6.22	102.00	4.18
Switzerland	—	—	—	—	12.10	1.01	—	0.95	31.80	1.30
United Arab Emirates	—	—	—	—	—	—	—	—	—	—
United Kingdom	131.14	17.33	96.60	12.97	155.52	12.96	—	12.23	311.04	12.74
United States	320.29	42.34	312.00	41.89	480.00	40.00	—	37.75	960.00	39.33
Venezuela	—	—	—	—	—	—	—	—	—	—
Yugoslavia	0.40	0.05	—	—	—	—	—	—	4.04	0.17
Unallocated	—	—	—	—	—	—	—	—	—	—
Total	756.56	100.00	744.73	100.00	1,200.10	100.00	71.42	100.00	2,440.87	100.00

Note: Total includes special contributions. See technical notes.

Fourth replenishment		Fifth replenishment		Special contributions		Sixth replenishment		Total	
Millions of dollars	Percentage of total	Millions of dollars	Percentage of total	Millions of dollars	Percentage of total	Millions of dollars	Percentage of total	Millions of dollars	Percentage of total
—	—	—	—	—	—	25.00	0.21	25.00	0.08
90.00	2.00	146.90	1.91	9.00	2.02	229.20	1.91	578.08	1.99
30.00	0.68	49.70	0.65	—	0.64	81.60	0.68	196.46	0.67
76.50	1.70	124.60	1.62	—	1.61	201.60	1.68	480.40	1.63
—	—	—	—	—	—	50.00	0.42	50.00	0.17
274.50	6.10	447.90	5.83	—	5.79	516.00	4.30	1,542.93	5.24
—	—	—	—	—	—	10.00	0.08	10.00	0.03
54.00	1.20	87.80	1.14	—	1.14	144.00	1.20	356.64	1.21
25.20	0.56	41.00	0.53	—	0.53	72.00	0.60	160.65	0.55
253.55	5.63	413.30	5.38	—	5.35	645.60	5.38	1,674.48	5.69
514.50	11.43	838.80	10.91	—	10.85	1,500.11	12.50	3,329.86	11.31
—	—	—	—	—	—	6.00	0.05	6.00	0.02
1.35	0.03	2.20	0.03	—	0.03	3.60	0.03	7.70	0.03
7.50	0.17	8.59	0.11	1.41	0.13	13.20	0.11	37.73	0.13
1.00	0.02	—	—	—	—	—	—	1.17	(.)
181.35	4.03	295.90	3.85	—	3.83	462.00	3.85	1,132.49	3.85
495.00	11.00	792.00	10.30	—	10.24	1,757.54	14.65	3,329.86	11.31
—	—	1.00	0.01	—	0.01	3.00	0.03	4.13	0.01
27.00	0.60	180.00	2.34	20.00	2.59	200.00	1.67	449.92	1.53
2.25	0.05	3.60	0.05	—	0.05	6.50	0.05	14.90	0.05
—	—	—	—	—	—	20.00	0.17	20.00	0.07
132.75	2.95	216.70	2.82	8.60	2.91	360.00	3.00	859.13	2.92
11.74	0.26	7.65	0.10	—	0.10	10.02	0.08	35.01	0.12
49.50	1.10	80.60	1.05	5.00	1.11	144.00	1.20	328.42	1.12
—	—	—	—	—	—	7.00	0.06	7.00	0.02
—	—	350.00	4.56	—	4.53	420.00	3.50	770.37	2.62
9.00	0.20	10.00	0.13	—	0.13	10.00	0.08	49.08	0.17
13.33	0.30	21.00	0.27	—	0.27	50.00	0.42	87.84	0.30
180.00	4.00	293.80	3.82	—	3.80	360.00	3.00	1,040.03	3.53
[66.18]	[1.47]	—	—	—	—	—	—	110.08	0.37
—	—	50.75	0.66	—	0.66	79.20	0.66	129.95	0.44
499.50	11.10	814.30	10.60	1.50	10.55	1,212.00	10.10	3,221.60	10.94
1,500.00	33.32	2,400.00	31.22	—	31.04	3,240.00	27.00	9,212.29	31.28
—	—	—	—	—	—	20.00	0.17	20.00	0.07
5.00	0.11	8.10	0.11	—	0.10	20.00	0.17	37.54	0.13
—	—	—	—	—	—	120.94	1.01	120.94	0.41
4,501.30	100.00	7,686.19	100.00	45.51	100.00	12,000.00	100.00	29,446.68	100.00

Table 4. IDA Flows and GNP per Capita, Population, Investment, and Total External Assistance

	GNP per capita (dollars) 1980	Population (millions)		Annual commitments per capita (dollars)		Disbursements per capita (dollars) 1980	IDA as a share of ODA (percent)		IDA as a share of investment (percent)	
		mid-1970	mid-1980	1969–71	1979–81		1970	1980	1970	1980
I. Current IDA recipients										
A. Pure IDA countries	220 w	274.4 t	411.8 t	0.5 w	2.8 w	1.3 w	7.0 w	7.2 w	1.8 w	4.5 w
Sub-Saharan Africa	270 w	142.9 t	185.8 t	0.6 w	3.3 w	1.5 w	7.3 w	6.0 w	1.8 w	3.8 w
South Asia	140 w	120.7 t	211.6 t	0.3 w	3.1 w	1.5 w	0.4 w	11.3 w	0.2 w	7.5 w
Others	360 w	10.8 t	14.4 t	0.4 w	1.4 w	0.8 w	—	6.0 w	0.6 w	2.8 w
Lao PDR	..	3.0	3.4	—	2.3	—	—	13.0	—	..
Chad	120	3.6	4.5	0.7	0.6	0.3	—	1.1	0.8	1.1
Bangladesh	130	67.2	88.5	0.3	3.2	1.7	—	12.3	—	13.1
Ethiopia	140	25.5	31.1	0.2	0.8	1.1	7.0	13.1	2.0	7.9
Nepal	140	11.4	14.6	0.1	3.1	1.6	0.4	—	0.2	9.4
Somalia	..	3.1	3.9	0.4	4.4	2.2	—	2.2	8.4	3.9
Guinea-Bissau	160	0.7	0.8	—	6.6	2.2	—	8.6	—	2.3
Burma	170	26.8	34.8	—	2.5	1.1	—	7.3	—	2.2
Afghanistan	..	12.3	15.9	0.4	1.5	—	—	—	0.6	3.5
Viet Nam	..	..	54.2	—	0.4	—	—	2.6	—	..
Mali	190	5.4	7.0	0.5	2.4	2.8	5.6	7.5	3.3	9.2
Burundi	200	3.4	4.1	0.2	7.6	2.4	2.2	9.4	4.5	10.0
Rwanda	200	3.8	5.2	0.8	3.8	2.1	0.4	6.6	0.6	5.7
Upper Volta	210	4.9	6.1	0.5	5.6	2.6	—	5.6	—	4.9
Zaïre	220	21.6	28.3	0.3	1.2	0.7	0.8	4.4	0.2	3.8
Gambia	250	0.4	0.6	1.6	2.8	5.7	—	9.6	—	7.7
Maldives	260	..	0.2	—	6.9	—	—	7.5	—	..
Haiti	270	4.2	5.0	—	2.5	2.3	—	12.4	—	5.0
Sierra Leone	280	2.7	3.5	0.8	3.2	0.5	—	2.6	—	1.4
Tanzania	280	12.9	18.7	0.9	5.1	1.8	18.4	4.4	2.8	3.1
Guinea	290	4.1	5.4	—	5.6	1.4	—	11.4	—	5.1
Central African Rep.	300	1.9	2.3	1.5	4.6	4.6	1.4	9.2	2.7	15.3
Comoros	300	0.2	0.4	—	9.6	6.0	—	4.6	—	..
Equatorial Guinea	..	0.3	0.3	—	—	—	—	—	—	—
Western Samoa	..	0.1	0.2	—	21.4	5.0	—	8.4	—	..
Uganda	300	9.8	12.6	0.9	2.3	0.1	16.4	0.6	3.9	0.5
Benin	310	2.6	3.4	1.0	5.8	3.7	0.7	13.5	2.1	5.6
Niger	330	4.0	5.3	1.0	6.0	2.5	6.9	10.6	2.5	2.7
Madagascar	350	6.8	8.7	0.9	5.4	2.0	10.3	12.3	3.3	2.5
Sudan	410	14.1	18.7	—	5.4	1.7	—	5.4	(.)	3.6
Ghana	420	8.6	11.7	0.8	2.9	0.4	6.6	2.4	1.2	1.1
Lesotho	420	1.1	1.3	—	8.7	2.6	—	5.9	—	3.1
Yemen, PDR	420	1.5	1.9	0.4	10.5	2.9	—	6.5	—	3.7
Yemen Arab Rep.	430	4.8	7.0	—	5.3	2.6	—	5.2	—	1.8
Mauritania	440	1.2	1.5	0.8	4.7	2.9	0.2	2.4	7.2	1.5
Solomon Islands	460	0.2	0.2	—	2.2	—	—	—	—	—
Djibouti	480	0.2	0.4	—	—	—	—	—	—	—
Dominica	620	..	0.1	—	—	—	—	—	—	—
B. IDA/IBRD blend countries	280 w	1,494.9 t	1,795.9 t	0.4 w	1.1 w	0.9 w	6.6 w	15.7 w	0.8 w	1.6 w
Sub-Saharan Africa	460 w	33.0 t	45.3 t	0.8 w	4.2 w	1.6 w	13.6 w	9.0 w	2.8 w	2.1 w
South Asia	240 w	620.5 t	770.1 t	0.4 w	2.1 w	0.9 w	6.5 w	19.0 w	0.7 w	1.6 w
Others	290 w	841.4 t	980.5 t	1.7 w	0.1 w	1.8 w	0.7 w	4.0 w	0.5 w	1.4 w
Malawi	230	4.5	6.1	0.9	7.0	2.5	26.0	10.0	9.7	4.3
India	240	547.6	673.2	0.4	2.0	0.8	7.2	28.2	0.6	1.6
Sri Lanka	270	12.5	14.7	0.6	8.7	1.3	2.0	4.5	0.3	1.5
China	290	838.3	976.7	—	(.)	—	—	—	—	—
Pakistan	300	60.4	82.2	0.6	2.2	0.9	5.5	6.3	1.7 .	1.8
Togo	410	2.0	2.5	0.6	7.1	3.9	6.6	13.7	2.6	3.7
Kenya	420	11.3	15.9	0.7	4.5	1.1	11.5	1.8	1.6	1.5

92

	GNP per capita (dollars) 1980	Population (millions)		Annual commitments per capita (dollars)		Disbursements per capita (dollars) 1980	IDA as a share of ODA (percent)		IDA as a share of investment (percent)	
		mid-1970	mid-1980	1969–71	1979–81		1970	1980	1970	1980
Senegal	450	4.4	5.7	1.2	6.7	2.3	8.7	4.5	2.1	5.4
Liberia	530	1.3	1.9	—	3.2	2.7	—	5.3	—	2.0
Zambia	560	4.2	5.8	—	1.5	0.2	—	0.5	—	0.2
Zimbabwe	630	5.3	7.4	—	0.7	—	—	—	—	—
Guyana	690	0.7	0.8	2.4	5.5	1.9	1.8	4.9	0.3	1.0
Papua New Guinea	780	2.4	3.0	1.5	6.7	1.7	0.5	3.8	0.6	1.5
II. Former IDA recipients	**840** *w*	**455.7** *t*	**582.6** *t*	**0.6** *w*	**1.3** *w*	**0.3** *w*	**2.3** *w*	**1.6** *w*	**0.5** *w*	**0.2** *w*
North Africa and Middle East	1,050 *w*	96.3 *t*	123.5 *t*	0.4 *w*	4.6 *w*	0.4 *w*	3.4 *w*	0.8 *w*	0.4 *w*	0.2 *w*
Sub-Saharan Africa	990 *w*	81.0 *t*	105.3 *t*	1.2 *w*	4.0 *w*	1.6 *w*	3.6 *w*	4.4 *w*	0.4 *w*	1.4 *w*
Latin America	1,230 *w*	57.0 *t*	73.0 *t*	0.8 *w*	2.7 *w*	0.7 *w*	7.4 *w*	3.5 *w*	0.8 *w*	0.5 *w*
East Asia	660 *w*	221.4 *t*	280.8 *t*	0.6 *w*	0.6 *w*	0.2 *w*	0.6 *w*	2.5 *w*	0.5 *w*	0.1 *w*
Indonesia	430	116.1	146.6	0.7	0.7	0.2	0.7	4.2	0.8	0.3
Honduras	560	2.6	3.7	1.0	2.3	1.4	10.2	17.4	1.1	1.9
Bolivia	570	4.3	5.6	1.2	2.1	0.3	5.8	0.9	1.1	0.6
Egypt	580	32.3	39.8	0.3	4.6	0.9	—	3.0	—	0.9
El Salvador	660	3.4	4.5	0.5	—	0.8	2.0	2.9	0.2	0.5
Cameroon	670	6.8	8.4	0.9	3.3	2.1	6.1	7.0	1.8	1.5
Thailand	670	36.5	47.0	—	0.4	0.1	—	1.0	—	0.1
Swaziland	680	0.4	0.6	—	—	0.3	—	0.6	—	2.1
Philippines	690	36.9	49.0	—	0.4	—	—	0.6	—	(.)
Nicaragua	740	1.9	2.6	—	4.6	2.5	—	3.9	—	2.7
Congo, People's Rep.	900	1.2	1.6	1.6	7.6	0.3	—	1.2	0.4	2.0
Morocco	900	15.0	20.2	0.2	—	—	2.2	0.1	0.4	(.)
Botswana	910	0.6	0.8	2.9	—	0.1	11.4	—	2.8	—
Nigeria	1,010	66.2	84.7	—	—	—	1.2	—	0.1	—
Mauritius	1,060	0.8	0.9	2.1	—	0.8	—	3.8	—	0.2
Ivory Coast	1,150	5.0	8.3	—	—	—	—	—	—	—
Dominican Rep.	1,160	4.1	5.4	0.7	—	0.1	—	—	—	0.1
Colombia	1,180	21.3	26.7	—	—	—	—	—	—	—
Ecuador	1,270	6.0	8.0	0.6	—	—	9.0	—	0.6	(.)
Paraguay	1,300	2.3	3.2	0.6	—	1.4	9.6	8.5	1.7	0.3
Tunisia	1,310	5.1	6.4	1.5	—	0.2	2.5	0.3	1.4	(.)
Syrian Arab Rep.	1,340	6.3	9.0	—	—	0.2	12.7	—	0.9	0.1
Jordan	1,420	2.3	3.2	0.9	—	3.5	0.8	0.7	..	..
Turkey	1,470	35.3	44.9	0.3	—	—	4.1	—	0.3	(.)
Korea, Rep. of	1,520	31.9	38.2	0.4	—	—	0.4	—	0.3	—
Costa Rica	1,730	1.7	2.2	—	—	—	—	—	—	—
Chile	2,150	9.4	11.1	—	—	—	—	—	—	—

Table 5. IDA Commitments by Country

(millions of dollars)

	1961–65	1966–70	1971–76	1977	1978	1979	1980	1981[a]	1982	Cumulative 1961–82[a,b]
I. Current IDA recipients										
A. Pure IDA countries	63.3 *t*	235.4 *t*	2,485.5 *t*	522.5 *t*	750.6 *t*	1,007.3 *t*	1,221.9 *t*	1,256.2 *t*	1,275.0 *t*	8,818.4 *t*
Sub-Saharan Africa	59.5 *t*	223.7 *t*	1,361.9 *t*	297.5 *t*	418.7 *t*	446.8 *t*	683.8 *t*	715.3 *t*	649.5 *t*	4,857.1 *t*
South Asia	—	1.7 *t*	853.6 *t*	176.0 *t*	211.7 *t*	353.0 *t*	460.0 *t*	451.2 *t*	521.0 *t*	3,028.3 *t*
Others	3.8 *t*	10.0 *t*	270.0 *t*	49.0 *t*	120.2 *t*	207.5 *t*	78.1 *t*	89.7 *t*	104.5 *t*	933.0 *t*
Lao PDR	—	—	—	—	8.2	10.4	13.4	—	15.0	47.0
Chad	—	5.9	23.3	20.0	21.7	7.6	—	—	—	78.5
Bangladesh	—	—	655.1	122.0	139.0	271.0	267.0	334.0	391.0	2,179.2
Ethiopia	13.5	21.5	252.1	57.0	24.0	—	—	75.0	30.0	473.1
Nepal	—	1.7	66.0	28.0	67.2	39.8	33.0	62.2	30.0	327.9
Somalia	6.2	2.9	67.0	12.0	17.0	24.0	18.0	10.2	15.0	172.4
Guinea-Bissau	—	—	—	—	—	9.0	—	6.8	—	15.8
Burma	—	—	132.5	26.0	5.5	39.0	160.0	55.0	100.0	518.0
Afghanistan	3.5	10.0	87.0	18.0	40.0	71.6	—	—	—	230.1
Viet Nam	—	—	—	—	—	60.0	—	—	—	60.0
Mali	—	16.8	76.4	26.0	25.0	21.0	8.0	20.7	20.0	213.9
Burundi	—	3.3	17.7	10.0	17.4	6.8	30.0	56.0	21.2	162.4
Rwanda	—	9.3	30.6	19.8	15.0	14.0	21.0	22.5	40.9	173.1
Upper Volta	—	0.8	55.8	23.6	17.4	—	35.0	62.0	33.0	227.7
Zaïre	—	11.0	155.5	26.0	9.0	46.0	29.5	29.3	100.8	407.1
Gambia	—	2.1	11.8	—	8.5	5.0	—	—	8.0	35.4
Maldives	—	—	—	—	—	3.2	—	—	—	3.2
Haiti	0.3	—	51.5	10.0	31.6	16.5	—	21.2	18.0	149.2
Sierra Leone	—	3.0	20.1	—	8.2	—	2.5	30.5	5.0	69.3
Tanzania	18.6	29.8	164.6	39.2	100.5	76.5	109.5	92.8	75.0	706.5
Guinea	—	—	21.0	—	—	21.6	23.4	46.0	19.0	131.0
Central African Rep.	—	8.5	3.9	—	—	18.0	—	9.4	18.0	57.8
Comoros	—	—	—	—	—	5.0	5.2	—	12.3	22.5
Equatorial Guinea	—	—	2.0	—	—	—	—	—	—	2.0
Western Samoa	—	—	4.4	—	—	—	8.0	2.0	—	14.4
Uganda	—	33.0	11.3	—	—	—	72.5	17.0	109.0	242.8
Benin	—	4.6	35.0	7.2	21.0	8.3	10.0	43.3	23.8	153.2
Niger	1.5	6.7	45.4	—	9.5	37.0	36.7	21.5	26.1	184.5
Madagascar	—	24.1	87.1	14.0	33.0	49.0	48.0	45.3	20.7	321.2
Sudan	13.0	8.5	172.0	25.0	78.0	56.0	170.0	73.0	56.0	651.5
Ghana	—	24.8	71.7	9.0	—	19.0	54.5	29.0	—	208.0
Lesotho	—	4.1	15.1	2.5	13.5	15.0	10.0	10.0	—	70.2
Yemen, PDR	—	—	38.4	—	11.4	14.0	22.2	24.0	19.5	129.5
Yemen Arab Rep.	—	—	88.7	21.0	29.0	35.0	34.5	41.0	42.0	291.3
Mauritania	6.7	3.0	22.5	6.2	—	8.0	—	15.0	12.7	74.2
Solomon Islands	—	—	—	—	—	—	—	1.5	5.0	6.5
Djibouti	—	—	—	—	—	—	—	—	3.0	3.0
Dominica	—	—	—	—	—	—	—	—	5.0	5.0
B. IDA/IBRD blend countries	765.1 *t*	1,363.3	3,445.0 *t*	689.2 *t*	1,259.8 *t*	1,591.2 *t*	2,068.6 *t*	2,000.8 *t*	1,394.3	14,350.5 *t*
Sub-Saharan Africa	10.3 *t*	92.4 *t*	282.2 *t*	72.0 *t*	142.6 *t*	142.2 *t*	204.1 *t*	215.8 *t*	173.3 *t*	1,335.1 *t*
South Asia	754.8 *t*	1,030.0 *t*	3,138.0 *t*	594.2 *t*	1,107.2 *t*	1,424.0 *t*	1,851.5 *t*	1,650.0 *t*	1,157.0 *t*	12,706.7 *t*
Others	—	13.9 *t*	24.8 *t*	23.0 *t*	10.0 *t*	25.0 *t*	13.0 *t*	135.0 *t*	64.0 *t*	308.7 *t*
Malawi	—	33.2	64.0	15.0	21.2	36.5	13.8	74.0	11.3	269.1
India	485.0	786.0	2,854.7	481.0	951.5	1,192.0	1,535.0	1,281.0	900.0	10,466.2
Sri Lanka	—	23.9	59.5	33.2	33.5	68.0	151.5	167.0	86.0	622.6
China	—	—	—	—	—	—	—	100.0	60.0	160.0
Pakistan[c]	269.8	220.1	223.8	80.0	122.2	164.0	165.0	202.0	171.0	1,617.9
Togo	—	3.7	24.2	10.0	19.8	16.2	11.0	25.7	5.5	116.1
Kenya	10.3	38.4	99.6	40.0	58.0	40.0	122.0	50.0	61.0	519.3
Senegal	—	17.1	77.4	—	26.3	24.5	42.3	47.1	19.5	254.3
Liberia	—	—	17.0	7.0	6.0	14.0	—	4.0	25.5	73.5
Zambia	—	—	—	—	11.3	11.0	15.0	—	50.5	87.8
Zimbabwe	—	—	—	—	—	—	—	15.0	—	15.0
Guyana	—	2.9	10.6	—	10.0	5.0	—	8.0	2.0	38.5
Papua New Guinea	—	11.0	14.2	23.0	—	20.0	13.0	27.0	2.0	110.2

	1961–65	1966–70	1971–76	1977	1978	1979	1980	1981[a]	1982	Cumulative 1961–82[a,b]
II. Former IDA recipients	**259.0**[c]	**363.1**	**1,336.7**	**95.8**	**302.6**[c]	**423.0**[c]	**537.0**[c]	**225.1**[c]	**17.0**[c]	**3,559.3**
North Africa and Middle East	87.7[c]	112.3[c]	498.8[c]	56.8[c]	115.0[c]	134.5[c]	215.0[c]	197.6[c]	—	1,417.7[c]
Sub-Saharan Africa	41.9[c]	33.7[c]	136.8[c]	24.0[c]	42.5[c]	30.0[c]	66.0[c]	22.5[c]	17.0[c]	414.4[c]
Latin America	100.1[c]	41.3[c]	154.1[c]	15.0[c]	14.0[c]	10.5[c]	82.0[c]	5.0[c]	—	422.0[c]
East Asia	29.3[c]	175.8[c]	547.0[c]	—	131.1[c]	248.0[c]	174.0[c]	—	—	1,305.2[c]
Indonesia	—	131.5	430.3	—	70.0	126.0	174.0	—	—	931.8
Honduras	12.5	12.1	23.6	5.0	5.0	—	25.0	—	—	83.2
Bolivia	15.0	10.8	34.5	—	9.0	10.5	25.0	—	—	104.8
Egypt	—	26.0	255.1	52.0	101.0	134.5	215.0	197.6	—	981.2
El Salvador	8.0	—	11.6	6.0	—	—	—	—	—	25.6
Cameroon	—	29.1	74.4	23.5	42.5	30.0	31.0	22.5	—	253.0
Thailand	—	—	32.0	—	33.1	60.0	—	—	—	125.1
Swaziland	2.8	—	5.0	—	—	—	—	—	—	7.8
Philippines	—	—	32.2	—	28.0	62.0	—	—	—	122.2
Nicaragua	3.0	—	20.0	—	—	—	32.0	5.0	—	60.0
Congo, People's Rep.	—	2.1	20.0	0.5	—	—	35.0	—	17.0	74.6
Morocco	—	18.3	32.5	—	—	—	—	—	—	50.8
Botswana	3.6	2.5	9.7	—	—	—	—	—	—	15.8
Nigeria	35.5	—	—	—	—	—	—	—	—	35.5
Mauritius	—	—	20.2	—	—	—	—	—	—	20.2
Ivory Coast	—	—	7.5	—	—	—	—	—	—	7.5
Dominican Rep.	—	—	22.0	—	—	—	—	—	—	22.0
Colombia	19.5	—	—	—	—	—	—	—	—	19.5
Ecuador	8.0	6.6	22.3	—	—	—	—	—	—	36.9
Paraguay	9.6	11.8	20.1	4.0	—	—	—	—	—	45.5
Tunisia	5.0	38.0	26.8	4.8	—	—	—	—	—	74.6
Syrian Arab Rep.	8.5	—	38.8	—	—	—	—	—	—	47.3
Jordan	8.5	3.0	59.8	—	14.0	—	—	—	—	85.3
Turkey	65.7	27.0	85.8	—	—	—	—	—	—	178.5
Korea, Rep. of	14.0	44.3	52.5	—	—	—	—	—	—	110.8
Costa Rica	5.5	—	—	—	—	—	—	—	—	5.5
Chile	19.0	—	—	—	—	—	—	—	—	19.0
Other	15.3	—	—	—	—	—	—	—	—	15.3
Grand total	1,087.5	1,735.0	7,267.8	1,307.5	2,313.0	3,021.5	3,837.5[d]	3,482.1	2,686.3	26,738.2

Note: Data are for fiscal years. Cape Verde, São Tomé and Principe, and Vanuatu are scheduled to receive their first IDA credits after fiscal 1982.
a. Includes $3,414.9 million, being the equivalent of commitments in SDR under IDA's sixth replenishment, translated at the rates applied at the time of negotiation.
b. Amounts may not add across because of rounding.
c. The figures after 1970 exclude $175.8 million which were replaced by commitments made to Bangladesh.
d. Includes development credits made to the Caribbean Development Bank and the Banque Ouest Africaine de Développement (total $10 million).

Table 6. IDA Disbursements by Country
(millions of dollars)

	1961–65	1966–70	1971–76	1977	1978	1979	1980	1981[a]	1982	Cumulative 1961–82[a]
I. Current IDA recipients										
A. *Pure IDA countries*	14.2 t	100.4 t	960.1 t	406.2 t	430.1 t	517.0 t	551.3 t	614.2 t	732.7 t	4,326.2 t
Sub-Saharan Africa	13.8 t	100.1 t	504.1 t	229.1 t	254.5 t	269.9 t	270.0 t	330.4 t	452.3 t	2,424.2 t
South Asia	—	—	397.9 t	115.7 t	117.0 t	198.9 t	211.9 t	220.3 t	229.6 t	1,613.6 t
Others	0.4 t	0.3 t	58.1 t	61.4 t	58.6 t	48.2 t	69.4 t	63.5 t	50.8 t	288.4 t
Lao PDR	—	—	—	—	—	0.1	3.0	5.4	3.6	12.1
Chad	—	0.3	12.8	7.2	7.0	9.6	1.2	0.2	—	38.3
Bangladesh	—	—	364.7	88.1	86.2	152.5	152.1	170.6	156.0	1,170.2
Ethiopia	3.8	17.4	64.7	37.3	26.9	43.8	33.4	33.5	27.4	288.2
Nepal	—	—	6.9	5.8	11.4	18.3	22.6	27.8	28.5	121.3
Somalia	—	5.5	25.6	9.6	8.3	8.3	8.7	15.5	17.1	98.6
Guinea-Bissau	—	—	—	—	—	0.1	1.8	4.8	4.4	11.1
Burma	—	—	26.3	21.8	19.4	28.1	37.2	19.8	45.0	197.6
Afghanistan	—	0.3	18.6	16.4	20.5	15.6	9.1	2.2	0.2	82.9
Viet Nam	—	—	—	—	—	—	24.5	6.6	3.8	34.9
Mali	—	5.6	39.6	11.7	15.7	15.6	19.6	19.2	17.1	144.1
Burundi	—	0.9	2.8	1.9	4.8	10.1	9.9	10.5	15.0	55.9
Rwanda	—	—	18.0	10.7	4.1	9.3	10.7	9.6	12.5	74.9
Upper Volta	—	—	15.3	8.4	14.9	18.3	15.0	10.3	8.1	90.3
Zaïre	—	0.3	43.8	20.5	32.4	29.0	21.0	18.1	27.3	192.4
Gambia	—	—	4.8	0.7	1.2	3.1	3.4	4.9	3.6	21.7
Maldives	—	—	—	—	—	—	—	2.1	0.1	2.2
Haiti	0.4	—	14.3	19.4	9.5	7.9	11.3	13.8	15.2	91.8
Sierra Leone	—	—	10.9	1.9	3.3	9.5	1.8	2.4	4.1	33.9
Tanzania	2.3	26.5	59.3	29.0	38.7	31.6	33.2	58.2	98.6	377.4
Guinea	—	—	0.4	3.4	8.3	6.8	7.4	11.5	11.5	49.3
Central African Rep.	—	0.1	8.7	0.6	0.9	3.5	10.6	3.9	5.3	33.6
Comoros	—	—	—	—	—	1.2	2.4	1.6	0.7	5.9
Equatorial Guinea	—	—	—	—	—	—	—	—	—	—
Western Samoa	—	—	1.8	0.7	1.1	0.7	1.0	1.6	1.0	7.9
Uganda	—	11.0	24.6	1.6	1.2	1.6	1.2	3.9	33.0	78.1
Benin	—	0.3	21.3	7.3	3.3	3.6	13.0	16.5	9.8	75.1
Niger	—	3.1	15.5	3.4	8.4	10.1	13.3	16.9	13.2	83.9
Madagascar	—	7.6	49.3	11.6	9.2	13.2	17.8	31.3	27.6	167.6
Sudan	7.7	4.6	36.6	35.3	34.1	28.7	32.2	42.2	85.6	307.0
Ghana	—	8.4	37.0	17.2	21.7	5.6	4.4	5.2	16.5	116.0
Lesotho	—	4.1	4.2	2.9	4.3	2.4	3.4	6.2	7.1	34.6
Yemen, PDR	—	—	7.3	5.7	7.0	6.8	5.5	8.4	12.1	52.8
Yemen Arab Rep.	—	—	16.1	19.2	20.5	17.1	15.0	25.5	14.8	128.2
Mauritania	—	4.4	8.9	6.9	5.8	4.9	4.6	4.0	6.8	46.3
Solomon Islands	—	—	—	—	—	—	—	—	0.1	0.1
Djibouti	—	—	—	—	—	—	—	—	—	—
Dominica	—	—	—	—	—	—	—	—	—	—
B. *IDA/IBRD blend countries*	323.1 t	1,015.4 t	2,097.1 t	652.4 t	441.8 t	541.6 t	723.1 t	1,030.2 t	1,053.5 t	7,878.2 t
Sub-Saharan Africa	0.1 t	49.5 t	151.5 t	42.9 t	46.3 t	70.3 t	61.7 t	142.3 t	96.0 t	660.6 t
South Asia	323.0 t	964.7 t	1,921.4 t	606.5 t	384.3 t	457.8 t	654.7 t	870.9 t	942.6 t	7,125.9 t
Others	—	1.2 t	24.2 t	3.0 t	11.2 t	13.5 t	6.7 t	17.0 t	14.9 t	91.7 t
Malawi	—	10.9	50.4	10.6	12.3	20.4	15.0	13.7	25.0	158.3
India	287.9	727.4	1,692.1	504.3	321.9	374.8	560.6	774.7	792.4	6,036.1
Sri Lanka	—	0.4	38.9	8.9	12.2	7.3	19.7	23.4	47.9	158.7
China	—	—	—	—	—	—	—	—	0.1	0.1
Pakistan	35.1	236.9	190.4	93.3	50.2	75.7	74.4	72.8	102.3	931.1
Togo	—	1.2	7.2	5.3	4.7	8.1	9.8	10.1	10.3	56.7
Kenya	0.1	29.7	51.4	13.2	18.5	22.7	17.7	68.8	15.6	237.7
Senegal	—	7.7	37.4	10.7	7.8	15.1	12.9	30.8	31.1	153.5
Liberia	—	—	5.1	3.1	3.0	4.0	5.1	6.3	6.7	33.3
Zambia	—	—	—	—	—	—	1.2	1.6	4.2	7.0
Zimbabwe	—	—	—	—	—	—	—	11.0	3.1	14.1
Guyana	—	0.2	4.6	0.4	2.8	7.3	1.5	2.0	6.8	25.6
Papua New Guinea	—	1.0	19.6	2.6	8.4	6.2	5.2	15.0	8.0	66.0

	1961–65	1966–70	1971–76	1977	1978	1979	1980	1981[a]	1982	Cumulative 1961–82[a]
II. Former IDA recipients	**77.4** *t*	**211.1** *t*	**921.2** *t*	**239.6** *t*	**189.9** *t*	**163.6** *t*	**136.7** *t*	**233.4** *t*	**278.4** *t*	**2,451.4** *t*
North Africa and Middle East	17.5 *t*	91.2 *t*	267.7 *t*	87.8 *t*	81.1 *t*	78.1 *t*	54.2 *t*	82.2 *t*	95.5 *t*	855.3 *t*
Sub-Saharan Africa	3.0 *t*	27.2 *t*	100.0 *t*	32.7 *t*	36.6 *t*	22.3 *t*	19.2 *t*	36.7 *t*	46.2 *t*	323.9 *t*
Latin America	30.6 *t*	76.8 *t*	103.7 *t*	18.1 *t*	22.2 *t*	25.5 *t*	22.5 *t*	52.3 *t*	32.9 *t*	384.7 *t*
East Asia	26.3 *t*	15.9 *t*	449.8 *t*	101.0 *t*	50.0 *t*	37.7 *t*	40.8 *t*	62.2 *t*	103.8 *t*	887.5 *t*
Indonesia	—	2.9	356.4	76.4	36.4	30.5	35.6	45.9	76.7	660.8
Honduras	5.4	8.9	13.3	2.0	5.2	8.5	5.1	22.2	6.9	77.5
Bolivia	2.2	14.6	30.8	3.0	3.6	3.5	1.8	7.7	15.2	82.4
Egypt	—	—	112.0	29.7	45.6	59.3	37.8	73.6	87.9	445.9
El Salvador	2.4	5.6	7.4	1.3	1.4	2.8	3.6	0.9	0.2	25.6
Cameroon	—	6.7	48.7	21.8	22.0	19.3	17.7	25.6	34.0	195.8
Thailand	—	—	6.6	8.9	6.3	5.0	3.4	11.6	21.5	63.3
Swaziland	2.8	—	0.1	0.4	2.6	0.8	0.2	0.3	0.5	7.7
Philippines	—	—	23.2	4.7	1.3	2.2	1.8	4.7	5.6	43.5
Nicaragua	2.4	0.6	12.6	5.6	1.4	0.2	6.9	16.0	8.4	54.1
Congo, People's Rep.	—	0.5	15.5	2.1	1.4	0.7	0.4	10.4	11.7	42.7
Morocco	—	2.1	29.0	4.1	0.8	0.2	0.8	1.0	0.7	38.7
Botswana	0.2	3.4	8.6	1.2	0.8	0.4	0.1	—	—	14.7
Nigeria	—	16.6	15.9	1.5	1.3	—	—	—	—	35.3
Mauritius	—	—	9.1	3.0	5.8	1.1	0.8	0.4	—	20.2
Ivory Coast	—	—	2.1	2.7	2.7	—	—	—	—	7.5
Dominican Rep.	—	—	9.8	0.9	0.8	5.5	0.6	2.9	1.5	22.0
Colombia	9.3	10.2	—	—	—	—	—	—	—	19.5
Ecuador	—	4.8	23.0	2.3	4.5	0.2	0.1	0.5	—	35.4
Paraguay	1.4	16.1	6.8	3.0	5.3	4.8	4.4	2.1	0.7	44.6
Tunisia	2.9	11.4	40.3	10.0	1.6	0.6	1.0	0.3	1.8	69.9
Syrian Arab Rep.	—	2.5	8.6	13.4	12.0	2.6	2.0	1.4	2.3	44.8
Jordan	2.9	6.0	24.8	5.4	10.5	9.2	11.2	5.8	2.8	78.6
Turkey	11.7	69.2	53.0	25.2	10.6	6.2	1.4	0.1	—	177.4
Korea, Rep. of	13.9	12.3	63.6	11.0	6.0	—	—	—	—	106.8
Costa Rica	2.1	2.4	—	—	—	—	—	—	—	4.6
Chile	5.4	13.6	—	—	—	—	—	—	—	19.0
Others	12.4	0.7	—	—	—	—	—	—	—	13.1
Grand total	*414.7*	*1,326.9*	*3,978.4*	*1,298.2*	*1,061.8*	*1,222.2*	*1,411.1*	*1,878.0*[b]	*2,067.1*	*14,658.4*

Note: Data are for fiscal years.
a. Includes $79.1 million, for fiscal 1981 and $376.2 million for fiscal 1982 being the equivalent of disbursements made under IDA's sixth replenishment credits, translated at the exchange rates on the dates of the disbursements.
b. Includes disbursements made under a development credit to the Caribbean Development Bank and to the Banque Ouest Africaine de Développement.

Table 7. IDA Commitments by Sector and Country

(millions of dollars)

	Agriculture and rural development	Development finance companies[a]	Education	Energy	Industry	Non-project	Population, health, and nutrition	Technical assistance and tourism	Telecommunications	Transport	Urbanization	Water supply and sewerage	Total
I. Current IDA recipients													
A. Pure IDA countries	3,024.5 t	470.9 t	677.8 t	790.2 t	217.0 t	1,044.1 t	47.0 t	172.7 t	229.2 t	1,740.4 t	76.7 t	327.9 t	8,818.4 t
Sub-Saharan Africa	1,700.9 t	294.3 t	455.9 t	312.2 t	58.0 t	272.5 t	—	126.0 t	124.2 t	1,318.9 t	61.7 t	132.5 t	4,857.1 t
South Asia	925.2 t	151.8 t	114.5 t	375.0 t	152.0 t	771.6 t	47.0 t	46.7 t	105.0 t	230.5 t	—	109.0 t	3,028.3 t
Others	398.4 t	24.8 t	107.4 t	103.0 t	7.0 t	—	—	—	—	191.0 t	15.0 t	86.4 t	933.0 t
Lao PDR	32.0	—	—	15.0	—	—	—	—	—	—	—	—	47.0
Chad	50.1	—	13.2	—	—	—	—	—	—	15.2	—	—	78.5
Bangladesh	466.8	141.3	94.5	245.0	136.0	771.6	47.0	39.5	27.3	148.0	—	—	2,179.2
Ethiopia	207.8	41.0	84.7	50.0	—	—	—	7.2	37.4	102.2	—	62.2	473.1
Nepal	152.2	10.5	20.0	—	—	—	—	—	21.7	19.5	—	46.8	327.9
Somalia	58.5	5.0	29.5	6.0	—	—	—	3.0	—	49.4	—	21.0	172.4
Guinea-Bissau	—	—	—	6.8	—	—	—	—	—	9.0	—	—	15.8
Burma	303.0	—	—	80.0	16.0	—	—	—	56.0	63.0	—	—	518.0
Afghanistan	125.5	2.0	30.5	10.0	—	—	—	—	—	36.6	—	25.5	230.1
Viet Nam	60.0	—	—	—	—	—	—	—	—	—	—	—	60.0
Mali	72.8	8.0	15.0	3.7	—	—	—	6.5	17.1	78.8	12.0	—	213.9
Burundi	52.6	8.6	25.0	—	4.0	—	—	4.0	7.7	44.4	15.0	1.1	162.4
Rwanda	64.4	9.2	18.0	—	—	—	—	5.0	7.5	69.0	—	—	173.1
Upper Volta	93.4	4.0	16.9	—	—	—	—	—	22.3	82.9	8.2	—	227.7
Zaire	82.2	75.0	27.5	19.0	—	—	—	7.9	—	156.0	—	39.5	407.1
Gambia	5.4	3.0	5.5	1.5	—	—	—	4.0	—	16.0	—	—	35.4
Maldives	3.2	—	—	—	—	—	—	—	—	—	—	—	3.2
Haiti	17.2	7.0	15.5	32.5	—	—	—	—	—	70.4	—	6.6	149.2
Sierra Leone	29.8	—	10.3	13.2	—	—	—	2.5	—	13.5	—	—	69.3
Tanzania	282.6	6.0	71.2	50.0	50.0	65.0	—	43.0	27.0	87.2	20.5	4.0	706.5
Guinea	34.9	19.0	8.0	29.6	—	—	—	—	—	27.0	—	12.5	131.0
Central African Rep.	2.5	—	4.8	—	—	—	—	4.0	—	46.5	—	—	57.8
Comoros	5.2	—	6.0	—	—	—	—	—	—	11.3	—	—	22.5
Equatorial Guinea	—	—	—	—	—	—	—	—	—	2.0	—	—	2.0
Western Samoa	10.0	—	—	—	—	—	—	—	—	4.4	—	—	14.4
Uganda	10.4	35.0	17.3	—	4.0	142.5	—	8.0	—	16.6	—	9.0	242.8
Benin	31.3	10.0	18.0	9.8	—	—	—	1.7	—	77.4	—	5.0	153.2
Niger	91.6	21.0	21.5	—	—	—	—	—	5.2	45.2	—	—	184.5
Madagascar	97.5	5.0	14.0	55.5	—	—	—	17.2	—	111.5	—	20.5	321.2
Sudan	323.0	11.0	18.5	88.0	—	65.0	—	10.0	—	136.0	—	—	651.5
Ghana	70.5	19.0	—	26.1	—	—	—	—	—	78.5	—	13.9	208.0
Lesotho	11.6	6.5	21.5	—	—	—	—	—	—	18.6	6.0	6.0	70.2
Yemen, PDR	41.3	—	15.4	21.5	—	—	—	—	—	33.4	—	17.9	129.5
Yemen Arab Rep.	112.4	14.3	41.0	24.0	7.0	—	—	—	—	41.2	15.0	36.4	291.3
Mauritania	22.8	8.0	9.5	3.0	—	—	—	6.2	—	24.7	—	—	74.2
Solomon Islands	—	1.5	5.0	—	—	—	—	—	—	—	—	—	6.5
Djibouti	—	—	—	—	—	—	—	3.0	—	—	—	—	3.0
Dominica	—	—	—	—	—	—	—	—	—	5.0	—	—	5.0

B. IDA/IBRD blend countries	5,582.8t	255.2t	433.1t	2,283.6t	796.7t	1,818.0t	134.2t	36.8t	664.2t	1,450.0t	320.0t	575.9t	14,350.5t
Sub-Saharan Africa	563.8t	16.5t	231.7t	26.1t	7.7t	100.0t	35.0t	26.8t	—	255.0t	51.0t	21.5t	1,355.1t
South Asia	4,898.3t	238.7t	78.5t	2,255.5t	789.0t	1,705.0t	99.2t	10.0t	664.2t	1,144.9t	269.0t	554.4t	12,706.7t
Others	120.7t	—	122.9t	2.0t	—	13.0t	—	—	—	50.1t	—	—	308.7t
Malawi	96.4	—	73.4	20.8	2.0	—	—	—	—	65.5	—	11.0	269.1
India	3,966.0	25.0	12.0	2,096.0	734.0	1,330.0	99.2	3.0	574.5	903.5	269.0	457.0	10,466.2
Sri Lanka	327.5	58.5	—	61.5	—	15.0	—	—	30.0	87.9	—	39.2	622.6
China	60.0	—	100.0	—	—	—	—	—	—	—	—	—	160.0
Pakistan	604.8	155.2	66.5	98.0	55.0	360.0	—	7.0	59.7	153.5	—	58.2	1,617.9
Togo	43.5	—	11.0	2.0	5.7	—	—	5.7	—	48.2	—	—	116.1
Kenya	243.6	10.0	76.1	—	—	55.0	35.0	4.5	—	62.1	8.0	—	519.3
Senegal	107.1	2.5	39.0	3.3	—	30.0	—	11.6	—	50.3	33.0	2.5	254.3
Liberia	41.7	4.0	7.2	—	—	—	—	—	—	2.6	10.0	8.0	73.5
Zambia	31.5	—	25.0	—	—	—	—	5.0	—	26.3	—	—	87.8
Zimbabwe	—	—	—	—	—	15.0	—	—	—	—	—	—	15.0
Guyana	12.2	—	6.9	2.0	—	—	—	—	—	4.4	—	—	38.5
Papua New Guinea	48.5	—	16.0	—	—	13.0	—	—	—	45.7	—	—	110.2
II. Former IDA recipients	1,344.6t	177.2t	408.8t	450.2t	85.1t	44.0t	129.5t	110.9t	95.8t	482.8t	80.3t	153.7t	3,559.3t
North Africa and Middle East	474.0t	79.0t	154.0t	247.9t	40.1t	35.0t	39.6t	55.4t	83.0t	74.1t	23.3t	112.3t	1,417.4t
Sub-Saharan Africa	135.7t	10.5t	53.2t	5.0t	2.5t	—	14.5t	—	—	187.0t	3.0t	3.0t	414.4t
Latin America	129.3t	6.2t	26.2t	86.3t	7.5t	9.0t	—	—	—	91.5t	54.0t	12.0t	422.0t
East Asia	605.6t	81.5t	175.4t	111.0t	35.0t	—	86.3t	41.0t	12.8t	130.2t	—	26.4t	1,305.2t
Indonesia	494.4	76.5	73.4	101.0	35.0	—	13.2	41.0	12.8	84.5	—	—	931.8
Honduras	28.2	—	8.0	29.5	—	—	—	—	—	17.5	—	—	83.2
Bolivia	29.7	6.2	—	44.4	7.5	—	—	—	—	8.0	—	9.0	104.8
Egypt	300.0	40.0	105.1	207.0	39.1	35.0	30.0	39.4	83.0	30.0	14.0	58.6	981.2
El Salvador	—	—	—	5.6	—	—	—	—	—	8.0	12.0	—	25.6
Cameroon	119.2	3.0	20.7	—	—	—	—	14.5	—	95.6	—	—	253.0
Thailand	37.5	—	54.5	—	—	—	33.1	—	—	—	—	—	125.1
Swaziland	—	—	5.0	—	—	—	—	—	—	2.8	—	—	7.8
Philippines	37.5	—	12.7	10.0	—	—	40.0	—	—	—	22.0	—	122.2
Nicaragua	10.0	—	—	—	—	5.0	—	—	—	42.0	3.0	—	60.0
Congo, People's Rep.	5.6	—	4.0	5.0	—	—	—	—	—	60.0	—	—	74.6
Morocco	24.0	—	19.5	—	—	—	—	—	—	7.3	—	—	50.8
Botswana	1.7	—	—	—	2.5	—	—	—	—	5.6	3.0	3.0	15.8
Nigeria	—	—	20.0	—	—	—	—	—	—	15.5	—	—	35.5
Mauritius	9.2	7.5	3.5	—	—	—	—	—	—	—	—	—	20.2
Ivory Coast	—	—	—	—	—	—	—	—	—	7.5	—	—	7.5
Dominican Rep.	18.0	—	4.0	—	—	—	—	—	—	—	—	—	22.0
Colombia	—	—	—	—	—	—	—	—	—	19.5	—	—	19.5
Ecuador	17.0	—	5.1	6.8	—	—	—	—	—	8.0	—	—	36.9
Paraguay	26.4	—	9.1	—	—	4.0	—	—	—	6.0	—	—	45.5
Tunisia	11.0	—	18.0	—	—	—	9.6	10.0	—	8.5	7.0	10.5	74.6
Syrian Arab Rep.	10.0	—	—	—	—	—	—	—	—	22.3	—	15.0	47.3
Jordan	13.5	4.0	11.4	15.2	1.0	—	—	6.0	—	6.0	—	28.2	85.3
Turkey	115.5	35.0	—	25.7	—	—	—	—	—	—	2.3	—	178.5
Korea, Rep. of	32.5	—	34.8	—	—	—	—	—	—	43.5	—	—	110.8
Costa Rica	—	—	—	—	—	—	—	—	—	5.5	—	—	5.5
Chile	—	—	—	—	—	—	—	—	—	19.0	—	—	19.0
Others	3.7	5.0	—	—	—	—	—	—	—	2.2	—	4.4	15.3
Grand total	9,951.9	910.3[b]	1,519.7	3,524.0	1,098.8	2,906.1	307.1	323.4[c]	989.2	3,673.2	477.0	1,057.5	26,738.2[b,c]

Note: Data are for fiscal 1961–82.

a. Includes small-scale enterprises.

b. Includes a development credit commitment made to the Caribbean Development Bank.

c. Includes a development credit commitment made to the Banque Ouest Africaine de Développement.

Table 8. IDA Commitments and Disbursements by Sector
(millions of dollars)

	1961–65	1966–70	1971–76	1977	1978	1979	1980	1981[a]	1982	Cumulative 1961–82[a]
Commitments										
Agriculture and rural development	221.1	412.3	2,340.8	670.1	1,340.7	953.7	1,758.0	1,357.0	898.2	9,951.9
Development finance companies	25.0	40.0	208.2	25.5	18.4	32.2	74.5	70.5	135.5	629.8
Education	46.1	133.2	389.7	78.5	83.0	250.5	80.0	360.7	98.0	1,519.7
Energy	96.7	70.2	615.2	167.0	246.2	512.4	936.3	136.0	744.0	3,524.0
Industry	—	32.5	414.1	16.0	27.0	121.5	29.0	409.7	49.0	1,098.8
Nonproject	90.0	565.0	1,265.6	90.0	75.0	105.0	242.5	223.0	250.0	2,906.1
Population, health, and nutrition	—	—	71.2	4.8	33.1	97.0	78.0	—	23.0	307.1
Small-scale enterprises	6.5	3.0	25.8	—	62.0	16.0	38.0	71.5	57.7	280.5
Technical assistance	—	4.0	36.0	15.4	9.3	29.7	13.0	81.6	47.7	236.7
Telecommunications	75.0	61.0	334.0	—	67.5	—	65.0	329.2	57.5	989.2
Tourism	—	—	40.2	—	—	46.5	—	—	—	86.7
Transport	464.2	396.9	1,217.8	172.0	174.8	473.5	239.5	299.8	234.7	3,673.2
Urbanization	—	—	97.8	30.0	146.2	12.0	99.0	42.0	50.0	477.0
Water supply and sewerage	62.9	16.9	211.4	38.2	29.8	371.5	184.7	101.1	41.0	1,057.5
Total	1,087.5	1,735.0	7,267.8	1,307.5	2,313.0	3,021.5	3,837.5	3,482.1	2,686.3	26,738.2

	1961–71	1972–76	1977	1978	1979	1980	1981[a]	1982[a]	Cumulative 1961–82[a]
Disbursements									
Agriculture and rural development	342.4	994.9	367.6	380.3	505.6	673.1	760.3	836.1	4,860.3
Development finance companies[b]	37.3	79.9	39.9	43.2	45.9	46.6	21.3	51.2	365.3
Education	66.0	149.3	72.6	70.7	87.0	70.5	82.0	93.9	692.0
Energy	122.9	221.9	123.4	115.9	110.6	150.1	330.7	321.6	1,497.1
Industry	17.0	170.9	96.2	57.3	55.6	88.0	115.6	156.3	756.9
Nonproject	595.9	1,033.9	257.4	74.2	105.7	66.8	167.7	182.6	2,484.2
Population, health, and nutrition	—	17.9	14.9	13.0	10.6	8.8	22.5	27.2	114.9
Technical assistance	3.7	7.1	2.3	5.8	13.3	14.3	16.4	16.2	79.1
Telecommunications	98.8	181.7	52.3	50.5	37.4	22.0	38.6	59.1	540.4
Tourism	—	5.6	9.3	3.0	4.1	4.4	6.7	8.2	41.3
Transport	671.7	788.9	217.2	187.7	156.2	166.0	192.5	205.1	2,585.3
Urbanization	—	41.8	18.7	22.8	33.5	40.5	53.6	42.0	252.9
Water supply and sewerage	21.0	49.5	26.4	37.4	56.7	60.0	70.1	67.6	388.7
Total	1,976.7	3,743.3	1,298.2	1,061.8	1,222.2	1,411.1	1,878.0	2,067.1	14,658.4

Note: Data are for fiscal years.
a. For commitments, includes $3,414.9 million, being the equivalent of commitments in SDRs under IDA's sixth replenishment, translated at the rates applicable at negotiation. For disbursements, includes $79.1 million for fiscal 1981 and $376.2 million for fiscal 1982, being the equivalent of disbursements made under IDA's sixth replenishment credit, translated at the exchange rates on the dates of the disbursements.
b. Includes small-scale enterprises.

Table 9. IDA Operations

Fiscal year	Number of credits	Number of countries receiving credits	Current dollars (millions)				1982 dollars (millions)	
			Commitments	Disbursements	Net transfer	Net income	Commitments	Disbursements
1961	4	4	101.0	—	—	0.4	452.9	—
1962	18	8	134.1	12.2	12.2	1.1	596.0	45.3
1963	17	9	260.1	56.2	56.1	1.0	1,140.8	209.7
1964	18	8	283.2	124.1	123.4	1.7	1,236.7	457.9
1965	20	11	309.1	222.2	220.4	2.6	1,338.1	802.2
1966	14	8	284.1	266.9	263.3	3.1	1,208.9	939.8
1967	18	13	353.6	342.1	336.7	4.6	1,437.4	1,187.8
1968	18	14	106.6	318.8	310.7	7.0	399.3	1,185.1
1969	38	28	385.0	255.8	245.5	10.4	1,287.6	943.9
1970	56	33	605.7	143.3	131.1	6.8	1,786.7	479.3
1971	52	34	584.1	235.0	221.5	7.1	1,493.9	723.1
1972	74	38	999.8	260.6	243.2	18.5	2,216.9	730.0
1973	89	43	1,357.0	492.9	460.7	5.7	2,660.8	1,156.8
1974	77	41	1,095.4	711.2	678.4	11.8	1,952.6	1,347.0
1975	80	39	1,576.2	1,026.3	984.7	8.0	2,567.1	1,699.3
1976	75	39	1,655.3	1,252.4	1,200.6	−6.4	2,441.4	2,036.4
1977	80	36	1,307.5	1,298.2	1,232.2	−8.1	1,762.1	1,946.3
1978	107	42	2,313.0	1,061.8	983.9	−42.9	2,927.8	1,344.1
1979	113	43	3,021.5	1,222.2	1,137.6	−45.9	3,644.8	1,384.1
1980	114	40	3,837.5	1,411.1	1,309.7	−52.5	4,395.8	1,451.7
1981	116	40	3,482.1	1,878.0	1,760.8	−63.0	3,728.2	2,025.9
1982	104	42	2,686.3	2,067.1	1,924.9	−82.2	2,686.3	2,067.1
Total	1,302	78[a]	26,738.2	14,658.4	13,837.6	−211.2[b]	43,362.1	24,162.8

a. The total is the number of countries that have received IDA credits from fiscal 1961 to 1982.
b. This excludes the adjustment resulting from the conversion of borrowings into grant contributions amounting to $43.6 billion.

Table 10. Basic Indicators

	Population (millions) mid-1980	Area (thousands of square kilometers)	GNP per capita — Dollars 1980	GNP per capita — Average annual growth rate (percent) 1960–80[a]	Average annual inflation rate (percent) 1960–70[b]	Average annual inflation rate (percent) 1970–80[c]	Adult literacy rate (percent) 1977[d]	Life expectancy at birth (years) 1980	Average index of food production per capita (1969–71 =100) 1978–80
I. Current IDA recipients	**2,207.7** t	**34,420** t	**270** w	**1.4** w	**3.7** m	**11.6** m	**50** w	**57** w	**104** w
A. *Pure IDA countries*	*411.8* t	*17,816* t	*220* w	*0.8* w	*3.1* m	*11.4* m	*41* w	*48* w	*92* w
Lao PDR	3.4	237	. .	. .	. .	. .	41	43	100
Chad	4.5	1,284	120	−1.8	4.6	7.8	15	41	91
Bangladesh	88.5	144	130	(.)	3.7	16.9	26	46	94
Ethiopia	31.1	1,222	140	1.4	2.1	4.2	15	40	83
Nepal	14.6	141	140	0.2	7.7	8.6	19	44	88
Somalia	3.9	638	. .	. .	4.5	12.4	60	44	84
Guinea-Bissau	0.8	36	160	1.0	. .	7.5	28	42	91
Burma	34.8	677	170	1.2	2.7	11.2	70	54	99
Afghanistan	15.9	648	. .	. .	11.9	. .	12	37	95
Viet Nam	54.2	330	. .	. .	. .	. .	87	63	107
Mali	7.0	1,240	190	1.4	5.0	10.1	9	43	88
Burundi	4.1	28	200	2.5	2.8	11.8	23	42	99
Rwanda	5.2	26	200	1.5	13.1	14.2	50	45	106
Upper Volta	6.1	274	210	0.1	1.3	10.1	5	39	95
Zaïre	28.3	2,345	220	0.2	29.9	32.2	58	47	88
Gambia	0.6	11	250	1.7	2.2	11.0	15	42	71
Maldives	0.2	(.)	260	1.3	. .	. .	82	47	. .
Haiti	5.0	28	270	0.5	4.0	9.4	23	53	92
Sierra Leone	3.5	72	280	(.)	2.7	11.6	. .	47	86
Tanzania	18.7	945	280	1.9	1.8	11.9	66	52	92
Guinea	5.4	246	290	0.3	1.5	4.4	20	45	86
Central African Rep.	2.3	623	300	0.9	4.1	9.7	39	44	101
Comoros	0.4	2	300	−0.1	. .	. .	. .	47	. .
Equatorial Guinea	0.3	28	. .	. .	3.7	11.6	. .	47	. .
Western Samoa	0.2	3	. .	. .	. .	. .	. .	68	. .
Uganda	12.6	236	300	−0.7	3.0	30.4	48	54	89
Benin	3.4	113	310	0.4	1.9	9.1	25	47	99
Niger	5.3	1,267	330	−1.6	2.1	12.2	5	43	93
Madagascar	8.7	587	350	−0.5	3.2	10.3	50	47	95
Sudan	18.7	2,506	410	−0.2	3.7	15.8	20	46	102
Ghana	11.7	239	420	−1.0	7.6	34.8	. .	49	82
Lesotho	1.3	30	420	6.1	2.7	11.6	52	51	91
Yemen, PDR	1.9	333	420	12.1	. .	. .	40	45	103
Yemen Arab Rep.	7.0	195	430	4.5	. .	16.1	21	42	94
Mauritania	1.5	1,031	440	1.6	1.6	9.6	17	43	76
Solomon Islands	0.2	28	460	1.0	3.0	. .	. .	. .	126
Djibouti	0.4	22	480	−5.3	. .	. .	14	45	. .
Dominica	0.1	1	620	−0.6	. .	. .	. .	. .	. .
B. *IDA/BRD blend countries*	*1,795.9* t	*16,604* t	*280* w	*1.6* w	*2.3* m	*9.8* m	*52* w	*58* w	*107* w
Malawi	6.1	118	230	2.9	2.4 ·	9.8	25	44	99
India	673.2	3,288	240	1.4	7.1	8.5	36	52	101
Sri Lanka	14.7	66	270	2.4	1.8	12.6	85	66	121
China	976.7	9,561	290	. .	. .	. .	66	64	116
Pakistan	82.2	804	300	2.8	3.3	13.5	24	50	101
Togo	2.5	56	410	3.0	1.3	9.8	18	47	81
Kenya	15.9	583	420	2.7	1.5	11.0	50	55	86
Senegal	5.7	196	450	−0.3	1.7	7.6	10	43	89
Liberia	1.9	111	530	1.5	1.9	9.6	25	54	98
Zambia	5.8	753	560	0.2	7.6	8.1	44	49	95
Zimbabwe	7.4	391	630	0.7	1.3	8.8	74	55	97
Guyana	0.8	215	690	0.9	2.3	10.8	. .	70	94
Papua New Guinea	3.0	462	780	2.8	3.6	8.8	32	51	106

| | Population (millions) mid-1980 | Area (thousands of square kilometers) | GNP per capita | | Average annual inflation rate (percent) | | Adult literacy rate (percent) 1977[d] | Life expectancy at birth (years) 1980 | Average index of food production per capita (1969–71 = 100) 1978–80 |
			Dollars 1980	Average annual growth rate (percent) 1960–80[a]	1960–70[b]	1970–80			
II. Former IDA recipients	**582.6** *t*	**12,238** *t*	**840** *w*	**3.9** *w*	**2.6** *m*	**13.1** *m*	**60** *w*	**57** *w*	**105** *w*
Indonesia	146.6	1,919	430	4.0	. .	20.5	62	53	110
Honduras	3.7	112	560	1.1	2.9	8.9	60	58	82
Bolivia	5.6	1,099	570	2.1	3.5	22.3	63	50	106
Egypt	39.8	1,001	580	3.4	2.6	11.5	44	57	93
El Salvador	4.5	21	660	1.6	0.5	11.3	62	63	119
Cameroon	8.4	475	670	2.6	4.2	10.2	. .	47	109
Thailand	47.0	514	670	4.7	1.8	9.9	84	63	128
Swaziland	0.6	17	680	6.2	2.2	10.8	65	47	114
Philippines	49.0	300	690	2.8	5.8	13.2	75	64	114
Nicaragua	2.6	130	740	0.9	1.8	13.1	90	56	95
Congo, People's Rep.	1.6	342	900	0.8	5.4	10.9	. .	59	79
Morocco	20.2	447	900	2.5	2.0	8.1	28	56	87
Botswana	0.8	600	910	9.2	2.4	10.5	35	50	89
Nigeria	84.7	924	1,010	4.1	2.6	18.2	30	49	87
Mauritius	0.9	2	1,060	2.3	2.2	15.4	85	65	91
Ivory Coast	8.3	322	1,150	2.5	2.8	13.2	41	47	107
Dominican Rep.	5.4	49	1,160	3.4	2.1	9.0	67	61	94
Colombia	26.7	1,139	1,180	3.0	11.9	22.0	. .	63	122
Ecuador	8.0	284	1,270	4.5	. .	14.4	81	61	95
Paraguay	3.2	407	1,300	3.2	3.1	12.4	84	65	111
Tunisia	6.4	164	1,310	4.8	3.6	7.7	62	60	120
Syrian Arab Rep.	9.0	185	1,340	3.7	2.6	11.4	58	65	157
Jordan	3.2	98	1,420	5.7	. .	. .	70	61	89
Turkey	44.9	781	1,470	3.6	5.6	29.7	60	62	111
Korea, Rep. of	38.2	98	1,520	7.0	17.4	19.8	93	65	130
Costa Rica	2.2	51	1,730	3.2	1.9	15.2	90	70	112
Chile	11.1	757	2,150	1.6	33.2	185.6	. .	67	93

a. Because data for the early sixties are not available, figures in italic are for periods other than that specified.
b. Figures in italic are for 1961–70, not 1960–70.
c. Figures in italic are for 1970–79, not 1970–80.
d. Figures in italic are for years other than those specified. See the technical notes.

Table 11. Growth of Production

	GDP		Agriculture		Industry		Manufacturing		Services	
	Average annual growth rate (percent)									
	1960–70[a]	1970–80[b]	1960–70[a]	1970–80[b]	1960–70[a]	1970–80[b]	1960–70[a]	1970–80[b]	1960–70[a]	1970–80[b]
I. Current IDA recipients	**4.4** w	**4.4** w	**2.2** m	**2.2** m	**5.4** m	**3.2** m	**6.3** m	**3.8** m	**4.0** m	**4.2** m
A. *Pure IDA countries*	*3.2* w	*2.6* w	*2.5* m	*2.0* m	*4.4* m	*3.0* m	*5.3* m	*3.6* m	*4.2* m	*4.7* m
Lao PDR	..	..	..	..	..	..	..	..	..	..
Chad	0.5	−0.2	..	−0.3	..	1.1	..	0.8	..	−0.8
Bangladesh	3.7	3.9	2.7	2.2	8.0	9.5	6.6	11.8	4.2	4.9
Ethiopia	*4.4*	*2.0*	*2.2*	*0.7*	*7.4*	*1.4*	*8.0*	*2.4*	*7.8*	*4.2*
Nepal	2.5	2.5	..	0.5	..	..	..	..	..	..
Somalia	1.0	3.4	−0.6	*3.0*	3.4	−2.6	4.0	−3.8	4.2	*6.9*
Guinea-Bissau	..	3.0	..	*0.9*	..	*1.6*	..	..	..	*7.9*
Burma	2.7	4.6	4.1	4.3	3.1	5.2	3.7	4.4	1.5	4.7
Afghanistan	2.0	4.5	..	..	..	..	..	..	..	..
Viet Nam	..	..	..	..	..	..	..	..	..	..
Mali	3.3	4.9	..	4.4	..	3.0	..	..	..	6.0
Burundi	4.4	2.8	..	1.8	..	7.8	..	5.3	..	3.0
Rwanda	2.7	4.1	..	..	..	..	..	..	..	..
Upper Volta	3.0	3.5	..	1.2	..	3.2	..	3.7	..	5.7
Zaïre	3.4	*0.1*	..	*1.2*	..	*−1.1*	..	*−1.5*	..	*0.7*
Gambia	5.4	2.9	4.6	5.9	2.1	3.1	7.8	..	6.6	0.5
Maldives	..	..	..	..	..	..	..	..	..	..
Haiti	−0.2	*4.0*	−0.6	*2.2*	0.1	*8.3*	−0.1	*7.1*	0.4	*3.7*
Sierra Leone	4.3	1.6	..	2.2	..	−3.8	..	3.8	..	4.2
Tanzania	6.0	*4.9*	..	*4.9*	..	*1.9*	..	*3.6*	..	*5.9*
Guinea	3.5	3.3	..	..	..	..	..	..	..	..
Central African Rep.	1.9	3.0	0.8	2.3	5.4	5.1	..	..	1.8	3.0
Comoros	..	..	..	..	..	..	..	..	..	..
Equatorial Guinea	..	−1.3	..	..	..	..	..	..	..	..
Western Samoa	..	..	..	..	..	..	..	..	..	..
Uganda	5.6	−1.7	..	−0.9	..	−9.6	..	−9.1	..	−0.8
Benin	2.6	3.3	..	..	..	..	..	..	..	..
Niger	2.9	2.7	3.3	−3.7	13.9	11.3	..	..	(.)	6.9
Madagascar	2.9	0.3	..	0.1	..	1.0	..	..	..	0.1
Sudan	1.3	4.4	..	2.6	..	3.1	..	1.3	..	6.4
Ghana	2.1	−0.1	..	*−1.2*	..	*−1.2*	..	*−2.9*	..	*1.0*
Lesotho	5.2	7.9	..	2.9	..	8.2	..	9.0	..	10.4
Yemen, PDR	..	..	..	..	..	..	..	..	..	..
Yemen Arab Rep.	..	9.2	..	3.7	..	14.7	..	12.2	..	12.5
Mauritania	..	1.7	..	−1.1	..	(.)	..	0.2	..	6.8
Solomon Islands	3.7	6.4	..	..	..	..	..	..	..	..
Djibouti	..	..	..	..	..	..	..	..	..	..
Dominica	2.1	−2.3	..	..	..	..	..	..	..	..
B. IDA/IBRD blend countries	*4.6* w	*4.8* w	*1.9* m	*2.3* m	*6.6* m	*4.0* m	*6.3* m	*4.2* m	*3.8* m	*3.7* m
Malawi	4.9	6.3	..	4.1	..	7.0	..	6.7	..	9.1
India	3.4	3.6	1.9	1.9	5.4	4.5	4.7	5.0	4.6	5.2
Sri Lanka	4.6	4.1	3.0	2.8	6.6	4.0	6.3	1.9	4.6	4.8
China	*5.2*	*5.8*	*1.6*	*3.2*	*11.2*	*8.7*	..	..	*3.1*	*3.7*
Pakistan	6.7	4.7	4.9	2.3	10.0	5.2	9.4	4.0	7.0	6.2
Togo	8.5	3.4	..	0.8	..	6.6	..	..	..	3.9
Kenya	6.0	6.5	..	5.4	..	10.2	..	11.4	..	5.8
Senegal	2.5	2.5	2.9	3.7	4.4	3.7	6.2	3.8	1.7	1.5
Liberia	5.1	1.7	..	4.7	..	−0.2	..	8.0	..	1.9
Zambia	5.0	0.7	..	1.8	..	0.1	..	0.4	..	1.2
Zimbabwe	4.3	*1.6*	..	*−0.5*	..	*1.8*	..	*2.8*	..	*2.1*
Guyana	3.4	0.9	1.4	−0.7	4.3	−0.8	2.5	4.3	3.8	3.5
Papua New Guinea	6.5	2.3	..	..	..	..	..	..	..	..

		GDP		Agriculture		Industry		Manufacturing		Services	
		1960–70[a]	*1970–80*[b]	*1960–70*[a]	*1970–80*[b]	*1960–70*[a]	*1970–80*[b]	*1960–70*[a]	*1970–80*[b]	*1960–70*[a]	*1970–80*[b]
II.	**Former IDA recipients**	**5.3** *w*	**6.4** *w*	**3.0** *m*	**3.1** *m*	**8.2** *m*	**8.3** *m*	**6.7** *m*	**7.2** *m*	**5.4** *m*	**7.0** *m*
	Indonesia	3.9	7.6	2.7	3.8	5.2	11.1	3.3	12.8	4.8	9.2
	Honduras	5.3	3.6	5.7	1.5	5.4	4.9	4.5	5.4	4.8	4.5
	Bolivia	5.2	4.8	3.0	3.1	6.2	4.3	5.4	6.0	5.4	5.7
	Egypt	4.3	*7.4*	2.9	2.7	5.4	6.8	4.8	*8.0*	4.7	*11.0*
	El Salvador	5.9	4.1	3.0	2.8	8.5	5.0	8.8	4.1	6.5	4.3
	Cameroon	3.7	5.6	. .	3.8	. .	8.6	. .	5.2	. .	5.7
	Thailand	8.4	7.2	5.6	4.7	11.9	10.0	11.4	10.6	9.1	7.3
	Swaziland	8.6	5.7	. .	. .	. .	. .	. .	. .	. .	. .
	Philippines	5.1	6.3	4.3	4.9	6.0	8.7	6.7	7.2	5.2	5.4
	Nicaragua	7.3	0.9	7.8	3.1	10.4	2.2	11.4	2.9	5.8	−0.9
	Congo, People's Rep.	2.7	3.1	1.0	1.7	7.0	4.0	6.8	. .	2.1	3.1
	Morocco	4.4	5.6	4.7	0.8	4.2	6.6	4.2	5.8	4.4	6.6
	Botswana	5.7	13.2	1.6	. .	12.6	. .	4.7	. .	7.6	. .
	Nigeria	3.1	6.5	−0.4	0.8	12.0	8.1	9.1	12.0	4.9	9.7
	Mauritius	1.0	7.1	. .	−5.7	. .	10.5	. .	7.3	. .	21.4
	Ivory Coast	8.0	6.7	4.2	3.4	11.5	*10.5*	11.6	7.2	9.7	7.0
	Dominican Rep.	4.5	6.6	2.1	3.1	6.0	8.3	5.0	6.4	5.0	7.0
	Colombia	5.1	5.9	3.5	4.9	6.0	4.9	5.7	6.3	5.7	7.0
	Ecuador	. .	8.8	. .	2.4	. .	12.1	. .	9.8	. .	9.4
	Paraguay	4.2	8.6	. .	6.9	. .	10.6	. .	7.9	. .	8.9
	Tunisia	*4.7*	7.5	*2.0*	4.9	*8.2*	9.0	*7.8*	11.2	*4.5*	7.8
	Syrian Arab Rep.	4.6	10.0	. .	8.2	. .	9.6	. .	7.9	. .	10.8
	Jordan	. .	. .	. .	. .	. .	. .	. .	. .	. .	. .
	Turkey	6.0	5.9	2.5	3.4	9.6	6.6	10.9	6.1	6.9	6.8
	Korea, Rep. of	8.6	9.5	4.4	3.2	17.2	15.4	17.6	16.6	8.9	8.5
	Costa Rica	6.5	5.8	5.7	2.5	9.4	8.3	10.6	7.9	5.7	5.9
	Chile	4.5	2.4	2.6	2.3	4.8	0.2	5.5	−0.5	4.6	4.1

a. Figures in italic are for 1961–70, not 1960–70.
b. Figures in italic are for 1970–79, not 1970–80.

Average annual growth rate (percent)

Table 12. Structure of Production

	GDP (millions of dollars)		Distribution of gross domestic product (percent)							
			Agriculture		Industry		Manufacturing[a]		Services	
	1960[b]	1980[c]	1960[b]	1980[c]	1960[b]	1980[c]	1960[b]	1980[c]	1960[b]	1980[c]
I. Current IDA recipients			**48** w	**35** w	**18** w	**33** w	**12** w	**14** w	**34** w	**32** w
A. Pure IDA countries			53 w	47 w	9 w	14 w	5 w	6 w	38 w	39 w
Lao PDR	. .	. .	. .	. .	. .	. .	. .	. .	. .	. .
Chad	180	500	52	57	12	5	4	4	36	38
Bangladesh	3,170	11,140	58	54	7	13	5	7	35	33
Ethiopia	900	3,690	65	51	12	16	6	11	23	33
Nepal	410	1,860	. .	57	. .	13	. .	4	. .	30
Somalia	160	1,130	71	60	8	11	3	7	21	29
Guinea-Bissau	. .	140	. .	53	. .	. .	. .	10	. .	. .
Burma	1,280	5,550	33	46	12	13	8	10	55	41
Afghanistan	1,190	. .	. .	. .	. .	. .	. .	. .	. .	. .
Viet Nam	. .	. .	. .	. .	. .	. .	. .	. .	. .	. .
Mali	270	1,410	55	42	10	10	5	6	35	48
Burundi	190	790	. .	55	. .	16	. .	9	. .	29
Rwanda	120	1,120	81	48	7	22	1	16	12	30
Upper Volta	200	980	62	40	14	18	8	13	24	42
Zaïre	130	6,160	30	32	27	23	13	4	43	45
Gambia	18	130	43	26	18	8	2	2	39	66
Maldives	. .	. .	. .	. .	. .	. .	. .	. .	. .	. .
Haiti	270	1,410	. .	. .	. .	. .	. .	. .	. .	. .
Sierra Leone	. .	930	. .	36	. .	20	. .	5	. .	44
Tanzania	550	4,350	57	54	11	13	5	9	32	33
Guinea	370	1,670	. .	37	. .	33	. .	4	. .	30
Central African Rep.	110	780	51	37	10	15	4	7	39	48
Comoros	. .	. .	. .	. .	. .	. .	. .	. .	. .	. .
Equatorial Guinea	. .	90	. .	. .	. .	. .	. .	. .	. .	. .
Western Samoa	. .	. .	. .	. .	. .	. .	. .	. .	. .	. .
Uganda	540	12,790	52	76	12	6	9	6	36	18
Benin	160	950	55	43	8	12	3	7	37	45
Niger	250	1,890	69	33	9	34	4	8	22	33
Madagascar	540	3,260	37	36	10	18	4	. .	53	46
Sudan	1,160	7,190	. .	38	. .	14	. .	6	. .	48
Ghana	1,220	15,390	. .	66	. .	21	. .	. .	. .	13
Lesotho	30	250	. .	31	. .	21	. .	5	. .	48
Yemen, PDR	. .	540	. .	13	. .	28	. .	14	. .	59
Yemen Arab Rep.	. .	2,610	. .	29	. .	16	. .	6	. .	55
Mauritania	70	490	59	26	24	33	3	8	17	41
Solomon Islands	18	120	. .	. .	. .	. .	. .	. .	. .	. .
Djibouti	. .	. .	. .	. .	. .	. .	. .	. .	. .	. .
Dominica	12	50	. .	. .	. .	. .	. .	. .	. .	. .
B. IDA/IBRD blend countries			46 w	33 w	21 w	38 w	14 w	18 w	33 w	29 w
Malawi	170	1,420	58	43	11	20	6	13	31	37
India	29,550	142,010	50	37	20	26	14	18	30	37
Sri Lanka	1,500	3,760	32	28	20	30	15	18	48	42
China	. .	252,230	. .	31	. .	47	. .	. .	. .	22
Pakistan	3,500	21,460	46	31	16	25	12	16	38	44
Togo	120	1,060	55	26	16	20	8	7	29	54
Kenya	730	5,990	38	34	18	21	9	13	44	45
Senegal	610	2,650	24	29	17	24	12	19	59	47
Liberia	220	1,040	. .	36	. .	31	. .	9	. .	33
Zambia	680	3,790	11	15	63	39	4	17	26	46
Zimbabwe	780	3,640	18	12	35	39	17	25	47	49
Guyana	150	520	26	23	31	36	10	13	43	41
Papua New Guinea	250	2,490	53	34	11	30	3	8	36	37

	GDP (millions of dollars)		Distribution of gross domestic product (percent)							
			Agriculture		Industry		Manufacturing[a]		Services	
	1960[b]	1980[c]	1960[b]	1980[c]	1960[b]	1980[c]	1960[b]	1980[c]	1960[b]	1980[c]
II. Former IDA recipients			**35** *w*	**21** *w*	**23** *w*	**35** *w*	**15** *w*	**17** *w*	**42** *w*	**44** *w*
Indonesia	8,670	69,800	54	26	14	42	8	9	32	32
Honduras	300	2,230	37	31	19	25	13	17	44	44
Bolivia	460	6,100	26	18	25	29	15	14	49	53
Egypt	3,880	22,970	30	23	24	35	20	28	46	42
El Salvador	570	3,390	32	27	19	21	15	15	49	52
Cameroon	550	6,010	. .	32	. .	22	. .	9	. .	46
Thailand	2,550	33,450	40	25	19	29	13	20	41	46
Swaziland	29	440	31	. .	23	. .	5	. .	46	. .
Philippines	6,960	35,490	26	23	28	37	20	26	46	40
Nicaragua	340	2,120	24	23	21	31	16	25	55	46
Congo, People's Rep.	130	1,750	23	12	17	45	10	6	60	43
Morocco	2,040	17,940	23	18	27	32	16	17	50	50
Botswana	35	820	54	. .	11	. .	8	. .	35	. .
Nigeria	3,150	91,130	63	20	11	42	5	6	26	38
Mauritius	120	860	22	16	27	30	13	18	51	54
Ivory Coast	570	7,030	43	34	14	22	7	11	43	44
Dominican Rep.	720	7,120	27	18	23	27	17	15	50	55
Colombia	4,010	29,570	34	28	26	30	17	22	40	42
Ecuador	960	11,380	29	13	19	38	13	8	48	49
Paraguay	300	4,450	36	30	20	25	17	17	44	45
Tunisia	770	7,300	24	17	18	35	8	13	58	48
Syrian Arab Rep.	890	12,900	. .	20	. .	27	. .	21	. .	53
Jordan	. .	2,190	. .	8	. .	32	. .	16	. .	60
Turkey	8,820	53,820	41	23	21	30	13	21	38	47
Korea, Rep. of	3,810	58,250	37	16	20	41	14	28	43	43
Costa Rica	510	4,850	26	17	20	29	14	20	54	54
Chile	3,730	28,080	10	7	51	37	29	21	39	56

a. Manufacturing is a part of the industrial sector, but its share of GDP is shown separately because it typically is the most dynamic part of the industrial sector.
b. Figures in italic are for 1961, not 1960.
c. Figures in italic are for 1979, not 1980.

Table 13. Growth of Consumption and Investment

	Public consumption		Private consumption		Gross domestic investment	
	1960–70[a]	1970–80[b]	1960–70[a]	1970–80[b]	1960–70[a]	1970–80[b]
I. Current IDA recipients	**5.2** *m*	**4.3** *m*	**3.4** *m*	**3.5** *m*	**4.9** *m*	**3.3** *m*
A. Pure IDA countries	*4.4 m*	*3.9 m*	*3.3 m*	*3.5 m*	*4.3 m*	*4.8 m*
Lao PDR	. .	. .	. .	. .	. .	. .
Chad	4.4	− 1.7	− 0.7	0.3	2.3	− 0.5
Bangladesh	c	c	3.4	4.0	11.2	1.8
Ethiopia	4.7	3.2	4.7	3.2	5.7	− 1.2
Nepal	. .	. .	. .	. .	. .	11.7
Somalia	3.7	*10.8*	0.4	*4.0*	4.3	*7.5*
Guinea-Bissau	. .	*8.8*	. .	*− 0.4*	. .	*− 2.2*
Burma	c	c	2.9	4.0	2.8	8.0
Afghanistan	c	. .	2.5	. .	− 1.0	. .
Viet Nam	. .	. .	. .	. .	. .	. .
Mali	6.2	7.5	2.8	5.3	4.9	3.3
Burundi	19.2	3.6	3.2	3.6	4.3	15.8
Rwanda	1.1	14.0	4.2	1.6	3.5	18.9
Upper Volta	. .	7.3	. .	3.4	. .	4.8
Zaïre	8.5	− 2.2	3.5	− 1.3	9.6	*1.1*
Gambia	4.9	5.6	4.9	4.6	6.1	4.7
Maldives	. .	. .	. .	. .	. .	. .
Haiti	c	c	− 1.0	3.5	1.7	11.1
Sierra Leone	. .	4.3	. .	1.0	. .	− 0.2
Tanzania	c	c	5.2	6.0	9.8	3.0
Guinea	. .	. .	. .	. .	. .	. .
Central African Rep.	2.2	− 2.6	3.0	5.8	1.3	− 10.6
Comoros	. .	. .	. .	. .	. .	. .
Equatorial Guinea	. .	. .	. .	. .	. .	. .
Western Samoa	. .	. .	. .	. .	. .	. .
Uganda	c	c	5.6	− 0.9	7.5	− 16.4
Benin	1.7	2.0	4.9	3.5	4.2	7.2
Niger	2.0	3.0	3.9	1.4	3.0	7.6
Madagascar	2.7	0.2	2.0	− 0.6	5.4	− 1.8
Sudan	12.1	− 4.2	− 1.6	6.6	− 1.3	6.7
Ghana	6.1	0.8	2.0	− 0.1	− 3.2	− 6.2
Lesotho	(.)	15.2	6.5	11.9	20.7	22.0
Yemen, PDR	. .	. .	. .	. .	. .	. .
Yemen Arab Rep.	. .	10.8	. .	10.0	. .	24.6
Mauritania	1.0	15.1	17.2	0.5	− 2.1	4.9
Solomon Islands	. .	. .	. .	. .	. .	. .
Djibouti	. .	. .	. .	. .	. .	. .
Dominica	. .	. .	. .	. .	. .	. .
B. IDA/IBRD blend countries	*6.5 m*	*3.6 m*	*3.7 m*	*4.1 m*	*6.9 m*	*2.6 m*
Malawi	4.6	2.5	4.1	6.4	15.4	2.6
India	− 0.2	4.2	3.7	3.2	5.3	4.8
Sri Lanka	c	c	2.1	2.7	6.6	9.8
China	c	c	2.7	5.4	9.8	6.8
Pakistan	7.3	4.3	7.1	4.9	6.9	2.4
Togo	6.7	10.1	7.6	5.7	11.1	10.5
Kenya	10.0	*9.0*	4.6	6.9	7.0	*1.2*
Senegal	− 0.2	3.0	3.2	2.7	1.1	2.4
Liberia	5.6	2.8	0.7	5.1	− 3.9	5.8
Zambia	11.0	1.4	6.8	1.5	10.6	− 10.9
Zimbabwe	. .	. .	. .	. .	. .	. .
Guyana	8.6	5.7	3.4	− 0.2	3.4	2.6
Papua New Guinea	6.5	− 0.6	6.1	2.3	*21.1*	− 5.9

	Average annual growth rate (percent)					
	Public consumption		Private consumption		Gross domestic investment	
	1960–70[a]	1970–80[b]	1960–70[a]	1970–80[b]	1960–70[a]	1970–80[b]
II. Former IDA recipients	**5.8** *m*	**7.9** *m*	**5.3** *m*	**6.0** *m*	**8.8** *m*	**9.6** *m*
Indonesia	0.9	12.9	4.1	8.1	4.6	14.4
Honduras	5.3	7.6	4.8	4.1	10.2	9.6
Bolivia	8.9	7.3	4.1	6.4	9.6	2.9
Egypt	c	c	6.7	5.1	3.1	16.5
El Salvador	6.4	6.1	6.1	5.3	3.5	5.2
Cameroon	6.1	5.8	2.7	5.0	9.3	8.5
Thailand	9.7	9.2	7.0	6.3	15.8	7.7
Swaziland	7.2	. .	13.6	. .	10.6	. .
Philippines	5.0	7.2	4.7	5.0	8.2	10.5
Nicaragua	2.2	9.7	7.6	0.6	10.9	2.5
Congo, People's Rep.	5.4	. .	−0.3	. .	2.9	2.7
Morocco	4.4	14.7	4.1	4.2	8.8	9.2
Botswana	10.8	. .	6.9	. .	25.3	. .
Nigeria	10.0	11.3	1.1	6.6	7.4	15.8
Mauritius	2.1	13.5	2.8	9.6	−6.7	16.5
Ivory Coast	11.8	8.1	8.0	7.6	12.7	13.2
Dominican Rep.	1.9	2.2	6.3	6.0	11.4	9.6
Colombia	5.5	4.9	5.5	5.8	4.5	5.4
Ecuador	. .	13.5	. .	9.8	. .	8.8
Paraguay	6.9	5.6	5.3	7.7	6.8	18.7
Tunisia	5.2	9.5	3.2	8.1	4.2	11.0
Syrian Arab Rep.	. .	16.1	. .	11.9	. .	16.7
Jordan	. .	. .	. .	. .	. .	. .
Turkey	6.7	6.4	5.1	4.2	8.8	9.4
Korea, Rep. of	5.5	8.3	7.0	7.5	23.6	13.4
Costa Rica	8.0	5.9	6.0	5.2	7.1	8.8
Chile	4.7	0.9	4.9	2.6	4.2	−1.8

a. Figures in italic are for 1961–71, not 1960–70.
b. Figures in italic are for 1970–79, not 1970–80.
c. Separate figures are not available for public consumption, which is therefore included in private consumption.

Table 14. Structure of Demand

	Distribution of gross domestic product (percent)											
	Public consumption		Private consumption		Gross domestic investment		Gross domestic saving		Exports of goods and nonfactor services		Resource balance	
	1960[a]	1980[b]	1960[a]	1980[b]	1960[a]	1980[b]	1960[a]	1980[b]	1960[a]	1980[b]	1960[a]	1980[b]
I. Current IDA recipients	**8** *w*	**11** *w*	**78** *w*	**67** *w*	**19** *w*	**25** *w*	**14** *w*	**22** *w*	**8** *w*	**10** *w*	**−5** *w*	**−3** *w*
A. Pure IDA countries	9 *w*	13 *w*	82 *w*	80 *w*	13 *w*	14 *w*	9 *w*	7 *w*	16 *w*	13 *w*	−4 *w*	−7 *w*
Lao PDR	..	..	..	..	..	..	..	..	..	..	..	..
Chad	13	18	82	96	11	13	5	−14	23	33	−6	−27
Bangladesh	6	7	86	91	7	17	8	2	10	8	1	−15
Ethiopia	8	15	81	80	12	10	11	5	9	15	−1	−5
Nepal	..	c	96	93	9	14	4	7	..	12	−5	−7
Somalia	8	19	86	78	10	16	6	3	13	15	−4	−13
Guinea-Bissau	..	52	..	71	..	32	..	−23	..	14	..	−55
Burma	c	c	89	82	12	24	11	18	20	8	−1	−6
Afghanistan	c	c	87	89	16	14	13	11	4	11	−3	−3
Viet Nam	..	..	..	..	..	..	..	..	..	..	..	..
Mali	12	22	79	81	14	15	9	−3	12	19	−5	−12
Burundi	3	12	92	88	6	14	5	(.)	13	8	−1	−14
Rwanda	10	12	82	85	6	16	8	3	12	14	2	−13
Upper Volta	10	16	94	93	10	18	−4	−9	9	14	−14	−27
Zaïre	18	12	61	75	12	11	21	13	55	29	9	2
Gambia	20	25	72	97	13	34	8	−22	59	52	−5	−56
Maldives	..	..	..	..	..	..	..	..	..	..	..	..
Haiti	c	c	93	91	9	18	7	9	20	19	−2	−9
Sierra Leone	..	17	..	77	..	15	..	6	..	23	..	−9
Tanzania	9	14	72	78	14	22	19	8	31	14	5	−14
Guinea	..	19	..	67	..	11	..	14	..	34	..	3
Central African Rep.	19	c	72	101	20	10	9	−1	23	29	−11	−19
Comoros	..	..	..	..	..	..	..	..	..	..	..	..
Equatorial Guinea	..	..	..	..	..	..	..	..	..	..	..	..
Western Samoa	..	..	..	..	..	..	..	..	..	..	..	..
Uganda	9	c	75	98	11	3	16	2	26	4	5	−1
Benin	16	15	75	80	15	24	9	5	12	28	−6	−19
Niger	9	9	79	70	13	29	12	21	9	25	−1	−8
Madagascar	20	17	75	74	11	21	5	9	12	15	−6	−12
Sudan	8	12	80	85	12	12	12	3	16	10	(.)	−9
Ghana	10	9	73	86	24	5	17	5	28	12	−7	(.)
Lesotho	17	20	108	158	2	30	−25	−78	12	18	−27	−108
Yemen, PDR	..	..	..	..	..	..	..	..	..	..	..	..
Yemen Arab Rep.	..	18	..	102	..	44	..	−20	..	7	..	−64
Mauritania	24	39	79	47	37	51	−3	14	18	38	−40	−37
Solomon Islands	..	..	..	..	..	..	..	..	..	..	..	..
Djibouti	..	..	..	..	..	..	..	..	..	..	..	..
Dominica	..	48	..	92	..	39	..	−40	..	31	..	−79
B. IDA/IBRD blend countries	8 *w*	11 *w*	77 *w*	64 *w*	20 *w*	27 *w*	15 *w*	25 *w*	7 *w*	9 *w*	−5 *w*	−2 *w*
Malawi	16	10	88	80	10	22	−4	10	21	22	−14	−12
India	7	10	79	70	17	23	14	20	5	..	−3	−3
Sri Lanka	13	8	78	78	14	36	9	14	44	31	−5	−22
China	c	11	77	59	23	31	23	30	4	6	(.)	−1
Pakistan	11	11	84	83	12	18	5	6	8	13	−7	−13
Togo	8	16	88	70	11	26	4	14	19	41	−7	−12
Kenya	11	20	72	65	20	22	17	15	31	26	−3	−7
Senegal	17	14	68	88	16	15	15	−2	40	31	−1	−17
Liberia	7	16	58	55	28	29	35	29	39	53	7	(.)
Zambia	11	28	48	54	25	23	41	18	56	38	16	−5
Zimbabwe	11	21	67	63	23	18	22	16	..	..	−1	−2
Guyana	12	29	69	56	28	30	19	15	49	68	−9	−15
Papua New Guinea	26	26	71	59	15	27	3	15	17	42	−12	−12

110

	Distribution of gross domestic product (percent)											
	Public consumption		Private consumption		Gross domestic investment		Gross domestic saving		Exports of goods and nonfactor services		Resource balance	
	1960[a]	1980[b]	1960[a]	1980[b]	1960[a]	1980[b]	1960[a]	1980[b]	1960[a]	1980[b]	1960[a]	1980[b]
II. Former IDA recipients	**11** w	**12** w	**75** w	**65** w	**15** w	**25** w	**14** w	**23** w	**13** w	**25** w	**−1** w	**−2** w
Indonesia	12	13	80	57	8	22	8	30	13	31	(.)	8
Honduras	11	13	77	67	14	28	12	20	22	37	−2	−8
Bolivia	7	10	86	75	14	13	7	15	13	17	−7	2
Egypt	17	19	71	65	13	31	12	16	20	32	−1	−15
El Salvador	10	15	79	75	16	12	11	10	20	31	−5	−2
Cameroon	. .	11	. .	66	. .	25	. .	23	. .	29	. .	−2
Thailand	10	12	76	66	16	27	14	22	17	25	−2	−5
Swaziland	18	. .	54	. .	13	. .	28	. .	47	. .	15	. .
Philippines	8	8	76	67	16	30	16	25	11	20	(.)	−5
Nicaragua	9	21	79	80	15	20	12	−1	24	24	−3	−21
Congo, People's Rep.	23	13	98	50	45	37	−21	37	21	. .	−66	(.)
Morocco	12	22	77	67	10	21	11	11	24	18	1	−10
Botswana	15	. .	88	. .	8	. .	−3	. .	23	. .	−11	. .
Nigeria	6	10	87	62	13	24	7	28	15	26	−6	4
Mauritius	15	14	79	69	30	27	6	17	32	48	−24	−10
Ivory Coast	10	18	73	59	15	28	17	23	37	33	2	−5
Dominican Rep.	13	8	68	78	12	24	19	14	24	17	7	−10
Colombia	6	8	73	67	21	25	21	25	16	17	(.)	(.)
Ecuador	10	14	75	63	15	25	15	23	18	24	(.)	−2
Paraguay	8	6	76	74	17	29	16	20	18	10	−1	−9
Tunisia	17	15	76	60	17	28	7	25	20	41	−10	−3
Syrian Arab Rep.	. .	23	. .	67	. .	25	. .	10	. .	18	. .	−15
Jordan	. .	33	. .	94	. .	48	. .	−27	. .	48	. .	−75
Turkey	11	13	76	69	16	27	13	18	3	7	−3	−9
Korea, Rep. of	15	13	84	64	11	31	1	23	3	37	−10	−8
Costa Rica	10	18	77	67	18	25	13	15	21	26	−5	−10
Chile	12	12	63	72	27	18	25	16	17	21	−2	−2

a. Figures in italic are for 1961, not 1960.
b. Figures in italic are for 1979, not 1980.
c. Separate figures are not available for public consumption, which is therefore included in private consumption.

Table 15. Commercial Energy

	Average annual growth rate (percent)				Energy consumption per capita (kilograms of coal equivalent)		Energy imports as a percentage of merchandise exports	
	Energy production		Energy consumption					
	1960–74[a]	1974–79	1960–74	1974–79	1960	1979	1960[b]	1979[c]
I. Current IDA recipients	**4.6** *w*	**8.1** *w*	**4.5** *w*	**7.5** *w*	**325** *w*	**415** *w*	**10** *w*	..
A. Pure IDA countries	6.6 *w*	6.5 *w*	9.2 *w*	1.2 *w*	49 *w*	75 *w*	7 *w*	..
Lao PDR	..	16.1	13.8	13.8	16	98	..	..
Chad	..	..	7.6	4.6	8	22	23	..
Bangladesh	..	10.1	..	6.6	..	40	..	27
Ethiopia	14.1	2.3	13.6	−5.3	9	20	11	26
Nepal	26.8	4.6	12.6	2.4	4	13	..	24
Somalia	..	..	8.7	13.1	16	74	4	..
Guinea-Bissau	..	..	6.6	0.7	17	51	..	..
Burma	5.6	12.4	3.7	5.8	55	67	4	..
Afghanistan	38.8	−2.8	10.3	6.6	23	88	12	..
Viet Nam	..	7.6	..	..	98	138	..	..
Mali	..	8.3	5.7	5.3	14	28	13	..
Burundi	..	22.0	..	7.0	..	17	..	14
Rwanda	..	3.5	..	10.2	..	28	..	..
Upper Volta	..	..	7.8	10.2	5	26	38	45
Zaïre	3.0	17.9	3.8	0.3	96	100	3	..
Gambia	..	..	9.0	17.7	27	117	..	..
Maldives	..	..	..	..	..	..	..	..
Haiti	..	13.7	1.5	20.8	34	63	..	15
Sierra Leone	..	..	9.0	−1.1	29	84	11	..
Tanzania	10.6	10.4	9.4	−2.8	41	51	..	30
Guinea	16.0	(.)	3.2	1.6	64	83	7	..
Central African Rep.	14.1	4.1	7.6	8.5	30	46	12	2
Comoros	..	..	9.5	6.2	22	48	..	..
Equatorial Guinea	6.9	..	−2.6	4.3	121	103	..	..
Western Samoa	4.1	2.6	5.6	15.2	77	263	..	..
Uganda	5.2	−4.4	9.1	−8.1	39	39	5	..
Benin	..	..	9.6	−0.5	37	65	16	..
Niger	..	..	14.8	12.9	5	46	6	..
Madagascar	6.7	4.1	9.0	3.9	39	89	9	10
Sudan	..	13.7	13.1	−0.9	52	133	8	3
Ghana	..	2.6	12.5	2.3	100	258	7	14
Lesotho	..	..	..	..	..	..	..	..
Yemen, PDR	..	..	8.7	7.1	210	509	..	..
Yemen Arab Rep.	..	..	12.9	16.0	7	58	..	..
Mauritania	..	..	21.3	5.5	18	196	39	..
Solomon Islands	..	..	14.0	8.2	48	197	..	..
Djibouti	..	..	8.6	5.2	274	282	..	..
Dominica	..	(.)	..	(.)	101	227	..	15
B. IDA/IBRD blend countries	4.6 *w*	8.1 *w*	4.3 *w*	7.8 *w*	371 *w*	492 *w*	11 *w*	28 *w*
Malawi	..	6.9	..	5.6	..	67	..	27
India	4.9	5.4	5.0	5.0	111	194	11	32
Sri Lanka	10.1	8.2	3.8	3.8	110	135	8	26
China	4.5	8.7	4.2	8.5	560	734	..	..
Pakistan	9.4	6.6	5.3	4.4	132	209	17	34
Togo	..	22.3	12.8	11.9	22	112	10	32
Kenya	9.6	17.6	3.3	3.6	144	172	18	38
Senegal	..	..	4.7	12.5	116	253	8	29
Liberia	31.8	−1.3	19.0	−0.9	83	425	3	19
Zambia	..	5.6	..	5.6	..	832	..	13
Zimbabwe	2.5	−3.1	2.4	−0.4	1,333	783	..	..
Guyana	..	..	8.2	5.1	554	1,168	..	..
Papua New Guinea	..	..	..	..	51	299	7	..

| | Average annual growth rate (percent) | | | | Energy consumption per capita (kilograms of coal equivalent) | | Energy imports as a percentage of merchandise exports | |
| | Energy production | | Energy consumption | | | | | |
	1960–74[a]	1974–79	1960–74	1974–79	1960	1979	1960[b]	1979[c]
II. Former IDA recipients	**13.3** *w*	**4.9** *w*	**7.9** *w*	**8.3** *w*	**171** *w*	**451** *w*	**9** *w*	**17** *w*
Indonesia	8.5	6.6	3.7	10.3	125	225	3	5
Honduras	29.4	6.4	7.7	1.7	149	238	10	*13*
Bolivia	17.1	−3.0	6.8	9.2	177	447	4	1
Egypt	9.4	27.0	3.6	10.5	283	539	12	2
El Salvador	5.1	24.3	7.7	8.4	143	338	6	9
Cameroon	1.1	45.0	3.8	7.6	85	143	7	12
Thailand	28.3	−0.2	16.2	7.4	60	353	12	31
Swaziland	4.8	33.0	4.8	33.0	35	267	. .	. .
Philippines	3.0	24.4	8.4	5.6	147	329	9	32
Nicaragua	26.4	−16.3	10.4	2.7	176	446	12	14
Congo, People's Rep.	15.8	5.1	5.4	6.9	120	195	25	3
Morocco	2.0	4.7	6.4	6.3	163	302	9	36
Botswana	. .	64.6	. .	64.6	. .	414	. .	. .
Nigeria	36.6	1.0	9.3	1.5	28	80	7	2
Mauritius	3.7	4.0	12.4	1.0	124	390	. .	. .
Ivory Coast	9.7	−12.2	14.3	5.5	71	230	5	11
Dominican Rep.	1.8	−5.1	14.4	−1.1	156	490	. .	37
Colombia	3.5	2.0	5.7	7.1	494	914	3	10
Ecuador	19.4	5.0	8.7	14.8	196	640	2	*1*
Paraguay	. .	6.7	8.3	10.7	80	234	. .	41
Tunisia	71.9	5.5	8.8	10.7	165	590	15	28
Syrian Arab Rep.	86.0	7.5	7.5	15.4	306	925	16	50
Jordan	. .	. .	5.9	13.3	186	522	79	90
Turkey	7.5	2.5	9.7	6.8	250	771	16	78
Korea, Rep. of	6.3	4.6	13.9	12.0	208	1,473	70	25
Costa Rica	9.5	3.5	10.1	7.5	304	812	7	20
Chile	3.9	0.1	6.1	0.7	797	1,153	10	24

a. Figures in italic are for 1961–74, not 1960–74.
b. Figures in italic are for 1961, not 1960.
c. Figures in italic are for 1978, not 1979.

Table 16. Balance of Payments and Debt Service Ratios

	Current account balance (millions of dollars)		Interest payments on external public debt (millions of dollars)		Debt service as a percentage of:			
					GNP		Exports of goods and services	
	1970	1980[a]	1970	1980	1970	1980[a]	1970	1980[a]
I. Current IDA recipients					**1.2** *w*	**1.5** *w*	**11.3** *w*	**10.2** *w*
A. *Pure IDA countries*					1.2 *w*	1.8 *w*	5.7 *w*	10.0 *w*
Lao PDR	..	..	..	..	..	..	..	..
Chad	2	..	(.)	4	1.0	3.1	3.9	..
Bangladesh	−60	−755	..	37	..	0.7	..	5.6
Ethiopia	−32	−228	6	19	1.2	1.1	11.4	7.6
Nepal	..	−53	(.)	2	0.3	0.2	..	1.5
Somalia	−5	−136	(.)	2	0.3	0.5	2.1	3.5
Guinea-Bissau	..	..	..	..	..	..	..	..
Burma	−64	−325	3	45	0.9	1.9	15.8	22.2
Afghanistan	..	..	9	23	2.5	..	..	..
Viet Nam	..	..	..	..	..	..	..	..
Mali	−2	−99	(.)	4	0.2	0.8	1.2	3.6
Burundi	2	..	(.)	2	0.3	0.6	..	..
Rwanda	6	−68	(.)	1	0.2	0.2	1.4	1.1
Upper Volta	9	..	(.)	7	0.6	1.2	4.0	..
Zaïre	−64	..	9	153	2.1	5.8	4.4	..
Gambia	(.)	−98	(.)	(.)	0.3	0.1	0.6	0.3
Maldives	..	..	..	(.)	..	..	..	..
Haiti	2	−77	(.)	5	1.0	1.1	5.8	4.2
Sierra Leone	−16	−168	2	8	2.9	4.2	10.1	18.4
Tanzania	−35	−548	6	31	1.2	1.0	8.2	7.3
Guinea	..	..	4	23	2.4	6.1	..	..
Central African Rep.	−11	7	(.)	2	1.1	1.0	3.3	4.5
Comoros	..	..	(.)	1	..	0.5	..	..
Equatorial Guinea	..	..	..	..	..	..	..	..
Western Samoa	−5	..	..	2	..	..	..	..
Uganda	20	−18	4	3	0.6	0.3	3.4	11.9
Benin	−1	..	(.)	2	0.7	0.6	2.2	..
Niger	(.)	..	1	16	0.6	2.2	3.8	2.3
Madagascar	10	−433	2	26	0.8	1.8	3.5	7.4
Sudan	−42	−196	13	16	1.7	1.8	10.7	14.4
Ghana	−68	−91	12	28	1.1	0.6	5.2	6.0
Lesotho	..	..	(.)	1	0.4	0.8	..	..
Yemen, PDR	−4	−35	..	7	..	1.5	..	1.5
Yemen Arab Rep.	..	−478	..	5	..	0.6	..	1.1
Mauritania	−5	−116	(.)	13	2.0	5.9	3.2	32.9
Solomon Islands	..	..	..	(.)	..	0.1	..	..
Djibouti	..	..	..	..	..	..	..	..
Dominica	..	−34	..	(.)	..	1.0	..	3.2
B. *IDA/IBRD blend countries*					1.2 *w*	1.4 *w*	14.8 *w*	10.3 *w*
Malawi	−35	−139	3	32	1.9	4.5	7.0	18.4
India	−394	3,163	189	372	0.9	0.6	20.9	8.9
Sri Lanka	−59	−664	12	32	2.0	2.0	10.3	6.0
China	..	..	..	..	..	..	..	..
Pakistan	−667	−928	76	242	1.9	2.4	23.6	11.3
Togo	3	..	1	54	0.9	14.4	3.0	..
Kenya	−39	−985	11	100	1.7	2.6	5.3	8.8
Senegal	−16	..	2	57	0.8	6.9	2.7	..
Liberia	..	..	6	27	5.5	4.2	..	..
Zambia	108	−508	23	98	3.2	9.5	5.6	24.4
Zimbabwe	−13	−255	5	10	0.6	0.9	..	2.6
Guyana	−21	−128	3	26	2.1	12.4	3.5	16.8
Papua New Guinea	..	−267	1	30	0.1	2.6	..	5.9

	Current account balance (millions of dollars)		Interest payments on external public debt (millions of dollars)		Debt service as a percentage of:			
					GNP		Exports of goods and services	
	1970	1980[a]	1970	1980	1970	1980[a]	1970	1980[a]
II. Former IDA recipients					**1.8** w	**2.9** w	**11.4** w	**10.6** w
Indonesia	−310	2,872	24	824	0.9	2.7	6.9	8.0
Honduras	−64	−321	3	55	0.8	3.9	2.8	9.9
Bolivia	−22	−115	6	157	2.3	4.7	11.0	25.9
Egypt	−154	−489	38	490	4.1	6.9	28.7	18.9
El Salvador	8	−86	4	24	0.9	1.2	3.6	3.5
Cameroon	−30	−129	4	103	0.8	3.1	3.2	7.7
Thailand	−250	−2,280	16	267	0.6	1.3	3.4	5.2
Swaziland	. .	−68	2	7	3.5	3.0	. .	3.1
Philippines	−48	−2,046	25	342	1.4	1.6	7.5	7.0
Nicaragua	−39	160	7	38	3.2	3.7	11.1	14.5
Congo, People's Rep.	−65	−172	3	39	3.3	6.1	8.9	9.3
Morocco	−124	−1,416	23	618	1.5	6.5	7.7	27.5
Botswana	. .	−29	(.)	6	0.7	1.5	. .	1.6
Nigeria	−368	2,915	20	394	0.7	0.5	4.2	1.9
Mauritius	8	−105	2	19	1.5	3.3	2.9	5.5
Ivory Coast	−37	−1,742	11	296	2.8	8.2	6.8	23.9
Dominican Rep.	−102	−341	4	97	0.8	2.3	4.5	21.5
Colombia	293	−25	44	282	1.7	1.7	11.6	9.6
Ecuador	−113	−575	7	230	1.5	3.8	9.1	14.0
Paraguay	−17	−282	4	35	1.8	1.8	11.8	11.3
Tunisia	−53	−324	18	191	4.5	4.7	18.5	12.2
Syrian Arab Rep.	−69	−640	6	95	2.0	3.2	11.0	14.5
Jordan	−17	374	2	58	. .	3.9	3.6	5.4
Turkey	−70	−2,762	42	589	1.3	1.7	16.3	15.8
Korea, Rep. of	−623	−5,326	70	1,310	3.1	4.9	19.4	12.2
Costa Rica	−74	−655	7	125	2.9	4.3	9.9	16.4
Chile	−91	−1,784	78	494	3.1	5.2	18.9	22.9

a. Figures in italic are for 1979, not 1980.

Table 17. Flow of Public External Capital
(millions of dollars)

	Gross inflow		Repayment of principal		Net inflow	
	1970	1980	1970	1980	1970	1980
I. Current IDA recipients						
A. Pure IDA countries						
Lao PDR	..	..	..	..	..	..
Chad	6	9	2	12	4	−3
Bangladesh	..	597	..	40	..	557
Ethiopia	27	132	15	16	12	116
Nepal	1	55	2	2	−1	53
Somalia	4	114	(.)	5	4	109
Guinea-Bissau	..	..	..	..	..	..
Burma	16	281	18	64	−2	217
Afghanistan	31	113	15	157	16	−44
Viet Nam	..	..	..	..	..	..
Mali	21	85	(.)	7	21	78
Burundi	1	43	(.)	4	1	39
Rwanda	(.)	34	(.)	1	(.)	33
Upper Volta	2	79	2	9	(.)	70
Zaïre	31	198	28	155	3	43
Gambia	1	35	(.)	(.)	1	35
Maldives	..	18	..	..	..	18
Haiti	4	55	4	11	(.)	44
Sierra Leone	8	88	10	34	−2	54
Tanzania	50	210	10	20	40	190
Guinea	90	122	10	72	80	50
Central African Rep.	2	43	2	6	(.)	37
Comoros	..	20	..	..	..	20
Equatorial Guinea	..	..	..	..	..	..
Western Samoa	..	10	..	2	..	8
Uganda	26	169	4	37	22	132
Benin	2	84	1	4	1	80
Niger	12	177	1	23	11	154
Madagascar	10	438	5	34	5	404
Sudan	54	749	22	132	32	617
Ghana	40	129	12	48	28	81
Lesotho	(.)	22	(.)	3	(.)	19
Yemen, PDR	1	101	..	6	1	95
Yemen Arab Rep.	..	399	..	13	..	386
Mauritania	4	153	3	17	1	136
Solomon Islands	..	4	..	(.)	..	4
Djibouti	..	..	..	..	..	..
Dominica	..	2	..	(.)	..	2
B. IDA/IBRD blend countries						
Malawi	38	160	3	35	35	125
India	890	2,477	307	636	583	1,841
Sri Lanka	61	296	27	49	34	247
China	..	..	..	..	..	..
Pakistan	484	1,199	114	363	370	832
Togo	5	222	2	97	3	125
Kenya	30	414	15	79	15	335
Senegal	15	283	5	123	10	160
Liberia	7	90	12	16	−5	74
Zambia	351	517	32	237	319	280
Zimbabwe	(.)	130	5	34	−5	96
Guyana	10	88	2	43	8	45
Papua New Guinea	25	134	(.)	35	25	99

	Gross inflow		Repayment of principal		Net inflow	
	1970	1980	1970	1980	1970	1980
II. Former IDA recipients						
Indonesia	441	2,592	59	953	382	1,639
Honduras	29	180	3	39	26	141
Bolivia	54	439	17	117	37	322
Egypt	302	2,982	247	1,246	55	1,736
El Salvador	8	124	6	17	2	107
Cameroon	28	571	4	79	24	492
Thailand	55	1,329	23	168	32	1,162
Swaziland	3	26	1	5	2	21
Philippines	132	1,390	73	220	59	1,170
Nicaragua	44	269	17	39	27	230
Congo, People's Rep.	35	230	6	58	29	172
Morocco	163	1,567	36	573	127	994
Botswana	3	18	(.)	6	3	12
Nigeria	62	1,526	36	84	26	1,442
Mauritius	2	85	1	13	1	72
Ivory Coast	77	1,426	27	534	50	892
Dominican Rep.	38	382	7	61	31	321
Colombia	235	1,005	75	264	160	741
Ecuador	42	749	16	179	26	570
Paraguay	15	158	7	44	8	114
Tunisia	87	431	45	222	42	209
Syrian Arab Rep.	59	509	30	297	29	212
Jordan	14	307	3	76	11	231
Turkey	328	2,222	128	399	200	1,823
Korea, Rep. of	440	3,548	198	1,452	242	2,096
Costa Rica	30	398	21	75	9	323
Chile	397	869	163	915	234	−46

Note: Data are for public and publicly guaranteed medium- and long-term loans.

Table 18. External Public Debt and International Reserves

	External public debt outstanding and disbursed				Gross international reserves		
	Millions of dollars		As a percentage of GNP		Millions of dollars		In months of import coverage
	1970	1980	1970	1980	1970	1980[a]	1980[a]
I. Current IDA recipients			*17.7 w*	**19.0** *w*			**5.1** *w*
A. Pure IDA countries			*16.7 w*	*22.6 w*			*3.2 w*
Lao PDR	..	..	..	..	..	..	..
Chad	32	159	11.8	31.7	2	11	..
Bangladesh	..	3,495	..	30.8	..	329	1.4
Ethiopia	169	728	9.5	17.8	72	263	3.6
Nepal	3	177	0.3	8.7	95	277	7.8
Somalia	77	688	24.4	45.3	21	27	0.6
Guinea-Bissau	..	..	..	..			
Burma	101	1,517	4.7	26.1	98	408	5.4
Afghanistan	454	1,094	48.2	..	50	943	..
Viet Nam	..	..	..	..	..	..	..
Mali	238	621	88.1	43.8	1	26	0.4
Burundi	7	137	3.1	15.6	15	105	..
Rwanda	2	158	0.9	15.1	8	186	5.8
Upper Volta	21	323	6.3	24.4	36	73	..
Zaïre	311	4,190	17.6	78.5	189	381	..
Gambia	5	85	14.1	53.1	8	6	0.4
Maldives	..	24	..	(.)	..	..	..
Haiti	40	258	10.3	18.5	4	28	0.7
Sierra Leone	59	344	14.3	34.3	39	31	1.3
Tanzania	248	1,360	19.4	27.6	65	20	0.2
Guinea	314	1,074	51.7	68.6	..	..	..
Central African Rep.	19	155	11.2	21.3	1	61	2.5
Comoros	1	50	..	46.0	..	..	..
Equatorial Guinea	..	..	..	..	..	..	..
Western Samoa	..	55	..	..	5	5	..
Uganda	128	669	9.8	4.8	57	17	0.5
Benin	41	262	16.0	23.4	16	14	..
Niger	32	399	8.7	22.1	19	132	2.1
Madagascar	93	1,035	10.8	31.6	37	5	0.1
Sudan	308	3,097	15.3	37.2	22	48	0.4
Ghana	489	1,011	22.6	8.0	58	344	2.9
Lesotho	8	71	7.8	11.1	..	..	..
Yemen, PDR	1	499	..	58.6	60	257	5.6
Yemen Arab Rep.	..	836	..	27.1	..	1,289	6.8
Mauritania	27	714	16.8	139.7	3	146	3.2
Solomon Islands	..	8	..	8.8	..	..	..
Djibouti	..	..	..	..	..	..	..
Dominica	..	14	..	29.2	..	..	..
B. IDA/IBRD blend countries			*18.0 w*	*17.2 w*			*5.5 w*
Malawi	122	634	39.1	42.6	29	75	1.6
India	7,936	17,358	14.9	10.0	1,023	12,007	8.3
Sri Lanka	317	1,337	16.1	32.5	43	282	1.5
China	..	..	..	..	..	10,144	6.2
Pakistan	3,059	8,775	30.5	34.7	194	1,569	2.8
Togo	40	907	16.0	86.7	35	84	..
Kenya	313	1,745	20.3	25.5	220	539	2.1
Senegal	98	906	11.6	34.9	22	25	..
Liberia	158	537	49.6	52.8	..	4	..
Zambia	581	1,815	34.6	51.2	515	207	1.3
Zimbabwe	233	698	15.8	13.8	59	373	2.4
Guyana	80	545	32.6	98.1	20	13	0.3
Papua New Guinea	36	507	5.8	20.3		459	3.6

	External public debt outstanding and disbursed				Gross international reserves		
	Millions of dollars		As a percentage of GNP		Millions of dollars		In months of import coverage
	1970	1980	1970	1980	1970	1980[a]	1980[a]
II. Former IDA recipients			**16.9** *w*	**21.6** *w*			**4.1** *w*
Indonesia	2,443	14,940	27.1	22.5	160	6,800	4.2
Honduras	90	892	12.8	36.9	20	161	1.5
Bolivia	479	2,124	47.1	36.4	46	554	5.4
Egypt	1,644	13,054	23.8	51.7	165	2,478	3.0
El Salvador	88	509	8.6	15.3	63	384	3.6
Cameroon	131	2,002	12.1	34.0	83	206	*0.9*
Thailand	328	4,063	5.0	12.4	911	3,028	3.3
Swaziland	37	163	39.8	40.3	(.)	162	3.8
Philippines	633	6,402	9.0	18.2	255	3,977	4.6
Nicaragua	155	1,698	20.7	83.0	50	. .	. .
Congo, People's Rep.	143	898	54.4	77.4	9	91	0.9
Morocco	711	7,098	18.0	38.6	141	811	1.7
Botswana	15	149	17.9	19.0	(.)	344	2.3
Nigeria	478	4,997	6.4	5.5	223	10,642	5.8
Mauritius	32	296	16.7	30.6	46	113	1.9
Ivory Coast	256	4,265	18.3	41.9	119	43	*0.4*
Dominican Rep.	212	1,186	14.5	17.5	32	278	*2.2*
Colombia	1,249	4,090	18.1	12.6	207	6,476	13.7
Ecuador	217	2,655	13.5	24.4	85	1,254	4.3
Paraguay	112	634	19.1	14.5	18	785	9.6
Tunisia	541	2,955	38.2	33.9	60	703	2.2
Syrian Arab Rep.	232	2,493	12.8	20.1	57	826	2.0
Jordan	118	1,266	. .	37.4	258	1,744	6.1
Turkey	1,854	13,216	14.4	22.4	440	3,497	4.6
Korea, Rep. of	1,797	16,274	20.9	28.8	610	3,101	1.3
Costa Rica	134	1,585	13.8	34.3	16	198	1.3
Chile	2,066	4,885	26.2	18.0	392	4,126	6.2

a. Figures in italic are for 1979, not 1980.

Table 19. Official Development Assistance from OECD and OPEC Members

	1960	1965	1970	1975	1976	1977	1978	1979	1980[a]	1981[a]
OECD (millions of U.S. dollars)										
Italy	77	60	147	182	226	198	376	273	683	670
New Zealand	..	..	14	66	53	53	55	67	72	67
United Kingdom	407	472	500	904	885	1,114	1,465	2,105	1,851	2,194
Finland	..	2	7	48	51	49	55	86	110	135
Australia	59	119	212	552	377	400	588	620	667	649
Japan	105	244	458	1,148	1,105	1,424	2,215	2,637	3,353	3,170
Canada	75	96	337	880	887	991	1,060	1,026	1,075	1,187
Austria	..	10	11	79	50	108	154	127	178	317
United States	2,702	4,023	3,153	4,161	4,360	4,682	5,663	4,684	7,138	5,760
Netherlands	35	70	196	608	728	908	1,074	1,404	1,630	1,510
France	823	752	971	2,093	2,146	2,267	2,705	3,370	4,162	4,022
Belgium	101	102	120	378	340	371	536	631	595	574
Norway	5	11	37	184	218	295	355	429	486	467
Denmark	5	13	59	205	214	258	388	448	474	405
Sweden	7	38	117	566	608	779	783	956	962	916
Germany, Fed. Rep.	223	456	599	1,689	1,593	1,717	2,347	3,350	3,567	3,182
Switzerland	4	12	30	104	112	119	173	207	253	236
Total	*4,628*	*6,478*	*6,967*	*13,847*	*13,953*	*15,733*	*19,992*	*22,420*	*27,256*	*25,461*
OECD (in national currencies)										
Italy (billions of lire)	48	38	92	119	188	175	319	227	585	762
New Zealand (millions of dollars)	..	..	13	54	53	55	53	65	74	77
United Kingdom (millions of pounds)	145	168	208	407	490	638	763	992	796	1,082
Finland (millions of markkaa)	..	6	29	177	197	197	226	335	410	583
Australia (millions of dollars)	53	106	189	421	308	361	514	555	585	565
Japan (billions of yen)	38	88	165	341	328	382	466	578	760	699
Canada (millions of dollars)	73	104	353	895	875	1,054	1,209	1,202	1,257	1,423
Austria (millions of schillings)	..	260	286	1,376	897	1,785	2,236	1,698	2,303	5,050
United States (millions of dollars)	2,702	4,023	3,153	4,161	4,360	4,682	5,663	4,684	7,138	5,760
Netherlands (millions of guilders)	133	253	710	1,538	1,925	2,229	2,324	2,816	3,241	3,768
France (millions of francs)	4,063	3,713	5,393	8,971	10,257	11,139	12,207	14,338	17,589	21,858
Belgium (millions of francs)	5,050	5,100	6,000	13,903	13,126	13,298	16,880	18,500	17,400	21,313
Norway (millions of kroner)	36	78	264	962	1,190	1,570	1,861	2,172	2,400	2,680
Denmark (millions of kroner)	35	90	443	1,178	1,294	1,549	2,140	2,357	2,671	2,885
Sweden (millions of kronor)	36	196	605	2,350	2,648	3,491	3,538	4,098	4,069	4,638
Germany, Fed. Rep. (millions of deutsche marks)	937	1,824	2,192	4,155	4,011	3,987	4,714	6,140	6,484	7,195
Switzerland (millions of francs)	17	52	131	268	280	286	309	344	424	463
OECD (as a percentage of donor GNP)										
Italy	.22	.10	.16	.11	.13	.10	.14	.08	.17	.19
New Zealand	..	..	.23	.52	.41	.39	.34	.33	.33	.29
United Kingdom	.56	.47	.41	.39	.39	.45	.46	.51	.35	.43
Finland	..	.02	.06	.18	.17	.16	.16	.21	.23	.28
Australia	.37	.53	.59	.65	.41	.42	.55	.52	.48	.41
Japan	.24	.27	.23	.23	.20	.21	.23	.26	.32	.28
Canada	.19	.19	.41	.54	.46	.50	.52	.46	.43	.43
Austria	..	.11	.07	.21	.12	.22	.27	.19	.23	.48
United States	.53	.58	.32	.27	.26	.25	.27	.20	.27	.20
Netherlands	.31	.36	.61	.75	.83	.86	.82	.93	1.03	1.08
France	1.35	.76	.66	.62	.62	.60	.57	.59	.64	.71
Belgium	.88	.60	.46	.59	.51	.46	.55	.56	.50	.59
Norway	.11	.16	.32	.66	.70	.83	.90	.93	.85	.82
Denmark	.09	.13	.38	.58	.56	.60	.75	.75	.73	.73
Sweden	.05	.19	.38	.82	.82	.99	.90	.94	.79	.83
Germany, Fed. Rep.	.31	.40	.32	.40	.36	.33	.37	.44	.43	.46
Switzerland	.04	.09	.15	.19	.19	.19	.20	.21	.24	.24

	1960	1965	1970	1975	1976	1977	1978	1979	1980[a]	1981[a]
OECD (net bilateral flow to low-income economies, as a percentage of donor GNP)										
Italy	.03	.04	.06	.01	.01	.02	.01	.01	.01	
New Zealand	. .	. .	. . .	.14	.06	.04	.03	.02	.02	
United Kingdom	.22	.23	.15	.11	.14	.11	.15	.16	.11	
Finland	. .	. .	. .	.06	.07	.06	.04	.06	.08	
Australia	. .	.08	.09	.10	.07	.07	.08	.09	.07	
Japan	.12	.13	.11	.08	.08	.06	.07	.11	.11	
Canada	.11	.10	.22	.24	.14	.13	.17	.13	.11	
Austria	. .	.06	.05	.02	.02	.01	.01	.02	.11	
United States	.22	.26	.14	.08	.05	.03	.04	.03	.03	
Netherlands	.19	.08	.24	.24	.26	.33	.34	.30	.35	
France	.01	.12	.09	.10	.10	.07	.08	.08	.09	
Belgium	.27	.56	.30	.31	.26	.24	.23	.28	.26	
Norway	.02	.04	.12	.25	.22	.30	.39	.34	.28	
Denmark	. .	.02	.10	.20	.21	.24	.21	.26	.27	
Sweden	.01	.07	.12	.41	.40	.44	.37	.40	.33	
Germany, Fed. Rep.	.13	.14	.10	.12	.09	.07	.10	.10	.09	
Switzerland	. .	.02	.05	.10	.07	.05	.08	.06	.08	
Total	*.18*	*.20*	*.13*	*.11*	*.09*	*.07*	*.09*	*.09*	*.09*	
OECD (summary)										
ODA (billions of U.S. dollars, nominal prices)	4.6	6.5	7.0	13.8	13.9	15.7	20.0	22.4	27.3	25.5
ODA as percentage of GNP	.51	.49	.34	.36	.33	.33	.35	.35	.38	.35
ODA (billions of U.S. dollars, constant 1978 prices)	13.1	16.7	14.9	17.9	17.4	18.0	20.0	20.4	22.7	21.2
GNP (trillions of U.S. dollars, nominal prices)	.9	1.3	2.0	3.9	4.2	4.7	5.7	6.5	7.2	7.2
ODA deflator[b]	.35	.39	.47	.77	.80	.87	1.00	1.10	1.20	1.20
OPEC (millions of U.S. dollars)										
Nigeria				14	83	65	38	30	42	
Algeria				41	54	47	44	272	83	
Iran				593	753	221	278	25	3	
Iraq				218	232	61	172	847	829	
Venezuela				31	103	52	109	83	130	
Libya				261	94	115	160	105	281	
Saudi Arabia				1,997	2,415	2,410	1,719	2,298	3,040	
Kuwait				976	621	1,517	1,270	1,055	1,188	
United Arab Emirates				1,046	1,059	1,238	717	1,115	1,062	
Qatar				339	195	197	106	277	319	
Total OAPEC[c]				*4,878*	*4,670*	*5,585*	*4,186*	*5,968*	*6,803*	
Total OPEC				*5,516*	*5,609*	*5,923*	*4,611*	*6,106*	*6,978*	
OPEC (as a percentage of donor GNP)										
Nigeria				.04	.19	.13	.07	.04	.05	
Algeria				.28	.37	.29	.22	1.08	.27	
Iran				1.12	1.16	.29	.37	.03	.00	
Iraq				1.65	1.45	.33	.76	2.53	2.12	
Venezuela				.11	.33	.14	.27	.17	.22	
Libya				2.31	.63	.65	.93	.45	.92	
Saudi Arabia				5.62	5.15	4.10	2.64	3.01	2.60	
Kuwait				8.11	4.56	10.02	7.37	4.09	3.88	
United Arab Emirates				11.68	9.21	8.49	5.05	5.87	3.96	
Qatar				15.62	7.95	7.91	3.57	5.89	4.80	
Total OAPEC[c]				*4.99*	*3.89*	*3.88*	*2.64*	*2.90*	*2.83*	
Total OPEC				*2.59*	*2.16*	*1.94*	*1.39*	*1.51*	*1.47*	

a. Preliminary estimates.   b. See the technical notes.   c. Organization of Arab Petroleum Exporting Countries.

Table 20. Population Growth, Actual and Projected

	Average annual growth rate of population (percent)			Projected population (millions)		Hypothetical size of stationary population (millions)[a]	Assumed year of reaching net reproduction rate of 1	Year of reaching stationary population
	1960–70	1970–80	1980–2000	1990	2000			
I. Current IDA recipients	**2.2** w	**2.1** w	**1.8** w	**2,677** t	**3,193** t			
A. *Pure IDA countries*	2.4 w	2.6 w	2.6 w	537 t	694 t			
Lao PDR	1.9	1.8	2.0	4	5	13	2045	2135
Chad	1.8	2.0	2.3	6	7	21	2045	2140
Bangladesh	2.4	2.6	2.3	113	141	321	2035	2125
Ethiopia	2.4	2.0	2.8	41	54	160	2045	2135
Nepal	1.8	2.5	2.1	18	22	54	2045	2135
Somalia	2.4	2.3	2.6	5	7	19	2040	2130
Guinea-Bissau	..	..	2.0	1	1	3	2040	2135
Burma	2.3	2.4	2.2	44	54	109	2030	2090
Afghanistan	2.2	2.5	2.0	19	24	58	2045	2160
Viet Nam	3.1	2.8	2.4	71	88	153	2015	2075
Mali	2.4	2.7	3.0	9	13	41	2040	2135
Burundi	1.6	2.0	2.5	5	7	18	2040	2130
Rwanda	2.6	3.4	3.5	7	10	38	2045	2110
Upper Volta	2.0	1.8	2.6	8	10	29	2040	2140
Zaïre	2.0	2.7	2.9	38	51	156	2040	2110
Gambia	3.2	2.9	2.8	1	1	3	2045	2135
Maldives	2.2	2.9	2.3	(.)	(.)	..	..	..
Haiti	1.5	1.7	2.0	6	7	14	2030	2090
Sierra Leone	2.2	2.6	2.9	5	6	19	2040	2110
Tanzania	2.7	3.4	3.3	26	36	111	2035	2100
Guinea	2.8	2.9	2.8	7	9	28	2040	2130
Central African Rep.	1.9	2.1	2.7	3	4	11	2040	2130
Comoros	3.2	3.6	3.1	..	1	2	2040	2130
Equatorial Guinea	1.2	1.3	2.6	(.)	1	2	2040	2130
Western Samoa	2.5	0.9	2.0	(.)	(.)	..	..	..
Uganda	2.9	2.6	3.3	17	24	73	2035	2100
Benin	2.5	2.6	3.1	5	6	21	2040	2110
Niger	3.3	2.8	3.2	7	10	34	2040	2130
Madagascar	2.1	2.5	3.1	12	16	51	2040	2110
Sudan	2.1	3.0	3.0	25	34	101	2040	2105
Ghana	2.4	3.0	3.4	16	23	70	2035	2105
Lesotho	2.0	2.3	2.8	2	2	6	2035	2105
Yemen, PDR	2.1	2.4	2.5	2	3	8	2040	2130
Yemen Arab Rep.	2.3	2.9	2.2	9	11	26	2040	2130
Mauritania	2.5	2.5	3.1	2	3	10	2045	2135
Solomon Islands	2.8	3.4	..	..	..	..	..	..
Djibouti	6.8	7.9	2.9	1	1	..	..	..
Dominica	4.4	2.8	..	..	..	..	..	..
B. *IDA/IBRD blend countries*	2.1 w	2.0 w	1.6 w	2,138 t	2,498 t			
Malawi	2.8	2.9	3.4	8	12	43	2040	2130
India	2.3	2.1	1.9	833	994	1,694	2020	2115
Sri Lanka	2.4	1.6	1.8	18	21	31	2010	2070
China	1.9	1.8	1.2	1,110	1,245	1,570	2005	2070
Pakistan	2.8	3.1	2.5	107	134	308	2035	2125
Togo	2.7	2.5	3.1	3	5	15	2040	2110
Kenya	3.2	3.4	4.1	24	36	128	2035	2100
Senegal	3.3	2.8	2.9	8	10	34	2045	2135
Liberia	3.1	3.4	3.7	3	4	13	2035	2100
Zambia	2.8	3.1	3.4	8	11	36	2035	2105
Zimbabwe	3.9	3.3	4.3	11	17	64	2035	2100
Guyana	2.4	1.1	2.1	1	1	2	2005	2065
Papua New Guinea	2.1	2.3	2.0	4	5	9	2035	2125

	Average annual growth rate of population (percent)			Projected population (millions)		Hypo-thetical size of station-ary popu-lation (millions)[a]	Assumed year of reaching net reproduc-tion rate of 1	Year of reaching stationary population
	1960–70	1970–80	1980–2000	1990	2000			
II. Former IDA recipients	**2.5** *w*	**2.4** *w*	**2.3** *w*	**742** *t*	**926** *t*			
Indonesia	2.0	2.3	2.0	180	216	376	2020	2110
Honduras	3.1	3.4	3.0	5	7	16	2030	2090
Bolivia	2.3	2.5	2.4	7	9	20	2035	2095
Egypt	2.2	2.1	2.1	50	60	104	2020	2080
El Salvador	2.9	2.9	2.7	6	8	15	2020	2080
Cameroon	1.8	2.2	2.6	11	14	41	2040	2110
Thailand	3.0	2.5	1.9	58	68	100	2005	2070
Swaziland	2.2	2.6	3.3	1	1	4	2040	2110
Philippines	3.0	2.7	2.3	63	77	127	2015	2075
Nicaragua	2.6	3.4	2.9	4	5	11	2030	2090
Congo, People's Rep.	2.4	2.8	3.4	2	3	10	2040	2100
Morocco	2.5	3.0	2.8	27	36	81	2030	2090
Botswana	2.2	2.6	3.6	1	2	6	2040	2105
Nigeria	2.5	2.5	3.4	119	169	528	2035	2105
Mauritius	2.2	1.4	1.7	1	1	2	2010	2075
Ivory Coast	3.7	5.0	2.9	11	15	47	2040	2110
Dominican Rep.	2.7	3.0	2.5	7	9	17	2015	2075
Colombia	3.0	2.3	2.0	33	39	60	2010	2070
Ecuador	3.0	3.0	2.7	11	14	27	2025	2085
Paraguay	2.5	3.2	2.4	4	5	9	2015	2075
Tunisia	1.9	2.1	1.9	8	10	18	2020	2080
Syrian Arab Rep.	3.2	3.6	3.0	12	16	33	2020	2080
Jordan	3.0	3.4	2.9	4	6	13	2025	2085
Turkey	2.5	2.4	2.0	56	67	108	2015	2075
Korea, Rep. of	2.5	1.7	1.6	45	52	70	2005	2065
Costa Rica	3.4	2.5	2.0	3	3	5	2005	2065
Chile	2.1	1.7	1.4	13	15	19	2005	2070

a. For the assumptions used in the projections, see the technical notes.

Table 21. Demography and Fertility

	Crude birth rate per thousand population		Crude death rate per thousand population		Percentage change in:		Total fertility rate 1980
					Crude birth rate 1960–80	Crude death rate 1960–80	
	1960[a]	1980	1960[a]	1980			
I. Current IDA recipients	**43** *w*	**31** *w*	**19** *w*	**12** *w*	**−27.3** *w*	**−36.4** *w*	**4.3** *w*
A. Pure IDA countries	48 *w*	44 *w*	25 *w*	17 *w*	−8.7 *w*	−31.3 *w*	6.1 *w*
Lao PDR	42	42	19	21	−1.0	8.9	6.1
Chad	45	44	29	23	−2.4	−19.6	5.9
Bangladesh	54	45	28	18	−15.3	−35.2	6.0
Ethiopia	51	49	28	24	−2.8	−14.8	6.7
Nepal	44	42	27	20	−3.4	−25.3	6.1
Somalia	47	46	28	20	−1.3	−27.1	6.1
Guinea-Bissau	41	40	32	22	−2.2	−29.4	5.4
Burma	43	37	21	14	−12.8	−35.7	5.3
Afghanistan	50	47	31	26	−6.5	−16.0	6.6
Viet Nam	47	36	21	9	−21.9	−59.4	5.2
Mali	50	50	27	21	−0.8	−20.1	6.7
Burundi	47	46	27	22	−3.0	−16.9	6.4
Rwanda	51	53	27	20	4.1	−26.1	8.3
Upper Volta	49	48	27	24	−1.2	−9.7	6.5
Zaïre	48	46	24	18	−4.6	−26.3	6.1
Gambia	48	47	27	22	−1.5	−16.2	6.4
Maldives	50	44	23	18	−12.0	−21.7	6.1
Haiti	39	36	20	14	−8.5	−29.2	4.8
Sierra Leone	47	46	27	18	−3.0	−31.6	6.1
Tanzania	47	46	22	15	−0.6	−32.6	6.5
Guinea	47	46	30	20	−2.1	−34.0	6.2
Central African Rep.	43	44	28	21	4.2	−25.2	5.9
Comoros	48	47	22	18	−1.7	−16.7	6.3
Equatorial Guinea	43	42	27	19	−1.6	−30.9	5.7
Western Samoa	. .	21	. .	3	. .	. .	3.6
Uganda	45	45	20	14	−0.9	−32.5	6.1
Benin	51	49	27	18	−3.8	−31.7	6.7
Niger	52	52	27	22	−0.6	−19.4	7.1
Madagascar	47	47	27	18	−0.2	−32.7	6.5
Sudan	47	47	25	19	0.9	−23.3	6.7
Ghana	49	48	24	17	−1.0	−31.0	6.7
Lesotho	41	43	23	16	4.9	−31.2	5.8
Yemen, PDR	50	46	29	20	−8.5	−31.3	6.7
Yemen Arab Rep.	50	47	29	23	−6.0	−21.1	6.5
Mauritania	51	50	27	22	−0.8	−20.7	6.9
Solomon Islands	. .	36	.	13	. .	. .	. .
Djibouti	. .	. .	. .	. .	. .	. .	. .
Dominica	44	21	14	5	−50.8	−61.3	. .
B. IDA/IBRD blend countries	42 *w*	28 *w*	17 *w*	11 *w*	−32.4 *w*	−38.6 *w*	3.9 *w*
Malawi	53	56	27	22	5.8	−17.6	7.8
India	44	36	22	14	−18.5	−37.6	4.9
Sri Lanka	36	28	9	7	−22.7	−19.6	3.6
China	40	21	14	8	−47.4	−42.6	2.9
Pakistan	51	44	24	16	−15.0	−34.2	6.1
Togo	51	48	27	18	−5.5	−32.5	6.5
Kenya	52	51	24	13	−0.8	−43.6	7.8
Senegal	48	48	27	21	−0.2	−19.6	6.5
Liberia	50	49	21	14	−2.6	−34.0	6.9
Zambia	51	49	24	17	−3.0	−32.4	6.9
Zimbabwe	55	54	17	13	−2.2	−21.2	8.0
Guyana	46	30	10	6	−34.7	−36.0	3.7
Papua New Guinea	44	37	23	15	−16.4	−34.9	5.2

	Crude birth rate per thousand population		Crude death rate per thousand population		Percentage change in:		Total fertility rate
					Crude birth rate	Crude death rate	
	1960	1980	1960	1980	1960–80	1960–80	1980
II. Former IDA recipients	**46** *w*	**37** *w*	**19** *w*	**12** *w*	**−20.7** *w*	**−40.5** *w*	**4.9** *w*
Indonesia	46	35	23	13	−22.7	−40.9	4.5
Honduras	51	45	19	11	−11.5	−41.0	6.8
Bolivia	46	43	22	16	−7.3	−26.7	6.1
Egypt	44	37	19	12	−15.9	−36.3	4.9
El Salvador	49	41	17	9	−16.6	−47.6	5.7
Cameroon	43	42	27	19	−1.4	−31.4	5.7
Thailand	44	30	15	8	−31.2	−47.0	4.0
Swaziland	49	51	27	18	4.1	−32.6	6.9
Philippines	46	34	15	7	−25.1	−50.0	4.6
Nicaragua	51	45	19	12	−11.2	−38.6	6.3
Congo, People's Rep.	40	42	18	10	5.5	−42.9	6.0
Morocco	52	44	23	13	−15.3	−45.7	6.5
Botswana	50	50	25	16	1.0	−33.7	6.5
Nigeria	52	50	25	17	−4.4	−32.8	6.9
Mauritius	41	27	9	7	−35.1	−18.0	3.0
Ivory Coast	50	47	26	18	−7.3	−33.2	6.7
Dominican Rep.	50	36	16	9	−28.2	−46.6	4.8
Colombia	46	30	14	8	−34.4	−41.9	3.8
Ecuador	47	40	17	10	−13.9	−41.0	6.0
Paraguay	43	36	13	7	−17.2	−42.5	4.9
Tunisia	49	35	21	9	−28.6	−56.2	5.4
Syrian Arab Rep.	47	45	18	8	−5.1	−53.1	7.0
Jordan	47	44	20	10	−6.3	−51.3	6.9
Turkey	43	32	16	10	−24.5	−38.5	4.4
Korea, Rep. of	43	24	13	7	−44.0	−47.0	3.0
Costa Rica	47	29	10	5	−37.6	−42.5	3.4
Chile	37	22	12	7	−40.7	−42.7	2.8

a. Figures in italic are for 1957, not 1960.

Table 22. Labor Force Structure

	Percentage of population of working age (15–64 years)		Percentage of labor force in:						Average annual growth rate of labor force (percent)		
			Agriculture		Industry		Services				
	1960	1980	1960	1980[a]	1960	1980[a]	1960	1980[a]	1960–70	1970–80	1980–2000
I. Current IDA recipients	**54** *w*	**59** *w*	**76** *w*	**71** *w*	**10** *w*	**14** *w*	**14** *w*	**15** *w*	**1.6** *w*	**2.2** *w*	**1.9** *w*
A. Pure IDA countries	54 *w*	53 *w*	86 *w*	75 *w*	5 *w*	10 *w*	9 *w*	15 *w*	1.8 *w*	2.2 *w*	2.7 *w*
Lao PDR	56	51	83	75	4	6	13	19	1.4	0.3	2.0
Chad	57	54	95	85	2	7	3	8	1.5	2.0	2.3
Bangladesh	53	55	87	74	3	11	10	15	2.1	2.4	2.7
Ethiopia	54	52	88	80	5	7	7	13	2.0	1.8	2.2
Nepal	57	55	95	93	2	2	3	5	1.5	2.0	2.1
Somalia	54	54	88	82	4	8	8	10	1.7	2.3	2.4
Guinea-Bissau	59	56	91	83	4	6	5	11	. .	. .	. .
Burma	59	55	. .	67	. .	10	. .	23	1.1	1.5	2.0
Afghanistan	55	52	85	79	6	8	9	13	2.0	1.8	2.5
Viet Nam	. .	54	. .	71	. .	10	14	19	. .	1.9	2.6
Mali	54	52	94	73	3	12	3	15	2.0	2.2	2.5
Burundi	55	53	90	84	3	5	7	11	1.2	1.6	2.3
Rwanda	53	51	95	91	1	2	4	7	2.4	2.5	2.8
Upper Volta	54	53	92	82	5	13	3	5	1.2	1.4	2.3
Zaïre	53	53	83	75	9	13	8	12	1.4	2.1	2.4
Gambia	54	53	85	79	7	9	8	12	2.6	2.4	2.6
Maldives	. .	53	. .	55	. .	26	. .	19	. .	. .	. .
Haiti	55	53	80	74	6	7	14	19	0.7	1.4	2.4
Sierra Leone	55	53	78	65	12	19	10	16	1.5	1.8	2.3
Tanzania	54	51	89	83	4	6	7	11	2.1	2.3	2.7
Guinea	55	53	88	82	6	11	6	7	2.5	2.2	2.1
Central African Rep.	58	55	94	88	2	4	4	8	1.7	1.6	2.3
Comoros	52	54	70	64	19	23	11	13	2.5	3.4	3.1
Equatorial Guinea	57	55	84	76	6	8	10	16	0.8	0.9	2.6
Western Samoa	49	50	. .	62	. .	8	. .	30	3.0	. .	. .
Uganda	54	52	89	83	4	6	7	11	3.3	2.5	2.5
Benin	53	51	54	46	9	16	37	38	2.1	2.2	2.1
Niger	53	51	95	91	1	3	4	6	3.0	2.6	2.9
Madagascar	55	53	93	90	2	3	5	7	1.7	2.0	2.3
Sudan	53	53	86	72	6	10	8	18	2.2	2.3	2.7
Ghana	53	51	64	53	14	20	22	27	1.6	2.4	2.9
Lesotho	57	55	93	87	2	4	5	9	1.6	1.9	2.1
Yemen, PDR	52	51	70	45	15	15	15	40	1.4	1.3	2.8
Yemen Arab Rep.	54	52	83	75	7	11	10	14	1.1	1.4	2.3
Mauritania	53	52	91	85	3	5	6	10	2.2	2.3	2.7
Solomon Islands	. .	49	. .	. .	. .	. .	. .	. .	. .	. .	. .
Djibouti	. .	. .	. .	. .	. .	. .	. .	. .	. .	. .	. .
Dominica	. .	. .	. .	. .	. .	. .	. .	. .	0.6	. .	. .
B. IDA/IBRD blend countries	54 *w*	60 *w*	73 *w*	70 *w*	11 *w*	15 *w*	16 *w*	15 *w*	1.6 *w*	2.1 *w*	1.8 *w*
Malawi	52	49	92	86	3	5	5	9	2.3	2.4	2.8
India	55	57	74	69	11	13	15	18	1.5	1.7	2.0
Sri Lanka	54	60	56	54	14	14	30	32	2.1	2.1	2.1
China	. .	64	. .	71	. .	17	. .	12	. .	1.9	1.4
Pakistan	52	51	61	57	18	20	21	23	1.9	2.5	2.9
Togo	53	51	80	67	8	15	12	18	2.2	2.1	2.6
Kenya	50	48	86	78	5	10	9	12	2.7	2.8	3.3
Senegal	54	53	84	76	5	10	11	14	1.9	1.9	2.2
Liberia	52	50	80	70	10	14	10	16	2.4	2.6	2.9
Zambia	53	50	79	67	7	11	14	22	2.3	2.4	2.8
Zimbabwe	52	50	69	60	11	15	20	25	3.2	2.6	3.0
Guyana	50	56	37	34	29	45	34	21	1.7	2.3	3.1
Papua New Guinea	57	55	89	82	4	8	7	10	1.6	1.9	2.0

126

	Percentage of population of working age (15–64 years)		Percentage of labor force in:						Average annual growth rate of labor force (percent)		
			Agriculture		Industry		Services				
	1960	1980	1960	1980	1960	1980	1960	1980	1960–70	1970–80	1980–2000
II. Former IDA recipients	**54** *w*	**55** *w*	**69** *w*	**52** *w*	**11** *w*	**17** *w*	**20** *w*	**31** *w*	**1.9** *w*	**2.4** *w*	**2.6** *w*
Indonesia	56	57	75	58	8	12	17	30	1.7	2.1	1.8
Honduras	52	50	70	63	11	15	19	22	2.5	3.0	3.3
Bolivia	55	53	61	50	18	24	21	26	1.7	2.4	2.9
Egypt	55	57	58	50	12	30	30	20	1.9	2.2	2.3
El Salvador	52	51	62	50	17	22	21	27	2.6	2.8	3.3
Cameroon	57	54	87	83	5	7	8	10	1.3	1.3	1.7
Thailand	53	55	84	76	4	9	12	15	2.0	2.9	2.3
Swaziland	54	52	89	74	4	9	7	17	1.7	2.0	3.1
Philippines	52	53	61	46	15	17	24	37	2.2	2.4	2.7
Nicaragua	50	50	62	39	16	14	22	47	2.6	3.3	3.6
Congo, People's Rep.	56	53	52	34	17	26	31	40	1.5	2.0	2.7
Morocco	53	51	62	52	14	21	24	27	1.6	2.9	3.3
Botswana	51	48	92	78	3	8	5	14	1.4	1.8	3.7
Nigeria	52	50	71	54	10	19	19	27	1.8	2.0	2.9
Mauritius	51	61	40	29	26	24	34	47	2.5	2.6	2.3
Ivory Coast	54	53	89	79	2	4	9	17	3.6	4.5	2.4
Dominican Rep.	49	52	67	49	12	18	21	33	2.3	3.4	3.3
Colombia	50	60	51	26	19	21	30	53	3.0	3.2	2.6
Ecuador	52	52	58	52	19	17	23	31	3.0	3.2	3.2
Paraguay	51	52	56	49	19	19	25	32	2.4	3.1	3.4
Tunisia	53	55	56	34	18	33	26	33	0.7	2.9	2.6
Syrian Arab Rep.	52	48	54	33	19	31	27	36	2.1	2.9	3.5
Jordan	52	51	44	20	26	20	30	60	2.8	2.9	3.2
Turkey	55	56	78	54	11	13	11	33	1.4	2.2	2.1
Korea, Rep. of	54	62	66	34	9	29	25	37	3.0	2.8	2.0
Costa Rica	50	58	51	29	19	23	30	48	3.5	3.6	2.7
Chile	57	62	30	19	20	19	50	62	1.4	2.6	2.1

a. Figures in italic are for 1979, not 1980.

Table 23. Life Expectancy and Mortality

	Life expectancy at birth (years)		Infant mortality rate (aged 0–1)		Child death rate (aged 1–4)	
	1960	1980	1960	1980	1960	1980
I. Current IDA recipients	**42** *w*	**57** *w*	**164** *w*	**93**	**28** *w*	**13** *w*
A. *Pure IDA countries*	*39 w*	*48 w*	*168 w*	*124 w*	*33 w*	*22 w*
Lao PDR	44	43	155	129	24	19
Chad	35	41	195	149	46	32
Bangladesh	37	46	159	136	25	20
Ethiopia	36	40	175	146	40	32
Nepal	38	44	195	150	33	23
Somalia	36	44	175	146	40	32
Guinea-Bissau	32	42	188	149	44	32
Burma	44	54	158	101	25	13
Afghanistan	33	37	233	205	41	35
Viet Nam	43	63	157	62	25	6
Mali	37	43	195	154	46	34
Burundi	37	42	150	122	33	25
Rwanda	37	45	147	137	32	29
Upper Volta	36	39	252	211	63	51
Zaïre	40	47	150	112	33	22
Gambia	37	42	222	198	54	47
Maldives	. .	47	. .	119	. .	21
Haiti	44	53	182	115	47	18
Sierra Leone	37	47	234	208	57	50
Tanzania	42	52	152	103	33	19
Guinea	35	45	208	165	50	37
Central African Rep.	36	44	195	149	46	32
Comoros	43	47	135	93	29	17
Equatorial Guinea	37	47	188	143	44	31
Western Samoa	. .	68	19	18	5	2
Uganda	44	54	139	97	29	18
Benin	37	47	206	154	49	34
Niger	37	43	191	146	45	31
Madagascar	37	47	109	71	21	11
Sudan	40	46	168	124	40	22
Ghana	40	49	143	103	31	19
Lesotho	42	51	144	115	31	23
Yemen, PDR	36	45	209	146	59	31
Yemen Arab Rep.	36	42	212	190	60	50
Mauritania	37	43	185	143	43	31
Solomon Islands	. .	. .	. .	. .	. .	. .
Djibouti	. .	45	69	30	23	10
Dominica	58	. .	107	20	19	. .
B. *IDA/IBRD blend countries*	*44 w*	*58 w*	*162 w*	*86 w*	*26 w*	*10 w*
Malawi	37	44	207	172	49	39
India	43	52	165	123	26	17
Sri Lanka	62	66	71	44	7	3
China	. .	64	. .	56	. .	5
Pakistan	43	50	162	126	25	18
Togo	37	47	182	109	42	21
Kenya	41	55	138	87	29	15
Senegal	37	43	182	147	42	32
Liberia	44	54	194	154	46	34
Zambia	40	49	151	106	33	20
Zimbabwe	49	55	118	74	23	12
Guyana	61	70	68	44	6	2
Papua New Guinea	41	51	165	105	26	14

	Life expectancy at birth (years)		Infant mortality rate (aged 0–1)		Child death rate (aged 1–4)	
	1960	*1980*	*1960*	*1980*	*1960*	*1980*
II. Former IDA recipients	**46** *w*	**57** *w*	**140** *w*	**89** *w*	**27** *w*	**13** *w*
Indonesia	41	53	150	93	23	11
Honduras	46	58	145	88	30	10
Bolivia	43	50	167	131	40	25
Egypt	46	57	128	103	34	14
El Salvador	51	63	136	78	26	7
Cameroon	37	47	162	109	36	21
Thailand	52	63	103	55	13	4
Swaziland	37	47	152	135	33	28
Philippines	53	64	106	55	14	4
Nicaragua	47	56	144	91	30	10
Congo, People's Rep.	48	59	171	129	39	27
Morocco	47	56	161	107	37	15
Botswana	40	50	115	83	23	14
Nigeria	39	49	183	135	42	28
Mauritius	59	65	71	35	11	3
Ivory Coast	37	47	173	127	39	26
Dominican Rep.	51	61	119	68	20	6
Colombia	53	63	93	56	11	4
Ecuador	51	61	140	82	28	8
Paraguay	56	65	86	47	9	3
Tunisia	48	60	159	90	36	10
Syrian Arab Rep.	50	65	132	62	25	5
Jordan	47	61	136	69	26	6
Turkey	51	62	190	123	50	21
Korea, Rep. of	54	65	78	34	9	2
Costa Rica	62	70	71	24	6	1
Chile	57	67	114	43	18	2

Table 24. Health and Nutrition

	Population per physician[a]		Population per nurse[a]		Percentage of population with access to safe water[a]	Daily per capita calorie supply, 1977	
	1960	1977	1960	1977	1975	Total	As a percentage of requirement
I. Current IDA recipients	**9,310** *w*	**5,810** *w*	**6,600** *w*	**4,700** *w*	**31** *w*	**2,282** *w*	**97** *w*
A. Pure IDA countries	*46,930 w*	*19,920 w*	*8,170 w*	*12,610 w*	*29 w*	*2,359 w*	*93 w*
Lao PDR	53,520	20,600	4,950	3,040	. .	2,082	94
Chad	72,190	41,940	5,780	3,820	26	1,762	72
Bangladesh	. .	12,690	. .	40,490	53	. .	. .
Ethiopia	100,470	74,910	14,920	5,320	6	1,754	78
Nepal	73,800	35,900	. .	13,510	9	2,002	89
Somalia	36,570	18,480	4,810	. .	33	2,033	88
Guinea-Bissau	. .	10,100	. .	2,300	11	. .	. .
Burma	15,560	5,260	8,550	4,400	17	2,286	103
Afghanistan	28,700	20,550	19,590	25,920	6	2,695	107
Viet Nam	. .	5,620	. .	2,470	. .	1,801	96
Mali	67,050	25,560	4,920	2,380	9	2,117	83
Burundi	96,570	45,020	4,530	6,180	. .	2,254	99
Rwanda	143,290	38,790	11,620	10,460	35	2,264	94
Upper Volta	81,650	50,000	4,090	3,650	25	1,875	93
Zaïre	37,620	15,530	3,510	1,620	16	2,271	102
Gambia	21,800	13,170	1,410	2,080	. .	2,217	93
Maldives	. .	15,670	. .	5,220	15	1,715	78
Haiti	9,230	5,940	4,020	2,940	14	2,100	92
Sierra Leone	20,420	. .	2,960	. .	. .	2,150	85
Tanzania	18,220	17,550	11,890	2,390	39	2,063	87
Guinea	26,900	16,630	3,260	2,490	10	1,943	78
Central African Rep.	49,610	20,280	3,280	1,540	16	2,242	92
Comoros	18,640	. .	3,110	. .	. .	1,900	81
Equatorial Guinea	5,810	58,000	610	840	. .	. .	. .
Western Samoa	2,270	2,940	450	630	43	2,206	83
Uganda	15,050	26,810	10,030	4,180	35	2,110	93
Benin	23,030	26,570	2,690	2,360	21	2,249	100
Niger	82,170	42,720	8,460	2,380	27	2,139	91
Madagascar	8,900	10,240	3,110	2,300	25	2,486	111
Sudan	33,420	8,780	3,030	850	46	2,184	96
Ghana	21,600	9,920	5,430	610	35	1,983	85
Lesotho	23,490	18,640	. .	14,900	17	2,245	95
Yemen, PDR	13,290	5,970	. .	1,330	24	1,945	81
Yemen Arab Rep.	130,010	11,670	. .	4,580	4	2,192	82
Mauritania	37,040	13,700	4,990	1,980	. .	1,976	94
Solomon Islands	. .	6,470	. .	740	31	2,058	77
Djibouti	. .	4,300	. .	510	. .	. .	. .
Dominica	7,370	4,560	. .	1,360	. .	. .	85
B. IDA/IBRD blend countries	*4,080 w*	*2,600 w*	*6,410 w*	*2,920 w*	*32 w*	*2,268 w*	*97 w*
Malawi	35,250	41,010	12,920	3,830	33	2,066	97
India	4,850	3,630	10,980	5,700	33	2,021	89
Sri Lanka	4,490	6,700	4,170	2,040	20	2,126	97
China	3,010	1,100	2,850	480	. .	2,441	103
Pakistan	5,400	3,780	16,960	10,030	29	2,281	99
Togo	35,760	18,160	5,340	1,740	16	2,069	92
Kenya	10,690	11,630	2,270	1,090	17	2,032	96
Senegal	21,970	15,710	2,840	1,390	37	2,261	95
Liberia	12,600	9,280	1,410	1,810	20	2,404	101
Zambia	9,540	10,410	9,920	1,970	42	2,002	90
Zimbabwe	4,790	7,030	1,010	1,170	. .	2,576	109
Guyana	3,860	7,350	1,730	660	81	2,655	117
Papua New Guinea	14,390	14,040	2,450	1,590	20	2,268	87

130

	Population per physician[a]		Population per nurse[a]		Percentage of population with access to safe water[a]	Daily per capita calorie supply, 1977	
	1960	1977	1960	1977	1975	Total	As a percentage of requirement
II. Former IDA recipients	**28,710** *w*	**8,340** *w*	**4,200** *w*	**3,590** *w*	**42** *w*	**2,333** *w*	**102** *w*
Indonesia	46,780	*13,670*	*4,520*	8,870	12	2,272	102
Honduras	12,610	*3,290*	. .	870	46	2,015	93
Bolivia	3,830	*1,850*	. .	3,070	34	1,974	87
Egypt	2,560	1,050	*1,930*	1,100	66	2,760	118
El Salvador	5,260	3,600	. .	950	53	2,051	94
Cameroon	*48,110*	16,500	3,280	1,150	26	2,069	106
Thailand	7,950	*8,220*	*4,860*	1,170	22	1,929	97
Swaziland	10,150	*9,190*	3,680	940	37	2,297	99
Philippines	. .	2,810	. .	3,170	43	2,189	107
Nicaragua	2,690	*1,590*	1,250	800	70	2,446	116
Congo, People's Rep.	16,100	*7,470*	1,300	600	17	2,284	99
Morocco	9,410	*11,040*	. .	1,830	. .	2,534	107
Botswana	25,350	*9,970*	5,410	1,320	45	2,105	91
Nigeria	73,710	15,740	4,040	2,880	. .	1,951	83
Mauritius	4,680	2,420	*2,100*	520	60	2,647	117
Ivory Coast	*29,190*	21,040	2,920	*1,590*	19	2,517	107
Dominican Rep.	8,220	. .	. .	. .	55	2,094	102
Colombia	2,640	1,970	4,220	1,250	64	2,364	98
Ecuador	2,670	1,570	2,360	. .	42	2,104	90
Paraguay	1,810	*2,190*	. .	2,290	13	2,824	119
Tunisia	10,030	*3,580*	. .	1,070	70	2,674	115
Syrian Arab Rep.	4,630	2,570	6,600	3,900	75	2,684	104
Jordan	5,800	*1,960*	*1,930*	820	61	2,107	62
Turkey	3,000	1,760	. .	920	75	2,907	116
Korea, Rep. of	3,540	1,980	3,250	490	71	2,785	117
Costa Rica	2,700	1,390	710	450	77	2,550	113
Chile	1,780	*1,930*	640	420	84	2,656	110

a. Figures in italic are for years other than those specified. See the technical notes.

Table 25. Education

| | Number enrolled in primary school as a percentage of age group | | | | | | Number enrolled in secondary school as a percentage of age group | | Number enrolled in higher education as a percentage of population aged 20–24 | | Adult literacy rate (percent) | |
| | Total | | Male | | Female | | | | | | | |
	1960	1979	1960	1979	1960	1979	1960	1979	1960	1978	1960	1977
I. Current IDA recipients	**76** w	**94** w	**68** w	**98** w	**34** w	**84** w	**14** w	**49** w	**2** w	**3** w	**26** w	**50** w
A. Pure IDA countries	*35* w	*71* w	*47* w	*81* w	*22* w	*58* w	*4* w	*21* w	*1* w	*2* w	*22* w	*41* w
Lao PDR	25	93	34	101	16	85	1	16	(.)	. .	28	41
Chad	17	35	29	51	4	19	(.)	3	. .	(.)	6	15
Bangladesh	47	65	66	79	26	49	8	25	1	2	22	26
Ethiopia	7	36	11	48	3	24	(.)	9	(.)	(.)	. .	15
Nepal	10	88	19	124	1	49	6	19	1	3	9	19
Somalia	9	50	13	64	5	36	1	7	(.)	1	2	60
Guinea-Bissau	25	96	35	133	15	60	3	8	. .	. .	5	28
Burma	56	84	61	87	52	81	10	20	1	4	60	70
Afghanistan	9	22	15	36	2	7	1	7	(.)	1	8	12
Viet Nam	. .	120	. .	124	. .	115	. .	56	. .	3	. .	87
Mali	10	28	14	36	6	20	1	9	. .	1	3	9
Burundi	18	23	27	28	9	18	1	2	(.)	1	14	23
Rwanda	49	70	68	74	30	67	2	2	. .	(.)	16	50
Upper Volta	8	21	12	26	5	15	(.)	3	. .	(.)	2	5
Zaïre	60	90	88	103	32	77	3	19	(.)	1	31	58
Gambia	12	42	17	56	8	28	3	12	. .	. .	6	15
Maldives	. .	36	. .	. .	. .	. .	. .	19	. .	. .	. .	82
Haiti	46	62	50	. .	42	. .	4	15	(.)	1	15	23
Sierra Leone	23	37	30	45	15	30	2	12	(.)	1	7	. .
Tanzania	25	104	33	113	18	94	2	4	. .	(.)	10	66
Guinea	30	34	44	45	16	24	2	15	. .	5	7	20
Central African Rep.	32	77	53	100	12	54	1	10	. .	1	7	39
Comoros	14	99	23	115	4	83	1	21	. .	. .	. .	. .
Equatorial Guinea	85	81	103	89	67	72	2	11	. .	. .	. .	. .
Western Samoa	121	. .	115	. .	127	. .	10	. .	. .	. .	. .	. .
Uganda	49	50	65	58	32	42	3	5	(.)	1	35	48
Benin	27	60	38	78	15	42	2	12	. .	1	5	25
Niger	5	23	7	29	3	17	(.)	4	. .	(.)	1	5
Madagascar	52	100	58	100	45	87	4	12	(.)	3	. .	50
Sudan	25	51	35	60	14	43	3	16	(.)	2	13	20
Ghana	38	71	52	80	25	62	5	36	(.)	. .	27	. .
Lesotho	83	104	63	84	102	123	3	17	(.)	2	. .	52
Yemen, PDR	13	70	20	99	5	42	5	31	. .	2	. .	40
Yemen Arab Rep.	8	34	14	59	(.)	9	(.)	4	. .	2	3	21
Mauritania	8	28	13	36	3	20	(.)	6	. .	(.)	5	17
Solomon Islands	. .	73	. .	87	. .	59	. .	15	. .	. .	. .	. .
Djibouti	. .	. .	. .	. .	. .	. .	. .	. .	. .	. .	. .	14
Dominica	121	. .	117	. .	125	. .	14	. .	. .	. .	. .	. .
B. IDA/IBRD blend countries	*83* w	*99* w	*77* w	*102* w	*38* w	*90* w	*18* w	*55* w	*3* w	*4* w	*28* w	*52* w
Malawi	. .	59	. .	70	. .	48	1	4	. .	(.)	. .	25
India	61	78	80	92	40	63	20	27	3	8	28	36
Sri Lanka	95	98	100	. .	90	. .	27	53	1	1	75	85
China	102	118	. .	111	. .	114	. .	79	. .	1	. .	66
Pakistan	30	56	46	81	13	31	11	16	1	2	15	24
Togo	44	110	63	136	24	85	2	32	. .	2	10	18
Kenya	47	99	64	105	30	94	2	18	(.)	1	20	50
Senegal	27	42	36	51	17	34	3	10	1	2	6	10
Liberia	31	67	45	83	18	51	2	22	(.)	. .	9	25
Zambia	42	95	51	101	34	89	2	17	. .	2	29	44
Zimbabwe	96	104	107	110	86	96	6	15	(.)	. .	39	74
Guyana	107	99	107	100	106	98	33	59	. .	3	. .	. .
Papua New Guinea	32	64	59	73	7	55	1	12	. .	. .	29	32

132

| | Number enrolled in primary school as a percentage of age group | | | | | | Number enrolled in secondary school as a percentage of age group | | Number enrolled in higher education as a percentage of population aged 20–24 | | Adult literacy rate (percent) | |
| | Total | | Male | | Female | | | | | | | |
	1960	1979	1960	1979	1960	1979	1960	1979	1960	1978	1960	1977
II. Former IDA recipients	**71** *w*	**93** *w*	**81** *w*	**102** *w*	**61** *w*	**89** *w*	**12** *w*	**34** *w*	**3** *w*	**8** *w*	**43** *w*	**60** *w*
Indonesia	71	*94*	86	*100*	58	89	6	*22*	1	*3*	39	62
Honduras	67	89	68	92	67	85	8	*21*	1	8	45	60
Bolivia	64	*82*	78	*87*	50	*76*	12	*35*	4	*13*	39	63
Egypt	66	75	80	88	52	61	16	48	5	15	26	44
El Salvador	80	82	82	83	77	81	13	26	1	8	49	62
Cameroon	65	*103*	87	*113*	43	*93*	2	17	. .	1	19	. .
Thailand	83	*82*	88	*85*	79	*78*	13	29	2	7	68	84
Swaziland	*58*	103	*58*	104	*58*	102	5	33	. .	*2*	. .	65
Philippines	95	98	98	. .	93	. .	26	63	13	27	72	75
Nicaragua	66	*85*	65	*83*	66	*88*	7	27	1	. .	. .	90
Congo, People's Rep.	78	156	103	163	53	148	4	69	1	*4*	16	. .
Morocco	47	75	67	93	27	56	5	22	1	*4*	14	28
Botswana	42	93	35	84	48	103	1	20	. .	1	20	35
Nigeria	36	79	46	. .	27	. .	4	10	(.)	1	15	30
Mauritius	98	99	103	99	93	99	24	52	. .	1	61	85
Ivory Coast	46	*74*	68	*91*	24	*58*	2	15	(.)	2	5	*41*
Dominican Rep.	98	*96*	99	*95*	98	*96*	7	28	1	. .	65	67
Colombia	77	128	77	127	77	129	12	46	2	10	63	. .
Ecuador	83	107	87	109	79	105	12	49	3	35	68	*81*
Paraguay	98	102	105	106	90	98	11	25	2	8	75	84
Tunisia	66	102	88	119	43	85	12	25	1	5	16	62
Syrian Arab Rep.	65	96	89	107	39	84	16	47	4	18	30	58
Jordan	77	102	94	106	59	99	25	74	1	. .	32	70
Turkey	75	*105*	90	*115*	58	*96*	14	34	3	8	38	60
Korea, Rep. of	94	111	99	112	89	111	27	76	5	12	71	93
Costa Rica	96	*107*	97	*108*	95	*106*	21	48	5	24	. .	90
Chile	109	119	111	120	107	118	24	55	4	12	84	. .

Note: Figures in italic are for years other than those specified. See the technical notes.

Technical Notes

This statistical annex provides economic data for periods of years and social data for selected years in a form suitable for comparing economies and groups of economies. Although the statistics and measures have been carefully selected to provide a comprehensive picture of development, readers are urged to exercise care in interpreting them. This is particularly true of comparing indicators across economies, because statistical methods, coverage, practices, and definitions differ widely. The statistical systems in many developing economies still are weak, and this affects the availability and reliability of data.

All growth rates shown are in real terms and, unless otherwise noted, have been computed by using the least-squares method. The least-squares growth rate, r, is calculated by regressing the annual values of the variable in the relevant period using the logarithmic form: $\log X_t = a + bt + e_t$ where X_t is the variable, t is time, e_t is the error term, and b is the slope coefficient. Then r is equal to (antilog b) $-$ 1, the least-squares estimate of the growth rate.

In each table, countries are listed in their group in ascending order of income per capita. Figures in colored bands are summary measures for groups of countries. The letter w after a summary measure indicates that it is a weighted average; the letter m, that it is a median value; the letter t, that it is a total. Figures in italic are for years or periods other than those specified. The Bank's fiscal year commences July 1 and ends June 30.

Other symbols used in the tables are:

.. Not available.
(.) Less than half the unit shown.
— Not applicable.

Table 1. IDA Voting Rights of Member Countries

IDA's Articles of Agreement provide for two categories of membership, Part I and Part II, largely reflecting levels of per capita income. Initial subscriptions were divided into a 10 percent component to be paid by all members in gold or convertible currency and a 90 percent component. For Part I countries, the 90 percent component was also payable in gold or convertible currency. Part II countries, however, were legally obligated to make only the 10 percent component available on a freely convertible basis. As of June 30, 1982, Part II members include the countries listed in Annex Table 4, plus the following countries: Algeria, Argentina, Belize, Bhutan, Brazil, Cape Verde, Cyprus, Fiji, Gabon, Greece, Grenada, Guatemala, Iran, Iraq, Israel, Kampuchea, Lebanon, Libya, Malaysia, Mexico, Oman, Panama, Peru, St. Lucia, São Tomé and Principe, Saudi Arabia, Spain, Trinidad and Tobago, Vanuatu, and Yugoslavia.

Iceland and Ireland, which were originally Part II members, became Part I members in 1971 and 1974, respectively. Memberships for Kuwait, New Zealand, and the United Arab Emirates were not provided for under the Articles of Agreement. They were later admitted as Part I members. The list of Part II donors includes Part II members contributing to the sixth replenishment.

It is assumed in Column (A), listing the voting rights under initial subscriptions, that all countries whose membership was provided for under the Articles of Agreement had become members. The votes include both membership and subscription votes. Initially there were 500 membership votes for each country. Currently, a country that has contributed to all replenishments has 9,900 membership votes.

Column (B) indicates the actual voting power for members as of June 30, 1982. The voting power of countries not shown separately on this table is published in the *World Bank Annual Report 1982*. In Column (C) the assumption is made that all members make all the subscriptions authorized for them in connection with the sixth and past IDA replenishments. Actual current numbers of votes of members as shown in Column (B) are lower than those in Column (C) because (1) one-third of the subscription votes to be accorded to each member on account of the sixth replenishment voting-rights adjustments will only become available November 8, 1982, and (2) some members have not participated in all replenishments or have not made all payments required under the sixth replenishment to get the full number of currently available votes.

Table 2. IDA Procurement by Supplying Country

There are three categories of procurement: (1) foreign, which applies to supplying members other than the borrowing countries; (2) local, which applies to supplying countries that are also borrowing countries; and (3) undetermined, which refers to supplying countries whose percentage of procurement cannot be determined. The amounts shown exclude exchange adjustments resulting from the devaluation of the U.S. dollar in May 1972 and February 1973. Disbursements made under the sixth replenishment are not included.

Table 3. Contributions to IDA by Country and by Replenishment

From the initial subscription through the third replenishment, contributions are expressed in 1960 U.S. dollars. Belgium and Luxembourg joined IDA in 1964; it was then agreed that their contributions would be divided equally between an initial subscription and a contribution to the first replenishment. The special contributions made by Sweden to the second replenishment include supplementary contributions spread over the period 1962–69.

Contributions to the fourth replenishment are expressed in U.S. dollar equivalents as of September 27, 1973. The intended loan from Switzerland was rejected in a referendum in June 1976.

The amounts shown for the fifth replenishment reflect the value of the U.S. dollar as of March 14, 1977. They include Saudi Arabia's contribution, which was increased from $250 million to $350 million in April 1978. They also include the "extra" contributions made by Japan and Kuwait amounting, respectively, to $144 million (1.8 percent of the total) and $136.1 million (1.77 percent of the total).

Contributions to the sixth replenishment are expressed in U.S. dollar equivalents, as of October 5, 1979, except for Colombia whose contribution is expressed in U.S. dollars as of September 1, 1980, following an agreement reached after the completion of the IDA-6 negotiations. The "extra" contributions of Japan and Germany and the "additional" contributions of Luxembourg and Saudi Arabia to the sixth replenishment are as follows: Japan, $317.54 million (2.65 percent of the total); Germany, $60 million (0.5 percent of the total); Luxembourg, $0.5 million (0.004 percent of the total); and Saudi Arabia, $30 million (0.25 percent of the total).

The cumulative column combines the 1960 dollar amounts for initial subscription through the third replenishment with the amounts for the fourth, fifth, and sixth replenishments expressed in dollars as of the date when the agreement was concluded.

Table 4. IDA Flows and GNP per Capita, Population, Investments, and Total External Assistance

The *GNP per capita* figures were calculated according to the *World Bank Atlas* method, using data for GNP as described in the technical notes to Table 10. The first step of this method is to convert the GNP series in constant market prices and national currency units to one measured in constant average 1978–80 prices. This is done by multiplying the original constant price series by the weighted-average domestic GNP deflator for the base period (that is, by the ratio of total GNP in current prices to total GNP in constant prices for the 1978–80 period). The second step is to convert the series measured in constant average 1978–80 prices in national currency to one in U.S. dollars by dividing that series by the weighted-average exchange rate for the base period. The weighted-average exchange rate is the ratio of the sum of GNP in current prices to the sum of the GNP divided by the annual average exchange rate in national currency per U.S. dollar for 1978, 1979, and 1980. The third step is to convert the series measured in constant average 1978–80 U.S. dollars to one measured in current U.S. dollars by multiplying that series by the implicit U.S. GNP deflator for 1978–80. The GNP per capita figures were obtained by dividing GNP at market prices in U.S. dollars by the population in mid-1980. The use of the three-year base period is intended to smooth the impact of fluctuations in prices and exchange rates. The estimates of population for mid-1970 and 1980 are primarily from the UN Population Division. In many cases the data for 1980 take into account the results of recent population censuses.

The *annual commitments per capita* were obtained by averaging the commitments for each three-year period and dividing the fiscal year 1969–71 average by the mid-1970 population and the fiscal year 1979–81 average by the mid-1980 population.

The *disbursements per capita* were calculated by dividing the disbursements for fiscal 1980 by the 1980 population.

IDA as a share of ODA represents net disbursements of IDA divided by the net disbursements of official development assistance (ODA) to the IDA recipients. See technical notes for Table 19. ODA for 1980 includes concessional flows from the Organization of Petroleum Exporting Countries (OPEC).

IDA as a share of investment was calculated by dividing the gross disbursements of IDA by the gross domestic investment of IDA recipients. See technical notes for Tables 13 and 14.

The four indicators cited above are all based on current prices. The average GNP per capita, annual commitments per capita, and disbursements per capita are weighted by population.

Tables 5 and 6. IDA Commitments and Disbursements by Country

The commitments are shown according to the fiscal year in which they were approved, and disbursements according to the fiscal year in which they were made. Until 1980 IDA commitments were expressed in U.S. dollar equivalents. Thereafter, Special Drawing Rights (SDRs) were used, and the dollar exchange rate for the SDRs at the time of negotiations determined the dollar equivalents of the commitments. In the case of disbursements, suppliers are normally paid in their own country's currency. However, if the suppliers import the goods required for the project, they are paid for in the currency of the country of the goods' origin.

Tables 7 and 8. IDA Commitments by Sector and Country; IDA Commitments and Disbursements by Sector

The major sectors for which IDA lends and disburses include the following categories of lending. *Agriculture* includes agricultural credit, agroindustry, area development, fisheries, forestry, irrigation and drainage, livestock, perennial crops, research and extension, and sector loans. *Energy* covers oil, gas, coal, and power. *Industry* comprises engineering, fertilizers and other chemicals, iron and steel, mining and other extraction, paper and pulp, textiles, and sector loans. *Transport* includes airlines and

airports, highways, pipelines, ports and waterways, railways, and sector loans.

Table 9. IDA Operations

The *number of credits* includes all credits approved by IDA as of the date of Board approval. IDA credits for projects financed jointly by IDA and the IBRD are included, but the amounts shown refer to the IDA portion only.

The *total number of countries receiving credits* represents in any given year the number of countries for which credits were approved during that year. The total represents the number of countries receiving credits at any time between 1961 and 1982.

Commitments and *disbursements* are explained in the technical notes to Tables 5 and 6.

Net transfer is the difference between disbursements and service payments, which include the repayments of principal and payments of service and other charges on the basis of book value.

Net income is the difference between IDA's income and administrative expenses as shown in IDA's financial statements, published in the *World Bank Annual Report*.

Commitments in 1982 dollars are calculated using the disbursement deflator (see below) and assuming that the credit will be disbursed as follows: 2.5 percent in the year the commitment was made, 16.7 percent, 24.7 percent, 22.8 percent, 16.8 percent, 10.7 percent, and 5.8 percent in the first, second, third, fourth, fifth, and sixth years respectively, following the commitment.

Disbursements in 1982 dollars were derived by using the unit value index of manufactured exports, c.i.f. (categories 5–8 of the Standard International Trade Classification) from developed market economies to developing countries, as published in the UN Monthly Bulletin of Statistics for the period 1961–80. The 1981 and 1982 indices are from the OECD.

Table 10. Basic Indicators

The data on *area* are from the Food and Agriculture Organization *Production Yearbook, 1979*.

Gross national product (GNP) measures the total domestic and foreign output claimed by residents. It comprises gross domestic product (see the technical notes for Table 11) and factor incomes (such as investment receipts and workers' remittances) accruing to residents from abroad, less the income earned in the domestic economy accruing to persons abroad. It is calculated without making deductions for depreciation. For some economies the estimates of GNP are adjusted from data on net material product.

The *GNP per capita* figures were calculated according to the *World Bank Atlas* method (see technical notes to Table 4).

The *average annual rate of inflation* was calculated from the implicit gross domestic product (GDP) deflator, which is calculated by dividing, for each year of the period, the value of GDP in current market prices by the value of GDP in constant market prices, both in national currency. This measure of inflation has limitations, especially for the oil-producing countries in the light of sharp increases in oil prices.

The *adult literacy rate* is the percentage of persons aged 15 and over who can read and write. These rates are based primarily on information from the UN Educational, Scientific, and Cultural Organization (Unesco), supplemented by World Bank data. Because such data are normally gathered in large-scale demographic surveys and censuses, they often are not available for the most recent year. For some countries the estimates are for years other than, but generally not more than two years distant from, those specified. Thus the series are not comparable for all countries.

Life expectancy at birth indicates the number of years newborn children would live if subject to the mortality risks prevailing for the cross section of population at the time of their birth. Data are from the UN Population Division, supplemented by World Bank estimates.

The *index of food production per capita* shows the average annual quantity of food produced per capita in 1978–80 in relation to that in 1969–71. The estimates were derived from those of the Food and Agriculture Organization (FAO), which are calculated by dividing indices of the quantity of food production by indices of total population. Food is defined as comprising cereals, starchy roots, sugar cane, sugar beet, pulses, edible oils, nuts, fruits, vegetables, livestock, and livestock products. Quantities of food production are measured net of animal feed, seeds for use in agriculture, and food lost in processing and distribution.

The weighted averages in Table 10 are weighted by population.

Tables 11 and 12. Growth and Structure of Production

Most of the definitions used are those of the UN *System of National Accounts.*

Gross domestic product (GDP) measures the total final output of goods and services produced by an economy—that is, by residents and nonresidents, regardless of the allocation to domestic and foreign claims. It is calculated without making deductions for depreciation. For most countries, GDP by industrial origin is measured at factor cost, but for some countries without complete national accounts series at factor cost, market price series were used. GDP at factor cost is equal to GDP at market prices, less indirect taxes net of subsidies. The figures for GDP are dollar values converted from domestic currency by using the average annual exchange rate for the year in question: that is, they were not calculated by using the *World Bank Atlas* method described in the technical notes

for Table 4 and thus are not comparable with the figures in that table.

The *agricultural sector* comprises agriculture, forestry, hunting, and fishing. The *industrial sector* comprises mining, *manufacturing,* construction, and electricity, water, and gas. All other branches of economic activity are categorized as *services.*

National accounts series in domestic currency units were used to compute the indicators in these tables. Whereas the growth rates in Table 11 were calculated from constant price series, the shares of GDP in Table 12 were calculated from current price series.

The average growth rates for the summary measures in Table 11 are weighted by GDP in 1970 dollars. The average sectoral shares in Table 12 are weighted by GDP in current dollars for the years in question.

Tables 13 and 14. Growth of Consumption and Investment; Structure of Demand

GDP is defined in the notes for Tables 11 and 12.

Public consumption (or general government consumption) includes all current expenditure for purchases of goods and services by all levels of government. Capital expenditure on national defense and security is regarded as consumption expenditure.

Private consumption is the market value of all goods and services purchased or received as income in kind by households and nonprofit institutions. It includes imputed rent for owner-occupied dwellings.

Gross domestic investment consists of the outlays for additions to the fixed assets of the economy, plus changes in the net value of inventories.

Gross domestic saving shows the amount of gross domestic investment financed from domestic output. Comprising public and private saving, it is gross domestic investment plus the net exports of goods and nonfactor services.

Exports of goods and nonfactor services represent the value of all goods and nonfactor services sold to the rest of the world; they include merchandise, freight, insurance, travel, and other nonfactor services. The value of factor services, such as investment receipts and workers' remittances from abroad, is excluded.

The *resource balance* is the difference between exports and imports of goods and nonfactor services.

National accounts series in domestic currency units were used to compute the indicators in these tables. Whereas the growth rates in Table 13 were calculated from constant price series, the shares of GDP in Table 14 were calculated from current price series.

The summary measures in Table 14 are weighted by GDP in current dollars for the years in question.

Table 15. Commercial Energy

The data on energy generally are from UN sources. They refer to commercial forms of primary energy: coal and lignite, petroleum, natural gas and natural gas liquids, and hydroelectric and nuclear power—all converted into coal equivalents. The use of firewood and other traditional fuels, though substantial in some developing countries, is not taken into account because reliable and comprehensive data are not available.

The summary measures of growth rates of *energy production* are weighted by volumes of production in 1974; those of growth rates of *energy consumption,* by volumes of consumption in 1974; those of *energy consumption per capita,* by population.

Energy imports refer to the dollar value of energy imports—Revised Standard International Trade Classification (SITC) Section 3—and are expressed as a percentage of earnings from merchandise exports. The summary measures are weighted by merchandise exports in current dollars.

Because data on energy imports do not permit a distinction between petroleum imports for fuel and for use in the petrochemicals industry, these percentages may be overestimates of the dependence on imported energy.

Table 16. Balance of Payments and Debt Service Ratios

The *current account balance* is the difference between (1) exports of goods and services plus inflows of unrequited official and private transfers and (2) imports of goods and services plus unrequited transfers to the rest of the world. *Interest payments on external public and publicly guaranteed debt* are those on the disbursed portion of outstanding public and publicly guaranteed medium- and long-term debt plus commitment charges on undisbursed debt. The current account estimates are from IMF data files; estimates of interest payments are from the World Bank Debt Reporting System.

Debt service is the sum of interest payments and repayments of principal on external public and publicly guaranteed medium- and long-term debt. Debt service data are from the World Bank Debt Reporting System. The ratio of debt service to exports of goods and services is one of several rules of thumb commonly used to assess the ability to service debt. The debt service ratios in the table do not cover unguaranteed private debt, which for some borrowers is substantial; the debt contracted for purchases of military equipment is also excluded because it usually is not reported. The average ratios of debt service to GNP for the groups are weighted by GNP in current dollars. The average ratios of debt service to exports of goods and services are weighted by exports of goods and services in current dollars.

Table 17. Flow of Public External Capital

Data on the *gross inflow* and *repayment of principal* (amortization) of public and publicly guaranteed medium- and long-term loans are from the World Bank Debt Re-

porting System. The *net inflow* is the gross inflow less the repayment of principal.

Net direct private investment is the net amount invested or reinvested by nonresidents in enterprises in which they or other nonresidents exercise significant managerial control. These net figures also take into account the value of direct investment abroad by residents. IMF data files were used in compiling these estimates.

Table 18. External Public Debt and International Reserves

External public debt outstanding represents the amount of public and publicly guaranteed loans that have been disbursed, net of canceled loan commitments and repayments of principal. The data refer to the end of the year indicated and are from the World Bank Debt Reporting System. In estimating external public debt as a percentage of GNP, GNP was converted from national currencies to dollars at the average official exchange rate for the year in question. The summary measures are weighted by GNP in current dollars.

Gross international reserves comprise holdings of gold, special drawing rights (SDRs), the reserve position of IMF members in the Fund, and holdings of foreign exchange under the control of monetary authorities. The gold component of these reserves is valued throughout at year-end London prices: that is, $37.37 an ounce in 1970 and $589.50 an ounce in 1980. The data on holdings of international reserves are from IMF data files. The reserve levels for 1970 and 1980 refer to the end of the year indicated and are in current dollars. The reserve holdings at the end of 1980 are also expressed in the number of months of imports of goods and services they could pay for, with imports at the average level for 1979 or 1980. The summary measures are weighted by imports of goods and services in current dollars.

Table 19. Official Development Assistance from OECD and OPEC Members

Official development assistance (ODA) consists of net disbursements of loans and grants made at concessional financial terms by official agencies of the members of the Development Assistance Committee (DAC) of the Organisation for Economic Co-operation and Development (OECD) and members of the Organization of Petroleum Exporting Countries (OPEC) with the objective of promoting economic development and welfare. It includes the value of technical cooperation and assistance. All data shown were supplied by the OECD.

Amounts shown are net disbursements to developing countries and multilateral institutions. The disbursements to multilateral institutions are now reported for all DAC members on the basis of the date of issues of notes; some DAC members previously reported on the basis of the date of encashment. *Net bilateral flows to low-income countries* exclude unallocated bilateral flows and all disbursements to multilateral institutions.

The nominal values shown in the summary for ODA from OECD countries were converted to 1978 prices using the dollar GNP deflator. This deflator is based on price increases in OECD countries (excluding Greece, Portugal, Spain, and Turkey) measured in dollars. It takes into account the parity changes between the dollar and national currencies. For example, when the dollar depreciates, price increases measured in national currencies have to be adjusted upward by the amount of the depreciation to obtain price increases in dollars.

The table, in addition to showing totals for OPEC, shows totals for the Organization of Arab Petroleum Exporting Countries (OAPEC). The donor members of OAPEC are Algeria, Iraq, Kuwait, Libya, Qatar, Saudi Arabia, and United Arab Emirates. ODA data for OPEC and OAPEC were also obtained from the OECD.

Table 20. Population Growth, Actual and Projected

The *growth rates of population* are period averages calculated from midyear populations. The summary measures are weighted by population in 1970.

The *projections of population* for 1990 and 2000, and to the year in which it will eventually become stationary, were made for each economy separately. Starting with information on total population by age and sex, fertility rates, and mortality rates in the base year 1980, these parameters were projected at five-year intervals on the basis of generalized assumptions until the population became stationary. The base-year estimates are from updated computer printouts of UN, *World Population Trends and Prospects by Country, 1950–2025,* and from the World Bank, the Population Council, the U.S. Bureau of the Census, and recent national censuses.

The *net reproduction rate* (NRR) indicates the number of daughters that a newborn girl will bear during her lifetime, assuming fixed age-specific fertility rates and a fixed set of mortality rates.

A *stationary population* is one in which age- and sex-specific mortality rates have not changed over a long period, while age-specific fertility rates have simultaneously remained at replacement level (NRR = 1). In such a population, the birth rate is constant and equal to the death rate, the age structure also is constant, and the growth rate is zero.

To make the projections, assumptions about future mortality rates were made in terms of female life expectancy at birth (that is, about the number of years a newborn girl would live if subject to the mortality risks prevailing for the cross section of population at the time of her birth). Economies were first divided according to whether their primary-school enrollment ratio for females was above or below 70 percent. In each group a set of annual increments in female life expectancy was assumed, depending on the female life expectancy in 1975–80. For a given life expectancy at birth, the annual increments during the projection period are larger in economies having a higher primary-school enrollment ratio in 1975–80 and a life expectancy of up to 60 years.

At higher life expectancies, the increments are the same.

To project the fertility rates, the first step was to estimate the year in which fertility would reach replacement level. These estimates are speculative and are based on information on trends in crude birth rates (defined in the notes for Table 21), total fertility rates (also defined in the notes for Table 21), female life expectancy at birth, and the performance of family planning programs. For most economies it was assumed that the total fertility rate would decline between 1980 and the year of reaching a net reproduction rate of 1, after which fertility would remain at replacement level. For Sub-Saharan Africa, total fertility rates were assumed to remain constant until 1990–95 and then to decline until replacement level was reached. In several industrial economies, fertility is already below replacement level. Because a population will not remain stationary if its net reproduction rate is other than 1, it was necessary to assume that fertility rates in these economies would regain replacement levels in order to make estimates of the hypothetical stationary population for them. For the sake of consistency with the other estimates, the total fertility rates in the industrial economies were assumed to increase to replacement level by 2000 and then to remain constant.

For all the projections, it was assumed that international migration would have no effect.

The estimates of the hypothetical size of the stationary population, the assumed year of reaching replacement-level fertility, and the year of reaching a stationary population are speculative. *They should not be regarded as predictions.* They are included to provide a summary indication of the long-run implications of recent trends on the basis of highly stylized assumptions. A fuller description of the methods and assumptions used to calculate the estimates is available from the Population, Health, and Nutrition Department of the World Bank.

Table 21. Demography and Fertility

The *crude birth and death rates* indicate the number of live births and deaths per thousand population in a year. They are from the same sources mentioned in the technical notes for Table 20. Percentage changes are computed from unrounded data.

The *total fertility rate* represents the number of children that would be born per woman, if she were to live to the end of her child-bearing years and bear children at each age in accord with prevailing age-specific fertility rates. The rates given are from the same sources mentioned in the technical notes for Table 20.

All summary measures are weighted by population.

Table 22. Labor Force Structure

The *population of working age* refers to the population aged 15–64. The estimates are based on the population estimates of the World Bank for 1980 and previous years. The summary measures are weighted by population.

The *labor force* comprises economically active persons, including the armed forces and the unemployed, but excluding housewives, students, and other economically inactive groups. *Agriculture, industry, and services* are defined in the same manner as in Table 11. The estimates of the sectoral distribution of the labor force in 1960 are from International Labour Office (ILO), *Labour Force Estimates and Projections, 1950–2000;* most of those for 1980 are geometric extrapolations of ILO estimates for 1960 and 1970 in the same source. The summary measures are weighted by labor force.

The *labor force growth rates* were derived from the Bank's population projections and ILO data on activity rates, again from the source cited above. The summary measures for 1960–70 and 1970–80 are weighted by labor force in 1970; those for 1980–2000, by projections of labor force in 1980.

The application of ILO activity rates to the Bank's latest population estimates may be inappropriate for some economies in which there have been important changes in unemployment and underemployment, in international and internal migration, or in both. The labor force projections for 1980–2000 should thus be treated with caution.

Table 23. Life Expectancy and Mortality

Life expectancy at birth is defined in the technical notes for Table 10.

The *infant mortality rate* is the number of infants who die before reaching one year of age, per 1,000 live births in a given year. The data are from a variety of sources—including different issues of the UN *Demographic Yearbook* and UN, "Infant Mortality: World Estimates and Projections, 1950–2025," *Population Bulletin of the United Nations,* no. 14 (forthcoming 1982)—and from the World Bank.

The *child death rate* is the number of deaths of children aged 1–4 per 1,000 children in the same age group in a given year. Estimates were based on the data on infant mortality and on the relation between the infant mortality rate and the child death rate implicit in the appropriate Coale-Demeny Model life tables; see Ansley J. Coale and Paul Demeny, *Regional Model Life Tables and Stable Populations* (Princeton, N.J.: Princeton University Press, 1966).

The summary measures in this table are weighted by population.

Table 24. Health and Nutrition

The estimates of *population per physician and per nurse* were derived from World Health Organization (WHO) data, some of which have been revised to reflect new information. They also take into account revised estimates

of population. Nurses include graduate, practical, assistant, and auxiliary nurses; this is the first year auxiliary nurses have been included, thus better estimating the availability of nursing care. Because definitions of nursing personnel vary—and because the data shown are for a variety of years, generally not more than two years distant from those specified—the data for these two indicators are not strictly comparable.

The *percentage of total population with access to safe water,* estimated by the WHO, is the proportion of persons with reasonable access to safe water, which is defined as including treated surface water and such untreated but uncontaminated water as that from boreholes, springs, and sanitary wells.

The *daily calorie supply per capita* was calculated by dividing the calorie equivalent of the food supplies in an economy by the population. Food supplies comprise domestic production, imports less exports, and changes in stocks; they exclude animal feed, seeds for use in agriculture, and food lost in processing and distribution. The *daily calorie requirement per capita* refers to the calories needed to sustain a person at normal levels of activity and health, taking into account age and sex distributions, average body weights, and environmental temperatures. Both sets of estimates are from the Food and Agriculture Organization.

The summary measures in this table are weighted by population.

Table 25. Education

The data in this table refer to a variety of years, generally not more than two years distant from those specified, and are mostly from Unesco.

The data on *number enrolled in primary school* refer to estimates of total, male, and female enrollment of students of all ages in primary school; they are expressed as percentages of the total, male, or female populations of primary-school age to give gross primary enrollment ratios. Although primary-school age is generally considered to be 6 to 11 years, the differences in country practices in the ages and duration of schooling are reflected in the ratios given. For countries with universal primary education, the gross enrollment ratios may exceed 100 percent because some pupils may be below or above the official primary-school age.

The data on *number enrolled in secondary school* were calculated in the same manner, with secondary-school age generally considered to be 12 to 17 years.

The data on *number enrolled in higher education* are from Unesco.

The *adult literacy rate* is defined in the technical notes for Table 10.

The summary measures in this table are weighted by population.

Bibliography of Data Sources

Contributions, voting rights of IDA members	World Bank data.
Procurement	World Bank data.
Financial data	World Bank data.
National accounts and economic indicators	*A System of National Accounts.* New York: UN Department of International Economic and Social Affairs, 1968. *Yearbook of National Accounts Statistics.* New York: UN Department of International Economic and Social Affairs, various issues. *Statistical Yearbook.* New York: UN Department of International Economic and Social Affairs, various issues. *Monthly Bulletin of Statistics.* New York: UN Department of International Economic and Social Affairs, various issues. *Production Yearbook.* Rome: FAO, various issues. *1981 World Bank Atlas.* Washington, D.C.: World Bank, 1982. World Bank data files.
Energy	*World Energy Supplies, 1950–74, 1972–76, and 1973–78.* UN Statistical Papers, Series J, nos. 19, 21, and 22. New York: UN Department of International Economic and Social Affairs, 1974, 1978, and 1979. *Yearbook of World Energy Statistics, 1979.* New York: UN Department of International Economic and Social Affairs, 1981.
Trade	*Direction of Trade.* Washington, D.C.: IMF, various issues. *International Financial Statistics.* Washington, D.C.: IMF, various issues. *Handbook of International Trade and Development Statistics.* New York: UN Conference on Trade and Development, various issues. *Monthly Bulletin of Statistics.* New York: UN Department of International Economic and Social Affairs, various issues. *Yearbook of International Trade Statistics.* New York: UN Department of International Economic and Social Affairs, various issues. United Nations trade tapes.

Balance of payments, capital flows, and debt	*Balance of Payments Manual.* 4th ed. Washington, D.C.: IMF, 1977. International Monetary Fund balance-of-payments data files. *Development Co-operation.* Paris: OECD, various annual issues. *Geographical Distribution of Financial Flows to Developing Countries.* Paris: OECD, various issues. World Bank Debt Reporting System.
Population	*World Population Trends and Prospects by Country, 1950–2025: Summary Report of the 1980 Assessment.* New York: UN Department of International Economic and Social Affairs, 1980. *Demographic Yearbook.* New York: UN Department of International Economic and Social Affairs, various issues. United Nations population tapes. *World Population: 1979.* Washington, D.C.: US Bureau of the Census, International Demographic Data Center, 1980. *1981 World Bank Atlas.* Washington, D.C.: World Bank, 1982. World Bank data files.
Labor force	*Labour Force Estimates and Projections, 1950–2000.* 2nd ed. Geneva: ILO, 1977. International Labour Office tapes. World Bank data files.
Social indicators	*Demographic Yearbook.* New York: UN Department of International Economic and Social Affairs, various issues. *Statistical Yearbook.* New York: UN Department of International Economic and Social Affairs, various issues. *Compendium of Social Statistics: 1977.* New York: UN Department of International Economic and Social Affairs, 1980 *Statistical Yearbook.* Paris: Unesco, various issues. *World Health Statistics Annual.* Geneva: WHO, various issues. *World Health Statistics Report.* Special Issue on Water and Sanitation, vol. 29, no. 10. Geneva: WHO, 1976. *Government Finance Statistics Yearbook, 1981.* vol. 5. Washington, D.C.: IMF, 1981. World Bank data files.